Apple
PRESS

Cyberdog Programmer's Kit

Addison-Wesley Publishing Company

Reading, Massachusetts   Menlo Park, California   New York
Don Mills, Ontario   Harlow, England   Amsterdam   Bonn
Sydney   Singapore   Tokyo   Madrid   San Juan
Paris   Seoul   Milan   Mexico City   Taipei

Apple Computer, Inc.
© 1996 Apple Computer, Inc.
All rights reserved.

No part of this publication may be reproduced, stored in a retrieval system, or transmitted, in any form or by any means, mechanical, electronic, photocopying, recording, or otherwise, without prior written permission of Apple Computer, Inc., except to make a backup copy of any documentation provided on CD-ROM. Printed in the United States of America.

No licenses, express or implied, are granted with respect to any of the technology described in this book. Apple retains all intellectual property rights associated with the technology described in this book. This book is intended to assist application developers to develop applications only for Apple-labeled or Apple-licensed computers.

Every effort has been made to ensure that the information in this manual is accurate. Apple is not responsible for printing or clerical errors.

Apple Computer, Inc.
1 Infinite Loop
Cupertino, CA 95014
408-996-1010

Apple, the Apple logo, AppleLink, LaserWriter, Macintosh, MacTCP, OpenDoc, and QuickTime are trademarks of Apple Computer, Inc., registered in the United States and other countries.

Apple Press, the Apple Press signature, and Finder are trademarks of Apple Computer, Inc.

Adobe, Acrobat, and PostScript are trademarks of Adobe Systems Incorporated or its subsidiaries and may be registered in certain jurisdictions.

Helvetica and Palatino are registered trademarks of Linotype-Hell AG and/or its subsidiaries.

ITC Zapf Dingbats is a registered trademark of International Typeface Corporation.

PowerPC is a trademark of International Business Machines Corporation, used under license therefrom.

QuickView™ is licensed from Altura Software, Inc.

SOM, SOMobjects, and System Object Model are registered trademarks of International Business Machines Corporation.

UNIX is a registered trademark of Novell, Inc. in the United States and other countries, licensed exclusively through X/Open Company, Ltd.

Simultaneously published in the United States and Canada.

ISBN 0-201-18375-7
1 2 3 4 5 6 7 8 9-MA-0099989796
First Printing, July 1996

Library of Congress Cataloging-in-Publication Data

Cyberdog programmer's kit   / Apple Computer, Inc.
    p. cm.
    Includes index.
    ISBN 0-201-18375-7
    1. Cyberdog. 2. Internet (Computer network) I. Apple Computer, Inc.
    TK5105.882.C93   1996
    005.7'1369—dc20
                            96-15566
                             CIP

Contents

Chapter 2   **Development Overview**   51

Chapter 7   Classes and Methods   197

Glossary

Index

Figures, Tables, and Listings

Chapter 5   Embedding a Cyberdog Display Part in a Navigator   145

Chapter 6   Types, Constants, and Global Functions   167

Chapter 7   Classes and Methods   197

About the Programmer's Kit

For users who wish to access network information, Cyberdog is a set of tools with which to search and browse the Internet, access Internet mail and newsgroups, and access content located on the Internet.

For developers who wish to provide such tools, Cyberdog is a collection of OpenDoc classes and extensions for creating OpenDoc parts that access and display remotely located content. This book and its accompanying CD-ROM make up the *Cyberdog Programmer's Kit*. It provides the tools you need and shows you how to develop Cyberdog components.

The Book

This book contains three parts, which contain overview information, programming examples, and reference documentation.

Part 1, "Basics," contains two chapters that you should read before reading any other parts of the book.

- Chapter 1, "Introduction to Cyberdog," provides an overview of Cyberdog features and introduces the key Cyberdog objects and the roles they play.

- Chapter 2, "Development Overview," introduces the Cyberdog class library and provides an example of how the key objects in Cyberdog collaborate to download and display network data. In addition, this chapter discusses the process of opening a Cyberdog item and the objects that play a role in that process.

Part 2, "Programming in Cyberdog," consists of three chapters that describe, with programming samples and tutorial-like steps, how to write Cyberdog components.

- Chapter 3, "Adding Cyberdog Features to an OpenDoc Part," describes how to use Cyberdog items and Cyberdog menus. The chapter illustrates a quick and simple way to provide Internet access from an OpenDoc part.

- Chapter 4, "Creating a Cyberdog Display Part," describes how to implement display capability for data located on the Internet. Although Cyberdog provides this capability for many kinds of data, this chapter shows you the steps to follow when developing this capability for your special kind of data or display needs.

- Chapter 5, "Embedding a Cyberdog Display Part in a Navigator," describes how to display Internet data in a display part that is embedded in a Cyberdog navigator and how to display progress during time-consuming operations, such as a download. It also shows additional techniques for using Cyberdog objects with navigators.

Part 3, "Cyberdog Reference," consists of two chapters that document the Cyberdog programming interface.

- Chapter 6, "Types, Constants, and Global Functions," describes the data types, constants, global functions, and programmer-defined functions you use when writing Cyberdog software.

- Chapter 7, "Classes and Methods," describes the classes and methods of the Cyberdog class library.

A glossary at the end of this book defines common terms used in Cyberdog programming.

OpenDoc documentation

Cyberdog is based on OpenDoc, the cross-platform component software architecture. To program with Cyberdog, you need to use and understand OpenDoc development techniques. See *OpenDoc Class Reference,* *OpenDoc Cookbook,* and *OpenDoc Programmer's Guide* for information and examples of OpenDoc programming. ◆

The CD-ROM

The CD-ROM that accompanies this book contains all the code, information, and development files you need to create Cyberdog part editors or network-service components. The CD-ROM includes these items, among others:

- installers for both OpenDoc and Cyberdog software

- critical development material, including header files, project files, and build instructions

- full documentation, including the complete text of this book in Adobe™ Acrobat™ format, QuickView™ format, and HTML format

  ☐ Acrobat provides a fully formatted book with page-numbered table of contents, index, and live hypertext cross-references. You can print all or portions of the book, and you can also view it online and use indexed search facilities.

  ☐ QuickView format is that used by the *Macintosh Programmer's Toolbox Assistant*. In this format, you can use full-text searching capabilities and ubiquitous hypertext jumps to find reference information quickly. You can even search for information and retrieve method templates from within development environments that can communicate with QuickView.

  ☐ HTML format allows you to read this book online, using any Internet browser software (including Cyberdog).

- complete source code for all samples documented in this book

- a tutorial (in HTML format) that takes you through step-by-step development of a simple Cyberdog display part

- executable samples, demos, and presentations that illustrate the range of possibilities for Cyberdog development

Formatting Conventions

This book uses various conventions to present certain types of information.

Special Fonts

All code listings, reserved words, and names of data structures, constants, fields, parameters, and functions are shown in Letter Gothic (`this is Letter Gothic`).

Types of Notes

There are several types of notes used in this book.

Note

A note formatted like this contains information that is interesting but possibly not essential to an understanding of the main text. ◆

IMPORTANT

A note like this contains information that is essential for an understanding of the main text. ▲

Code Presentation

Prototypes for methods of Cyberdog classes are in the System Object Model™ (SOM™) Interface Definition Language (IDL). As an example of what IDL prototypes look like, here is the prototype for the SetCyberItem method:

```
void SetCyberItem (in CyberItem item, in ParameterSet openParams);
```

In IDL method declarations, each parameter declaration is preceded by a directional attribute ("in", "out", or "inout") that denotes whether the parameter is used as an input, or as a result, or as both.

Listings of implementation code are in C++. In implementation listings, every call to a method of a SOM-based class (as all Cyberdog classes are) includes an extra parameter, the environment parameter (ev), that does not appear in the method's IDL prototype. Here is an example (in C++) of a call to the SetCyberItem method:

```
somSelf → SetCyberItem (ev, item, openParams);
```

For More Information

Further information about Cyberdog is available via World Wide Web pages linked to the Cyberdog home page at the following universal resource locator (URL) address:

`http://cyberdog.apple.com`

The *Apple Developer Catalog* (ADC) is Apple Computer's worldwide source for hundreds of development tools, technical resources, training products, and information for anyone interested in developing applications on Apple computer platforms. Customers receive the *Apple Developer Catalog* featuring all current versions of Apple development tools and the most popular third-party development tools. ADC offers convenient payment and shipping options, including site licensing.

To order products or to request a complimentary copy of the *Apple Developer Catalog*, contact

Apple Developer Catalog
Apple Computer, Inc.
P.O. Box 319
Buffalo, NY 14207-0319

Telephone	1-800-282-2732 (United States)
	1-800-637-0029 (Canada)
	716-871-6555 (International)
Fax	716-871-6511
AppleLink	ORDER.ADC
Internet	order.adc@applelink.apple.com

Basics

The chapters in this part provide an overview of Cyberdog features and the Cyberdog class library. You should read these two chapters before reading any other parts of this book.

- Chapter 1, "Introduction to Cyberdog," provides an overview of Cyberdog features and introduces the key Cyberdog objects and the roles they play.

- Chapter 2, "Development Overview," introduces the Cyberdog class library and provides an example of how the key objects in Cyberdog collaborate to download and display network data. In addition, this chapter discusses the process of opening a Cyberdog item and the objects that play a role in that process.

Introduction to Cyberdog

Contents

21

This chapter provides an introduction to Cyberdog, an OpenDoc-based solution that provides network access. Cyberdog provides a collection of OpenDoc classes and extensions developers can use to create OpenDoc parts that access and display remotely located content.

This chapter gives a brief overview of Cyberdog features and then introduces the key Cyberdog objects and the roles they play in Cyberdog. Whether you are interested in modifying an existing OpenDoc part to display Internet content or you want to extend Cyberdog to support new network services, read this chapter to gain an overall understanding of Cyberdog concepts.

What Is Cyberdog?

Cyberdog is an extensible architecture for searching and browsing networks, accessing Internet mail and newsgroups, and embedding network content in OpenDoc documents and container applications. Cyberdog uses OpenDoc to allow the user to combine network content with other content smoothly.

Figure 1-1 shows the Cyberdog Starting Point window, the interface through which most users access Cyberdog. The Cyberdog Starting Point window, which is actually an OpenDoc document window, contains buttons for accessing the primary Cyberdog features.

Figure 1-1   The Cyberdog Starting Point window

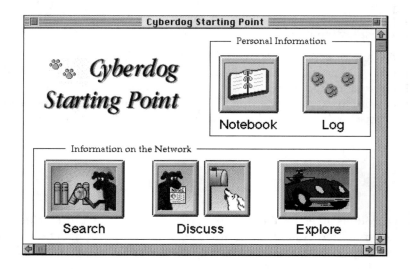

Cyberdog provides a variety of fully implemented tools for accessing networks, such as tools for sending and receiving Internet mail, including a message editor and mail trays for organizing incoming and outgoing mail, as shown in Figure 1-2. Cyberdog uses the POP/SMTP protocol to access mail servers.

Figure 1-2   Cyberdog mail

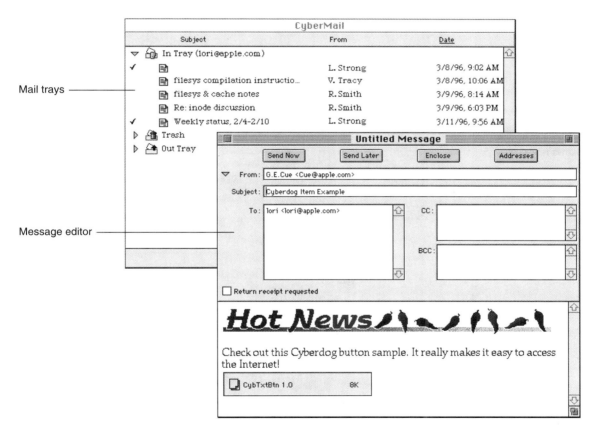

Mail trays

Message editor

Cyberdog provides components for connecting to newsgroups and reading news. It also provides handlers for filtering news, as shown in Figure 1-3. Cyberdog uses the NNTP protocol to access news servers.

Figure 1-3   Cyberdog news

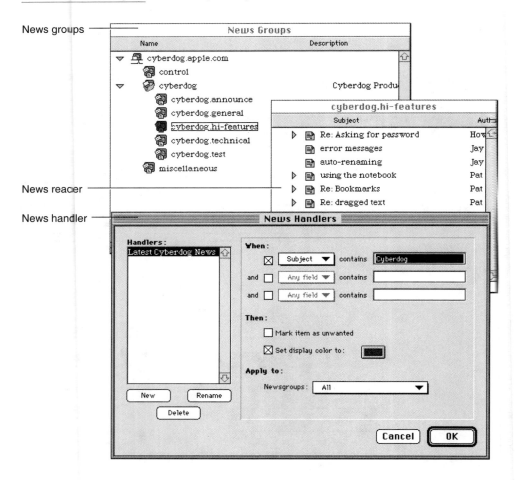

Cyberdog provides built-in access to network data using a variety of protocols, including Gopher, FTP, Telnet, and HTTP. The Cyberdog Connect To dialog box allows the user to enter information for connecting to a remote location using a particular protocol. The Cyberdog Preferences dialog box allows the user to specify usage preferences for a particular protocol.

Cyberdog supplies part editors that are enhanced to download and display information located on a network (Figure 1-4). Cyberdog provides display parts for a variety of formats including text, JPEG images, QuickTime movies, and so on. A Cyberdog display part may be embedded in other OpenDoc documents, displayed in its own window, or displayed embedded in a Cyberdog navigator. The navigator is a tool that makes it easy for the user to browse the Internet, moving from one location to another without opening many windows.

Figure 1-4   Navigating to and displaying network content

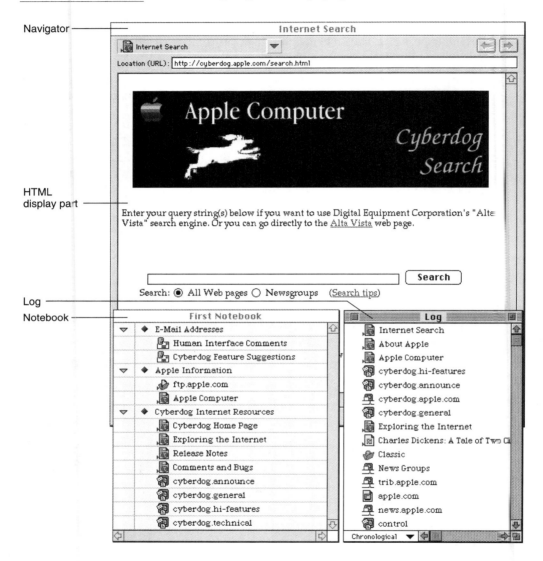

The Cyberdog log provides users with a simple but useful way of looking at the locations they have visited during a session. Each location is represented by a Cyberdog item, a reference to remotely located data. Notebooks provide a

place for users to store Cyberdog items that refer to network locations that they might want to visit again. The log and notebook windows are always available, regardless of which Cyberdog features the user is currently working with.

Developing With Cyberdog

From an architectural perspective, Cyberdog is a collection of OpenDoc classes and concrete parts that provides a flexible, extensible framework for accessing remotely located information.

Using the Cyberdog class library, you can

- modify an existing OpenDoc part or create a new OpenDoc part that can download and display content located on the Internet. For example, you might develop a QuickTime VR or VRML part.

- add network access to an existing application. For example, you might extend an application for creating multimedia presentations to allow the user to browse and download videos stored in an Internet database.

- add support for a new network service to Cyberdog. For example, you might extend Cyberdog to support a videoconferencing service.

- replace a Cyberdog-provided part, such as the Cyberdog text display part, the log, or the navigator, with your own custom part.

Cyberdog display parts that you develop are indistinguishable from those supplied by Cyberdog; the components in Cyberdog communicate using the same public IDL interfaces available to developers. Likewise, the services shipped with Cyberdog are not implemented in any special way; they load through the same interfaces that are available to developers. You add support for new services into the Cyberdog class library by creating new subclasses.

Data Types and Network Protocols

The Cyberdog class library is organized to address two issues: data type and protocol. To address these issues, Cyberdog has independent sets of objects: objects that understand different data types and objects that understand different protocols. Keeping the two dimensions independent improves code independence and reuse, since a display part for any data type can be combined with objects that provide data from any protocol.

If you wish to add support for a new network protocol, you can create
Cyberdog subclasses to support the new protocol. When a Cyberdog display
part needs to access data using a particular network protocol, Cyberdog
dynamically chooses the appropriate objects to retrieve the data, insulating the
display part from details about the protocol that was used to download it.

If you develop a display part for a particular type of network data (a
QuickTime VR display part, for example), you can concentrate on how your
part editor displays its content. Cyberdog relies on OpenDoc to dynamically
select the right display part to display data as the need arises, leaving Cyberdog's
protocol objects to locate and download the data. This insulates the protocol
objects from details about which display part is displaying the data.

Key Classes

The Cyberdog class library is built around a few key classes that you, as a
developer, work with to create Cyberdog display parts and services. Each class
defines the public interface for an area of responsibility within Cyberdog. There
are five key Cyberdog classes.

- A **Cyberdog item** is a reference to data stored at a remote location, such as
  on a local network or on the Internet.

- A **Cyberdog display part** displays the data referenced by a Cyberdog item.

- A **Cyberdog stream** downloads the data referenced by a Cyberdog item. A
  Cyberdog display part can use a Cyberdog stream to download data
  referenced by a Cyberdog item.

- A **Cyberdog service** implements network access for a particular network
  protocol.

- A **Cyberdog session** is a single, global object that represents a user's
  access to Cyberdog. The Cyberdog session keeps track of the supported
  Cyberdog services.

The Cyberdog class library includes a number of other classes you can use to
implement Cyberdog features. The entire Cyberdog class library is outlined in
"Cyberdog Class Library" (page 53).

Cyberdog Items

A Cyberdog item stores the location of data. The Cyberdog item does not store the data itself; instead, the item stores enough information about the location and protocol of the data to access the data on demand.

There is a different kind of Cyberdog item for each protocol that Cyberdog supports. There are web items, FTP items, Gopher items, Telnet items, and so on. Each kind of Cyberdog item understands how to address information for that protocol. Cyberdog items are not distinguished by the type or format of the data to which they refer. Cyberdog FTP items, for example, are used to address any data located on an FTP server, regardless of whether the data is an FTP directory, an image, audio, or text.

In addition to its address information, a Cyberdog item has an associated icon and a default display name. The user can select a Cyberdog item and choose the Get Info command from the Edit menu to display an Item Info window for the Cyberdog item. For most Cyberdog items, the Item Info window displays the Cyberdog item's icon, display name, and URL.

A Cyberdog item defines its opening behavior. What happens when a user opens a Cyberdog item depends on the implementation of the Cyberdog item. When a Cyberdog item is opened, it is responsible for determining the kind of data it references and creating a display part appropriate for displaying the data. If a Cyberdog item references a downloadable file, the Cyberdog item is responsible for producing a Cyberdog stream that can be used to download the data.

A Cyberdog item is persistent; it has a kind and can be stored in a storage unit. By convention, when a Cyberdog item is stored in a storage unit, it is written in a minimum of two formats in decreasing order of fidelity: the Cyberdog item kind (kCyberItemKind) and the URL text.

The user can drag a Cyberdog item to the Finder. When the user drags a Cyberdog item icon to the Finder, Cyberdog downloads the content that the item references and saves it as an OpenDoc document. In the Finder, the file is represented by a part icon, as shown in Figure 1-5. When the user drags a Cyberdog item to the Finder using Option-drag, Cyberdog saves the Cyberdog item as a reference to content stored on a network. In the Finder, the file is represented by a **reference icon**.

Figure 1-5   Cyberdog item icons in the Finder

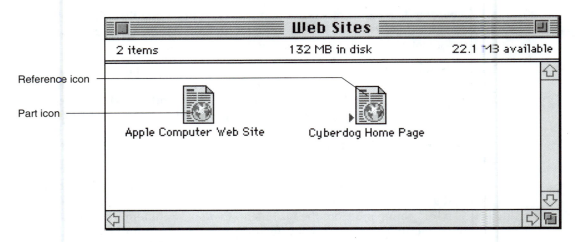

Reference icon

Part icon

Cyberdog Display Parts

A Cyberdog display part is an OpenDoc part that has been enhanced to display the content referenced by a Cyberdog item. In particular, a Cyberdog display part knows how to use a Cyberdog stream to download data referenced by a Cyberdog item. Like any OpenDoc part, a Cyberdog display part can be embedded in an OpenDoc document.

Cyberdog display parts are distinguished by the type of data that they display. For example, a Cyberdog JPEG part can display JPEG data, whether the source of the JPEG data is a Gopher server or an HTTP server.

Like any OpenDoc part, each Cyberdog display part has associated part kinds that describe the types of data it can display. When a Cyberdog item needs to create a part to display the content it references, OpenDoc uses the kind of the data to determine which part editor is appropriate. Cyberdog uses MIME media types to create corresponding OpenDoc kind strings.

As an OpenDoc part, a Cyberdog display part can add menu items of its own to the menu bar and modify the standard OpenDoc menus. In particular, a Cyberdog display part may replace the standard Document menu with a Document menu customized for parts whose data is not stored on disk. Cyberdog services can also add menus to the menu bar. A Cyberdog display part can choose to display Cyberdog service-related menus as well as its own menus. For example, when the Cyberdog FTP display part is active, the FTP service adds an FTP menu to the menu bar.

The simplest Cyberdog display parts display content that does not contain links to other content (a JPEG display part, for example). Figure 1-6 shows the Cyberdog text display part displayed in its own window.

Figure 1-6   A Cyberdog text part

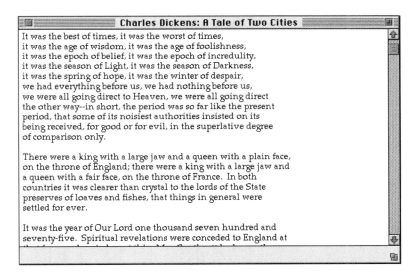

Some Cyberdog display parts, such as FTP, Gopher, and HTML display parts, display content that includes links to other content, as shown in Figure 1-7. By convention, such display parts display themselves embedded in a navigator. A navigator is an OpenDoc part that can embed Cyberdog display parts. It provides a user interface that allows the user to navigate easily from location to location on the network without opening many windows.

If a display part displays content that includes links to other data, the display part must parse its content to find references to other content. For each reference, the display part creates a corresponding Cyberdog item and holds it in its content model. When the user clicks on a link, the display part opens the corresponding Cyberdog item.

Figure 1-7 Gopher display part

Cyberdog navigator

Gopher display part

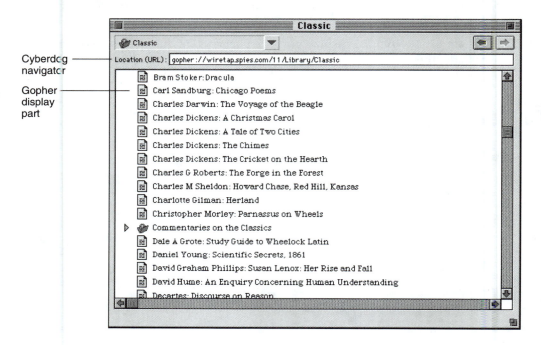

Cyberdog Streams

A Cyberdog stream is an object used to retrieve data at a location described by a Cyberdog item. A Cyberdog stream downloads data for a given protocol. For any type of Cyberdog item that refers to data stored on a file server, there is usually a corresponding stream that is used to download data for the given protocol.

To download data, the stream object must fulfill three conditions:

1. Get enough addressing information from its creating Cyberdog item to locate the network resource desired.

2. Negotiate with the server to retrieve the data.

3. Clean up the downloaded data by removing extraneous information such as headers, pad bytes, and so on. For example, Cyberdog stream implementations should delete the line-feed from carriage-return/line-feed pairs in text data.

A stream object's ability to provide data as a uniform, clean byte stream accounts, in part, for Cyberdog's flexibility. A Cyberdog display part can dynamically access data from a Gopher server, a web server, or a local file. The display part requests a stream from a Cyberdog item, initiates the download, and retrieves data from the stream as it becomes available. The item/stream pair insulates the display part from details of where the data came from or how it was downloaded.

Cyberdog includes stream objects for downloading data for common protocols such as HTTP, FTP, Gopher, and so on. A Cyberdog item and Cyberdog stream for a particular protocol are associated with a corresponding Cyberdog service object.

When a display part is ready to download the content referenced by a Cyberdog item, the display part requests a Cyberdog stream from the item. The item creates a stream that the display part can use to download the data. When the data is downloaded, the Cyberdog display part deletes the stream. Unlike Cyberdog items, Cyberdog streams are transitory. A Cyberdog stream is used to download data from a location one time; the stream is never reused, even to download data referred to by the same Cyberdog item a second time. If a stream object encounters an error, it is permanently broken.

Downloading Data

The Cyberdog stream interface is structured so that the stream can read data efficiently in its own thread. When a display part requests a Cyberdog stream to initiate a download, the stream is free to begin the download. The display part polls the stream periodically to check on the status of the download operation. The Cyberdog stream provides an interface that the display part can use to monitor the progress and the status of the download operation and determine when data is available for display.

A Cyberdog stream has memory buffers that it uses to hold data as it is downloaded. When the stream has data available, the display part can retrieve a buffer of data from the stream. When the display part is done reading a buffer, it can release it back to the stream. This scheme minimizes the repeated copying of data during the downloading process and allows the stream to proceed with the downloading instead of waiting for the display part to retrieve data from it.

When the stream detects that the downloading operation is complete, it closes the connection on its own.

Using a separate stream object to download data provides flexibility; however, in some cases, that flexibility is not always necessary. For example, the Telnet display part does not use a separate stream object to get its data because the Telnet display part always gets its data from a Telnet server that uses the Telnet protocol. The Telnet display part is specialized to download data using the Telnet protocol itself rather than relying on a separate Telnet stream.

When opened, the Telnet display part asks its creating Cyberdog item for the URL to be downloaded and proceeds with the Telnet download operation itself. Contrast this situation with a JPEG display part that might get its data from any number of sources. As a practical matter, almost all the services supported by Cyberdog are implemented with corresponding Cyberdog streams.

Cyberdog Services

A Cyberdog service provides Internet access using a particular network protocol. A Cyberdog service acts as the coordinating object for the set of objects that collectively implement a protocol. This set of objects may include

- the Cyberdog item that references data accessed using the protocol

- the Cyberdog stream that downloads data using the protocol

- a service-specific panel to be embedded in the Connect To dialog box

- a service-specific panel to be embedded in the Preferences dialog box

In addition, a service may add its own service-specific menus to the menu bar.

You can use any of the fully implemented services that come with Cyberdog or you can extend Cyberdog to support new network services. When Cyberdog is initialized, it creates a Cyberdog service object for each supported service. Cyberdog selects the appropriate service object as needed to access network data.

If you are developing a Cyberdog display part, you should not need to access Cyberdog service objects directly. In most cases, other objects in Cyberdog mediate between Cyberdog display parts and service objects. Cyberdog service objects are mainly of interest to developers who want to implement their own services.

Cyberdog Menu

When a user uses Cyberdog, three menus are always available: the Document menu, the Edit menu, and the Cyberdog menu. Most menu items in the Document and Edit menus provide standard OpenDoc functionality. Cyberdog display parts should always add the Document and Edit menus. Cyberdog display parts that are not embedded in an OpenDoc document should replace the standard Document menu with a custom Document menu for parts whose data is not stored on disk.

The Cyberdog menu contains items that provide access to Cyberdog supporting parts such as the Connect To dialog box, the log, the notebook, and so on. These supporting parts may add their own menus to the menu bar. For example, when a navigator is activated, it adds a Navigate menu to the menu bar. Following OpenDoc conventions, these part-specific menus appear and disappear from the menu bar as their parts are activated and deactivated. In addition, each Cyberdog service can add its own service-specific menus to the menu bar.

A Cyberdog display part can choose to include the Cyberdog menu and service-specific menus in its menu bar. To do so, the display part creates a **Cyberdog service menu** object, which represents the Cyberdog menu and all of the menus added to the menu bar by all Cyberdog services.

Connect To Dialog Box

The Cyberdog **Connect To dialog box** allows the user to specify the information needed to connect to a remote location. The Connect To dialog box displays a selectable list of services, as shown in Figure 1-8. When the user selects a service, the service's **Connect To panel** is displayed and the user enters the connection information.

The format for specifying connection information varies from service to service. For example, the Connect To panel for a Gopher service might allow the user to specify a host name, whereas a Connect To panel for a Telnet service might allow the user to specify a terminal type. In addition to the service-specific Connect To panels, Cyberdog provides a general-purpose Connect To panel that allows the user to specify a URL.

Figure 1-8   The Connect To dialog box

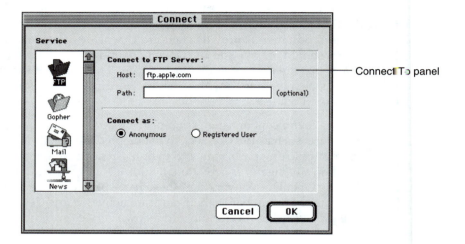

If you add a new service to Cyberdog, you may need to create a Connect To panel, a part that is embedded in the Connect To dialog box. Your custom panel should contain user interface elements that allow the user to specify connection information for the new service.

Preferences Dialog Box

The Cyberdog **Preferences dialog box** allows the user to specify usage preferences for a particular service. The Preferences dialog box displays a selectable list of services, as shown in Figure 1-9. When the user selects a service, the service's **Preferences panel** is displayed and the user enters preferences specific to that service.

The preferences that the user can specify vary from service to service. For example, the Preferences panel for an FTP service might allow the user to specify whether UNIX® hidden files should be shown, whereas the Preferences panel for a World Wide Web service might allow the user to specify the colors used to display links.

Cyberdog stores preferences using Internet Config, software that many Internet access programs use to store and recall user preferences. For more information on Internet Config, see the Internet Config documentation located at the FTP site `ftp://redback.cs.uwa.edu.au//Others/PeterLewis/InternetConfig1.2.sit` or search on the Internet for "Internet Config".

Figure 1-9   The Preferences dialog box

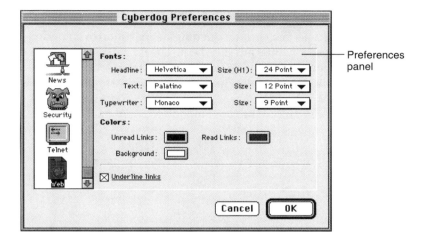

If you add a new service to Cyberdog, you may need to create a Preferences panel, a part that is embedded in the Preferences dialog box. Your custom panel should contain user interface elements that allow the user to specify preferences for the new service.

Cyberdog Session

The Cyberdog session is a global object that represents a single user's access to Cyberdog. A single Cyberdog session object exists in each process in which Cyberdog is running. The Cyberdog session keeps track of the

■ services that are available to the session

■ notebook

■ log

■ Connect To dialog box

■ Preferences dialog box

■ Cyberdog session document

The Cyberdog session represents the user's opening of and access to a single, nonpersistent **Cyberdog session document.** The Cyberdog session document is an OpenDoc document whose root part never displays itself.

Figure 1-10 shows the various documents that share a Cyberdog process and the storage relationships among them. The Cyberdog Starting Point, notebook, log, and session document are all separate OpenDoc documents. The session document contains all navigators and display parts that Cyberdog opens to display network content. The Cyberdog session document does not contain Cyberdog display parts that are embedded in other OpenDoc documents.

Figure 1-10   Storage relationships in a Cyberdog process

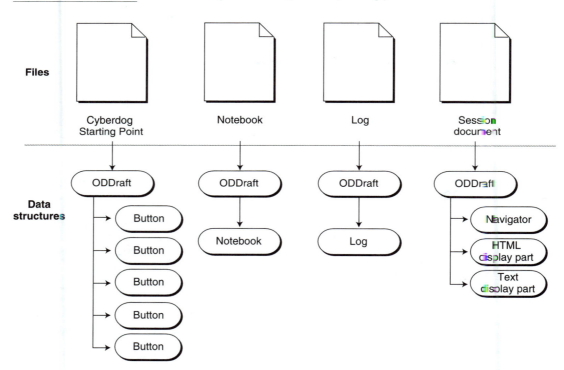

The Cyberdog session also provides access to a number of global Cyberdog utilities.

Supporting Parts

There are a number of OpenDoc parts provided with Cyberdog, such as the log and the notebook, that support the user when using Cyberdog. This section describes the roles these Cyberdog supporting parts play. As a developer, you can continue to use the supporting parts supplied by Cyberdog, or you can subclass the extensions in the Cyberdog class library to create your own custom parts.

Log

As the user navigates from location to location, Cyberdog automatically maintains a **log** that shows all the locations the user has visited. The log is an OpenDoc part, extended with a subclass of the Cyberdog log extension, that exists as a separate document and opens in its own document window.

When the user visits a remote location, the Cyberdog item that references the location is added to the log. The log is persistent; the user can specify the maximum number of Cyberdog items stored in the log in the preferences. The user may choose to view items in the log hierarchically, alphabetically, or chronologically. The **log finger** indicates the user's current location. Figure 1-11 shows a log with the items viewed hierarchically.

Figure 1-11   The Cyberdog log

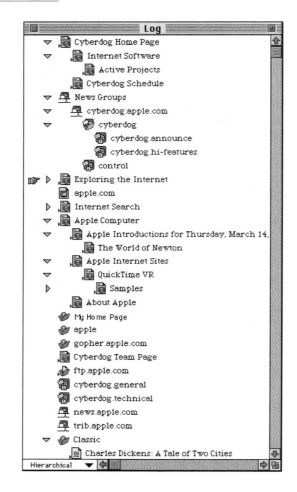

The log serves three main purposes:

- It provides the user with a way to return to a location of interest quickly.

- It helps the user develop a mental model of the physical relationships among locations on the Internet.

- It allows the user to place Cyberdog items of interest in a notebook or in containers in the Finder.

A Cyberdog display part is responsible for adding the Cyberdog item it is displaying to the log and setting the log finger to point to it. The log is associated with the Cyberdog session object; Cyberdog display parts access the log using Cyberdog session methods.

In most cases, developers creating Cyberdog software will continue to use the log supplied by Cyberdog. However, you can extend Cyberdog by creating your own custom log part.

Notebooks

A **notebook** is a part in which users can store Cyberdog items that reference network locations they have visited and found interesting. For example, the user might use the notebook to store a reference to a particular directory on a Gopher server, a specific document page on a web server, an image on an FTP server, and some e-mail addresses.

Users can drag Cyberdog items to the notebook from any source of Cyberdog items (such as the list in the log), from the banner of any Cyberdog window, or from the Finder. In addition to Cyberdog items, the user can create categories to organize items in the notebook (Figure 1-12).

Figure 1-12   The Cyberdog notebook

Categories ———

Cyberdog
Items ———

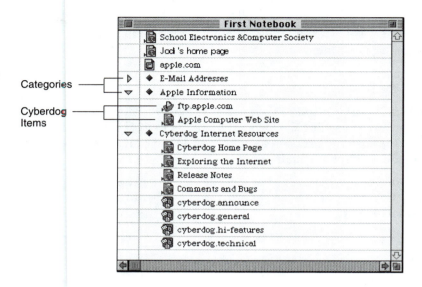

Notebooks are OpenDoc parts, extended with a subclass of the Cyberdog notebook extension, that exist as separate documents and open in their own document windows. The notebook is associated with the Cyberdog session object; developers access the notebook using Cyberdog session methods.

A notebook is represented in the Finder by a document icon. If the user double-clicks on a notebook icon in the Finder, the Finder launches the notebook document, which opens the notebook window. A user may have any number of notebooks and may add Cyberdog items to any notebook; however, the user designates only one notebook at a time as the default notebook that is displayed by Cyberdog.

E-mail addresses and newsgroups are represented by Cyberdog items; as with any Cyberdog item, the user can store them in a notebook. The address browser, opened by Cyberdog mail, displays a selectable list of e-mail addresses and newsgroups from the user's default notebook (Figure 1-13). The user can select addresses in the browser and add them to address fields in a mail message.

Figure 1-13   The address browser

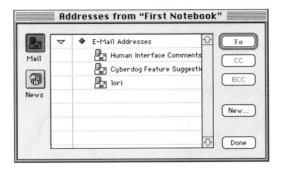

In most cases, developers creating Cyberdog software will continue to use the notebook supplied by Cyberdog. However, you can extend Cyberdog by creating your own custom notebook part.

Navigator

Many kinds of Internet information, such as HTML documents, Gopher directories, and FTP directories, contain links to other information. A **navigator** is a part that assists the user in navigating from location to location quickly and accurately. A navigator is an OpenDoc container part, extended with a subclass of the Cyberdog navigator extension, that embeds Cyberdog display parts, as shown in Figure 1-14.

A Cyberdog display part can choose to display itself in its own window or embedded in a navigator. By convention, display parts whose content includes links to other content are usually displayed embedded in a navigator. The FTP, Gopher, and web display parts supplied with Cyberdog are displayed embedded in a navigator. The user can control whether the same navigator window should be used for all display parts that are opened or whether a new navigator window should be opened for each new display part that is opened by enabling or disabling the Browse in Place menu item in the Navigate menu.

Figure 1-14   The Cyberdog navigator

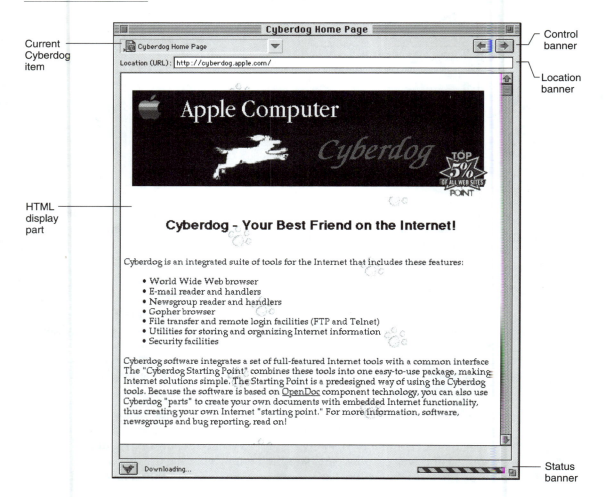

A navigator maintains a **visitation history**; when the user visits an Internet location using a navigator, the Cyberdog item that references the location and the associated Cyberdog display part are added to the navigator's visitation history. The navigator provides a user interface that allows the user to view a list of the items in the visitation history, to move from item to item in the history, and to revisit an item in the history.

The name and icon of the Cyberdog item currently displayed in a navigator is shown in the navigator's control banner. The name of the Cyberdog item also appears in the title of the navigator window. The user can save the Cyberdog item by dragging the icon into a notebook or into the Finder. The control banner contains a pop-up menu that displays the navigator's visitation history and buttons that allow the user to navigate forward and backward in the visitation history.

When the Cyberdog item whose content is being displayed represents a connection to a secure site, the navigator enables a Secure button in the control banner. When the user clicks the Secure button, a Security Info window that contains information about the connection is displayed.

A navigator's location banner contains an editable text field for specifying a URL. The field displays the URL of the current Cyberdog item. The status banner displays status and progress as a Cyberdog item's content is downloaded.

Whenever the navigator is active, a Navigate menu is available in the menu bar to allow the user to perform navigator-related commands such as displaying the visitation history, navigating to the next item or previous item in the visitation history, or refreshing the current display.

In most cases, developers creating Cyberdog software will continue to use the navigator supplied by Cyberdog. However, you can extend Cyberdog by creating your own custom navigator.

Opener Part

When a Cyberdog item is opened with certain protocols, it cannot determine the type of the content referenced by the item until downloading begins. However, in some cases—for instance, when the user drags a Cyberdog item to the Finder or embeds a Cyberdog item in a document—OpenDoc needs to create a part right away, even though the data type to be displayed by the part is not yet known.

In such cases, Cyberdog creates an **opener part,** a transient part used as a substitute during the opening process until the appropriate Cyberdog display part can be opened and switched into the opener part's place. The opener part is an OpenDoc part extended with a subclass of the Cyberdog opener part extension. The opener part can display progress and status information to the user until the appropriate Cyberdog display part can be opened.

In most cases, developers creating Cyberdog software will use the opener part supplied by Cyberdog. However, you can extend Cyberdog by creating your own custom opener part.

Progress Part

A **progress part** displays the progress of an asynchronous process to the user (Figure 1-15). By convention, a progress part is used to display progress when a Cyberdog item is being resolved or when data is downloaded. A progress part is an OpenDoc part extended with a subclass of the Cyberdog progress part extension. The opener part extension and the navigator extension are subclassed from the progress part extension; both the navigator and the opener part can display progress.

Figure 1-15　　An opener part, an example of a progress part

Cyberdog provides two classes of objects to assist a progress part in monitoring and displaying progress: a **progress broadcaster** object and a **progress receiver** object. These two objects work in conjunction with a progress part to monitor and display progress to the user.

A progress broadcaster object represents an asynchronous process, such as a download operation, and its progress toward completion. When a display part initiates an asynchronous process, such as downloading with a stream, it can also create a progress broadcaster object to keep track of the progress of the process. The broadcaster keeps track of the total amount of work to be performed by the process and the amount that has been performed so far.

The display part attaches its broadcaster to the progress part that will display the progress. The progress part has an associated progress receiver object; the progress part attaches its progress receiver to the progress broadcaster.

The display part polls the stream for the status and progress of the download operation and updates the settings of the broadcaster, as shown in Figure 1-16. The broadcaster sends changes to its attached receiver. The progress part gets status and progress from its receiver and displays it to the user.

Figure 1-16   Monitoring and displaying progress

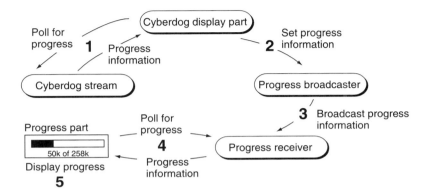

The Cyberdog navigator and opener parts are both progress parts that have their own associated progress receivers. To display the progress of a process, a display part need only create a progress broadcaster, attach it to the progress part, and call the broadcaster's accessor methods to change its progress settings. In most cases, developers creating Cyberdog software will use the progress-part capabilities provided by the navigator and opener part. However, you can extend Cyberdog by creating your own custom progress part and progress receiver.

Download Part

In Cyberdog, a **download part** is a part that is used to download the content referenced by a Cyberdog item and save it to disk. A download part is used in two situations:

- When a user drags a Cyberdog item from a Cyberdog display part to the Finder, the display part creates a download part to download the content referenced by the Cyberdog item and save it to disk.

- If a Cyberdog item is opening and cannot find an appropriate Cyberdog display part editor to bind to, it can bind the data to the download part editor. The download part downloads the content referenced by the Cyberdog item, saves it to disk, and notifies the opener part to open the resulting file.

In both cases, the download part requests a stream from the Cyberdog item and uses the stream to download the data.

Note
Typically, a Cyberdog display part does not use a download part when it downloads content referenced by a Cyberdog item for display. The Cyberdog display part requests a stream from the Cyberdog item; the stream downloads the data. ◆

A download part is provided with Cyberdog. In most cases, developers creating Cyberdog software will continue to use this Cyberdog-supplied download part. However, you can extend Cyberdog by creating your own custom download part.

Development Overview

Contents

This chapter introduces the Cyberdog class library and provides an example of how the key objects in Cyberdog collaborate to download and display network data. In addition, this chapter discusses the process of opening a Cyberdog item and the objects that play a role in that process. For more detailed descriptions of the public Cyberdog classes and methods, see Chapter 7, "Classes and Methods."

Cyberdog Class Library

Cyberdog is a set of classes built on top of OpenDoc. Like OpenDoc, Cyberdog is an object-oriented library that is largely platform independent. As with OpenDoc, you can write a Cyberdog part editor in procedural code and use it within the OpenDoc and Cyberdog class structures. You can easily enhance existing OpenDoc parts to work with Cyberdog. Cyberdog is extensible, and many of its components are replaceable, allowing for innovation by developers at both the system and application levels.

Cyberdog and OpenDoc are implemented as shared libraries consisting of a set of classes constructed using **System Object Model (SOM),** a specification for object binding at runtime. Because Cyberdog and OpenDoc both use SOM, Cyberdog parts and components that have been created with different compilers or in completely different programming languages can nevertheless communicate properly with each other. Furthermore, they can be independently revised and extended and still work together.

The interfaces to all of Cyberdog's classes are specified in the **Interface Definition Language (IDL),** a programming-language-neutral syntax for creating interfaces. IDL interfaces are typically compiled separately from implementation code, using a SOM compiler.

For more information on SOM and using the SOM compiler on the Mac OS platform, see *OpenDoc Cookbook for the Mac OS* and *OpenDoc Programmer's Guide for the Mac OS.* For a more detailed description of IDL and instructions on programming with SOM, see *SOMObjects Developer Toolkit Users Guide* and *SOMObjects Developer Toolkit Programmers Reference Manual* from IBM.

Class Hierarchy

Cyberdog classes create objects that cooperate in referencing, downloading, and displaying remotely located content. Because the Cyberdog class library builds on the OpenDoc class library, you must use both class libraries to create Cyberdog components.

All Cyberdog classes are derived from the OpenDoc superclass `ODObject`, itself a subclass of `somObject`, the fundamental SOM superclass. The Cyberdog classes can be divided into three groups according to their uses:

- classes that you use when you create a Cyberdog display part

- classes that you use when you create a Cyberdog service

- classes that you use when you create a custom Cyberdog supporting part, such as a log or notebook

Two additional Cyberdog classes, `CyberSession` and `CyberExtension`, are used more generally. An object of class `CyberSession` represents a single Cyberdog process; the `CyberSession` interface provides access to a number of Cyberdog utilities. Class `CyberExtension`, a subclass of class `ODExtension`, is the abstract superclass for all Cyberdog-specific extensions.

Classes for Cyberdog Display Parts

The classes shown in Figure 2-1 are classes you subclass or use to create a Cyberdog display part. The figure shows these categories of classes:

- Names in bold represent abstract superclasses that you are likely to subclass when creating a Cyberdog display part.

- Names in italics represent classes whose objects you may create when creating a Cyberdog display part.

- Names in plain text represent classes whose objects you call but typically never have to create; they are created for you by Cyberdog.

Figure 2-1   Classes for creating a Cyberdog display part

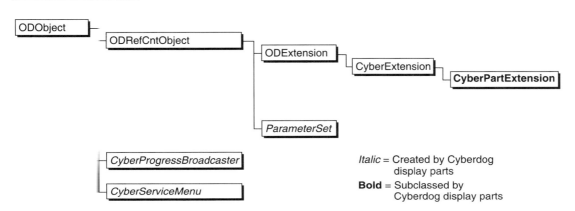

Italic = Created by Cyberdog
display parts
Bold = Subclassed by
Cyberdog display parts

A Cyberdog display part is an OpenDoc part (an object of an ODPart subclass) with an extension subclassed from the CyberPartExtension class. The CyberPartExtension object provides the Cyberdog-specific public interface for a Cyberdog display part.

The CyberPartExtension class is an abstract superclass with 12 methods, all of which you can override. At a minimum, Cyberdog display part developers usually override the OpenCyberItem method in their CyberPartExtension subclass. OpenCyberItem is called to notify the Cyberdog display part that it is being opened by a Cyberdog item, rather than in some other way, such as being restored from disk. Your implementation of OpenCyberItem depends on the desired behavior of your Cyberdog display part; a common behavior involves opening the display part and creating and opening a Cyberdog stream to download the content referenced by its Cyberdog item.

CyberProgressBroadcaster is an implemented class that a Cyberdog display part can instantiate directly to represent the progress of an asynchronous process, such as a download operation. If you display your display part embedded in a navigator, you can use the navigator and its associated progress receiver to display progress. However, if you want to implement your own progress part, you must subclass and implement the CyberProgressPartExtension and CyberProgressReceiver classes.

In addition, if you want your display part to include the Cyberdog service-related menus in its menu bar, you must create and initialize an object of the fully implemented CyberServiceMenu class. When your display part handles a menu event, adjusts its menus, and acquires or loses the menu focus, it should call the appropriate `CyberServiceMenu` methods to allow the service-related menus to handle their menu commands, adjust menus, and show and hide menus.

The `ParameterSet` class is a Cyberdog utility class. An object of class `ParameterSet` defines an arbitrary collection of objects. Parameter sets are general purpose objects; you can use them in any way you want. In Cyberdog, a parameter set is used during the opening of a Cyberdog item. For example, if a client wants a Cyberdog item to open embedded in a navigator, it can add, to the parameter set that is passed to the opening Cyberdog item, a pointer to the navigator.

Classes for Cyberdog Services

The classes shown in Figure 2-2 are classes you subclass or use to create a Cyberdog service.

Figure 2-2   Classes for creating a Cyberdog service

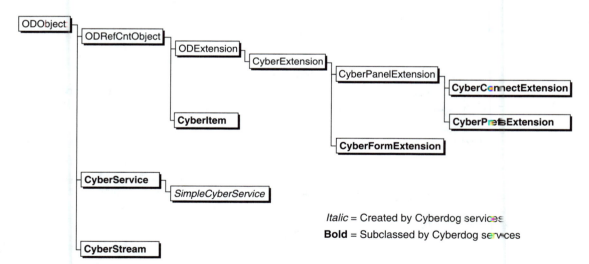

If you are adding a new service to Cyberdog, you will subclass the following abstract superclasses:

■ The class `CyberService` represents a Cyberdog service. A `CyberService` object acts as the representative object for the suite of objects that collectively implement a network protocol. `CyberService` is an abstract superclass with 12 methods, most of which you may override. The class `SimpleCyberService` is an implemented subclass of `CyberService`. The `SimpleCyberService` class is a simple, resource-driven service that you can instantiate or subclass.

■ The class `CyberItem` represents a Cyberdog item. `CyberItem` is subclassed by protocol; each subclass understands how to address information for that protocol. `CyberItem` has 24 methods, most of which you must override when you subclass `CyberItem` to support a new protocol.

■ The class `CyberStream` represents a Cyberdog stream. `CyberStream` is subclassed by protocol; each subclass understands how to download data for that protocol. If you add support for a new protocol and you intend to use a Cyberdog stream to download data, you must subclass the `CyberStream` class. `CyberStream` has 11 methods, most of which you must override.

■ The class `CyberConnectExtension` is a subclass of class `CyberPanelExtension`. A subclass of `CyberConnectExtension` represents an object you can use to create a part to use as a panel in the Connect To dialog box. Your custom panel should contain user interface elements that allow the user to specify the appropriate connection information for the new service. `CyberConnectExtension` has one method, which returns the Cyberdog item specified by the user; you must override this method.

■ The class `CyberPrefsExtension` is a subclass of class `CyberPanelExtension`. A subclass of `CyberPrefsExtension` represents an object you can use to create a part to use as a panel in the Preferences dialog box. Your custom panel should contain user interface elements that allow the user to specify meaningful preferences for the new service. `CyberPrefsExtension` has methods for saving and restoring preferences; you must override these methods.

■ The class `CyberFormExtension`, when subclassed, represents an object you can use to extend a Cyberdog item so that it can submit an HTML form. If you intend to develop a service for accessing data using HTTP protocol, you must subclass the `CyberFormExtension` class. `CyberFormExtension` has five methods, all of which you must override.

Classes for Supporting Parts

Cyberdog provides a number of classes, shown in Figure 2-3, that you can subclass and implement to replace Cyberdog supporting parts, such as the log or the notebook, with your own custom parts.

Figure 2-3   Classes for creating supporting parts

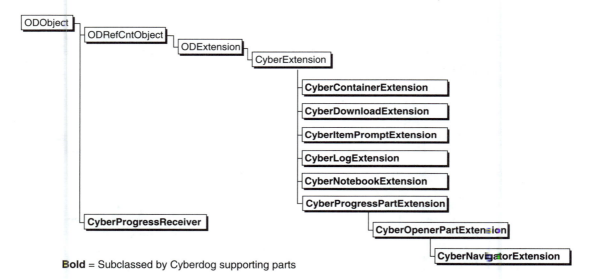

Bold = Subclassed by Cyberdog supporting parts

- To create a custom log part, you must subclass and implement the `CyberLogExtension` class.

- To create a custom notebook part, you must subclass and implement the `CyberNotebookExtension` class.

- To create a custom navigator part, you must subclass and implement the `CyberNavigatorExtension` class.

- The classes `CyberProgressPartExtension` and `CyberProgressReceiver` can be used together to implement a progress part that monitors and displays the progress of any asynchronous process. The Cyberdog navigator and opener parts are progress parts; you can use them to display progress. To create a custom progress part, you must subclass and implement both

`CyberProgressPartExtension` and `CyberProgressReceiver`. An object of class `CyberProgressBroadcaster` broadcasts progress information to a progress part's receiver. You can directly instantiate `CyberProgressBroadcaster`.

■ To create a custom opener part, you must subclass and implement the `CyberOpenerPartExtension` class.

■ To create a custom download part, you must subclass and implement the `CyberDownloadExtension` class.

■ To create a custom Connect To or Preferences dialog box, you must subclass and implement the `CyberContainerExtension` class. To extend a Connect To dialog box to allow it to return the Cyberdog item entered by the user, you must also subclass and implement the `CyberItemPromptExtension` class.

Note
In addition to the extensions described above, the Cyberdog-supplied download part, opener part, and navigator part are also extended with a subclass of class `CyberPartExtension`. ◆

Runtime Object Relationships

The runtime state of Cyberdog involves relationships among a variety of objects instantiated from Cyberdog classes. Taken together, the diagrams in this section show the principal runtime relationships among the major Cyberdog objects. The details of the interactions among the objects are explained elsewhere in this book.

The Cyberdog Session

Figure 2-4 shows a runtime object diagram depicting the relationships among the key objects in a Cyberdog session.

Figure 2-4   Object relationships of the Cyberdog session

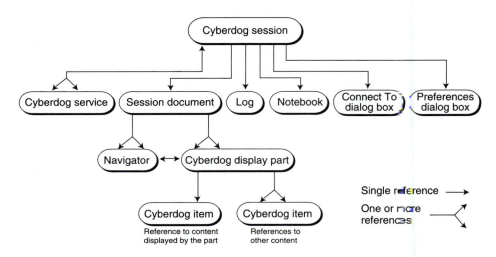

All of the objects in a Cyberdog session share the same process. The Cyberdog session has multiple Cyberdog service objects, one for each supported service. The Cyberdog session maintains references to the log, notebook, Connect To dialog box, and Preferences dialog box.

In addition, the Cyberdog session has a single session document that contains all open navigators. The session document also contains all open Cyberdog display parts, some of which may be embedded in navigators.

A Cyberdog display part displays the content referenced by a Cyberdog item; the display part may also keep track of other Cyberdog items that correspond to other remotely located content.

Note

In Figure 2-4, the log, notebook, navigator, Preferences dialog box, and Cyberdog display part are all actually composed of two objects: an object of an `ODPart` subclass extended with the appropriate extension object. For example, the log is an object of an `ODPart` subclass extended with an object of a `CyberLogExtension` subclass. The Connect To dialog box is an object of an `ODPart` subclass with two extensions: an extension subclassed from `CyberContainerExtension` and an extension subclassed from `CyberItemPromptExtension`. ◆

Display Part Objects

Figure 2-5 shows the runtime object relationships among the objects involved with a Cyberdog display part.

Figure 2-5   Object relationships of Cyberdog display parts

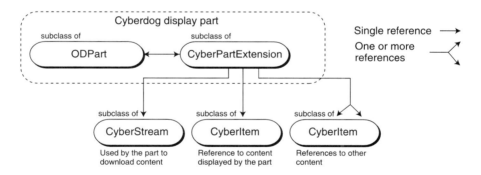

A Cyberdog display part is composed of an object of an `ODPart` subclass extended with a subclass of `CyberPartExtension`. A Cyberdog display part displays the content referenced by its Cyberdog item (an object of a `CyberItem` subclass). If the displayed content includes links to other network data, the Cyberdog display part creates and caches a Cyberdog item for each link.

When the Cyberdog display part needs to download the content referenced by its Cyberdog item, it creates a Cyberdog stream (an object of a `CyberStream` subclass) and uses it to download the data. When the data is finished downloading, the Cyberdog display part deletes the Cyberdog stream.

Note
Figure 2-5 shows the part extension maintaining the references to the Cyberdog items and the Cyberdog stream. In fact, the references can also be maintained by the part itself. Whether the references are maintained in a Cyberdog display part or its extension depends on the implementation. ◆

Progress Monitoring Objects

Figure 2-6 shows the runtime object relationships among objects used to monitor and display the progress of an asynchronous process.

Figure 2-6   Object relationships of progress monitoring objects

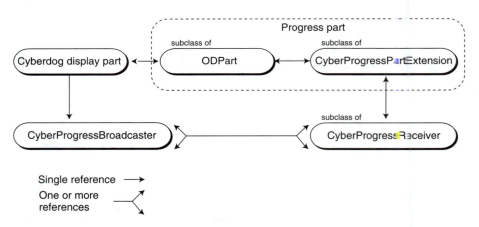

When a Cyberdog display part initiates an asynchronous process, it creates a progress broadcaster object. The display part acquires a progress part (the navigator, for example) and attaches the progress broadcaster to the progress part. The progress part has an associated progress receiver. The progress part attaches its progress receiver to the progress broadcaster.

The Cyberdog display part monitors the asynchronous process and updates the progress values in the progress broadcaster accordingly. The broadcaster notifies its attached receiver of the updates. The progress part retrieves progress information from its receiver and updates its display.

Typically, a single broadcaster is attached to a single receiver. However, it is possible to attach multiple receivers to a broadcaster or multiple broadcasters to a receiver.

Log and Notebook Objects

Figure 2-7 shows the runtime object relationships among objects used to create the Cyberdog log and notebook.

Figure 2-7   Object relationships of the log and notebook

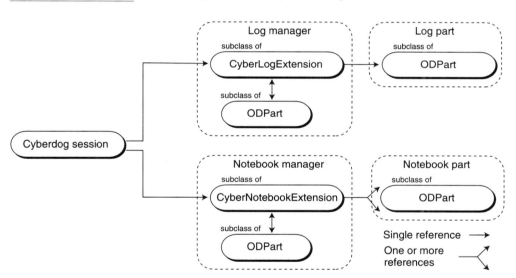

The Cyberdog session maintains references to the Cyberdog log and the Cyberdog notebook.

The Cyberdog log implementation is divided between two parts: a log manager and a log part. The Cyberdog log manager (kLogManagerKind) is composed of an object of an ODPart subclass extended with a subclass of

CyberLogExtension. The log manager does not provide a user interface. The log user interface is provided by the log part (kLogKind). The log part is an object of an ODPart subclass.

Similarly, the Cyberdog notebook implementation is divided between two parts: a notebook manager and a notebook part. The Cyberdog notebook manager (kNotebookManagerKind) is composed of an object of an ODPart subclass extended with a subclass of CyberNotebookExtension. The notebook manager does not provide a user interface. The notebook user interface is provided by the notebook part (kNotebookKind). The notebook part is an object of an ODPart subclass.

Service Menu Objects

Figure 2-8 shows the runtime object relationships among objects used to display service-related menus for a Cyberdog display part.

Figure 2-8   Object relationships of service menu objects

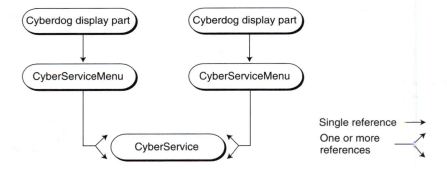

A Cyberdog display part may choose to display the Cyberdog menu and Cyberdog service-related menus when the part gets the focus. To do this, the Cyberdog display part creates a single CyberServiceMenu object. When the Cyberdog display part adjusts its menu bar, receives a menu event, or acquires or loses the menu focus, it notifies the CyberServiceMenu object. The CyberServiceMenu object iterates through all of the Cyberdog services, giving each service the opportunity to handle its menus.

Dialog Box Objects

This section describes the runtime object relationships among objects used to create the Cyberdog Preferences and Connect To dialog boxes.

Preferences Dialog Box

Figure 2-9 shows the runtime object relationships among objects used to create the Cyberdog Preferences dialog box.

Figure 2-9   Object relationships of the Preferences dialog box

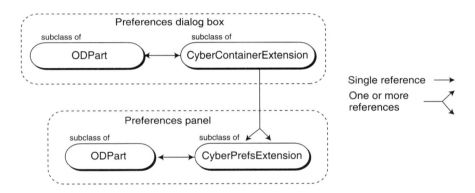

The Cyberdog Preferences dialog box is composed of an object of an ODPart subclass extended with a subclass of CyberContainerExtension. The Preferences dialog box embeds multiple Preferences panels. Each Preferences panel is composed of an object of an ODPart subclass extended with a subclass of CyberPrefsExtension.

Connect To Dialog Box

Figure 2-10 shows the runtime object relationships among objects used to create the Cyberdog Connect To dialog box.

Figure 2-10   Object relationships of the Connect To dialog box

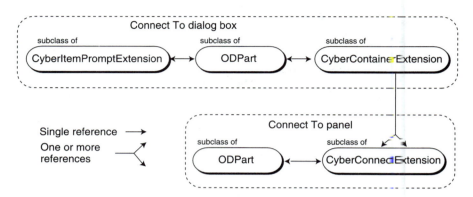

The Cyberdog Connect To dialog box is composed of an object of an ODPart subclass and two extensions: a subclass of CyberContainerExtension and a subclass of CyberItemPromptExtension. The Connect To dialog box embeds multiple Connect To panels. Each Connect To panel is composed of an object of an ODPart subclass extended with a subclass of CyberConnectExtension.

A Cyberdog Example

This section describes an example that illustrates how the key Cyberdog objects cooperate at runtime to access and display Internet data. The example includes two Cyberdog display parts:

■ The Gopher display part displays the contents of a Gopher directory from a Gopher server. The Gopher display part is displayed embedded in the navigator.

■ The text display part displays a text item stored on a Gopher server. The text display part is displayed in its own window.

Gopher Display Part

The Cyberdog Gopher display part, shown in Figure 2-11, displays Gopher directories; it knows how to interpret data coming from a Gopher server and how to display Gopher directories in a meaningful way. In particular, the

Gopher display part knows that the Gopher directory entries represent links to other data located on the Gopher server and displays those links differently from other content. When the user clicks on a link, the Gopher display part initiates retrieving the content referenced by the link.

Figure 2-11   The Gopher display part embedded in the navigator

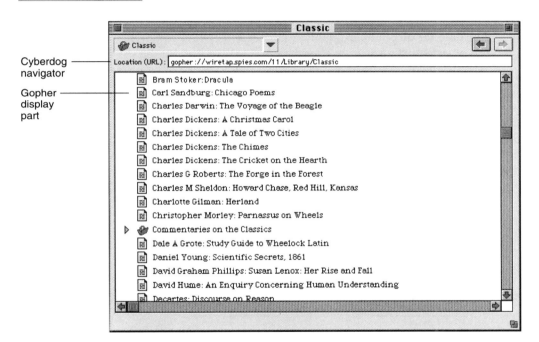

Cyberdog navigator

Gopher display part

In addition to displaying the contents of a Gopher directory, the Gopher display part must be able to

■ download Gopher directories using a stream

■ display status information while downloading

■ add its menu items to the menu bar

■ interact with the log and the notebook

■ embed itself in a navigator

In addition to its Cyberdog-specific features, the Gopher display part retains all the features of an ordinary OpenDoc part. It can display content, be embedded in other parts, store its content, and so on.

The Gopher display part is embedded in the Cyberdog navigator; both the Gopher display part and the navigator are contained in the Cyberdog session document. The Gopher display part has an extension subclassed from `CyberPartExtension`. The extension receives Cyberdog-related messages; the part and its extension cooperate to respond to those messages.

The Gopher display part displays the content referenced by a `GopherItem` object (an object subclassed from class `CyberItem`). In addition, the Gopher display part caches a `GopherItem` object for each link in the Gopher directory. The Gopher display part is responsible for initiating a response when the user clicks on a link. The runtime object relationships of the Gopher display part are shown in Figure 2-12.

Figure 2-12   Gopher display part runtime object relationships

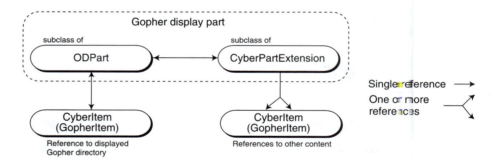

Creating and Opening the Text Display Part

When the user clicks on one of the links shown in Figure 2-11, the Gopher display part calls the corresponding Cyberdog item's `Open` method. The `Open` method does two things:

- It creates a Cyberdog text display part because the Cyberdog item the user clicked on references text data.

- It calls the text display part's `OpenCyberItem` method to notify the text display part it is being opened by a Cyberdog item.

The Cyberdog text display part is an OpenDoc part whose part editor can display text and has been extended with a `CyberPartExtension` subclass. The text display part is created in the Cyberdog session document. The part editor for the Cyberdog text display part is shown in Figure 2-13.

Figure 2-13   The text display part

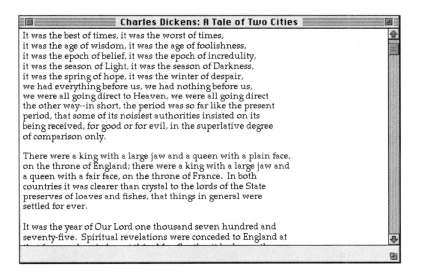

Once the text display part has been created, the Cyberdog item's `Open` method calls the text display part's `OpenCyberItem` method, passing the text display part the `CyberItem` object to be opened. The default implementation of `OpenCyberItem` does two things:

- It calls `SetCyberItem` to cache the `CyberItem` object in the text display part's extension.

- It calls the text display part's `Open` method, which opens the part.

Developers of Cyberdog display parts usually override `OpenCyberItem` to receive notification that the part is opening; typically, in addition to the implementation described above, `OpenCyberItem` creates a Cyberdog stream, initiates the download operation, and adds the Cyberdog item to the log.

Downloading Content to the Text Display Part

Once the text display part has been created, it needs to download the content referenced by its Cyberdog item. The Cyberdog item relies on a Cyberdog stream to download the data for the text display part.

In its `OpenCyberItem` method, the text display part requests a stream object from its Cyberdog item by calling the Cyberdog item's `CreateCyberStream` method. The Cyberdog item returns a `GopherStream` object (an object subclassed from class `CyberStream`), initialized to download the data referenced by the Cyberdog item from the Gopher server. Then, `OpenCyberItem` calls the stream's `Open` method to initiate the download operation.

Figure 2-14 shows the runtime relationships between the text display part, the Cyberdog item, and the Cyberdog stream.

Figure 2-14   Downloading object relationships

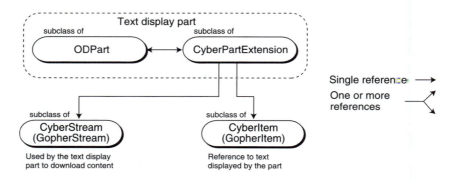

The stream's `Open` method signals the stream to start downloading. `Open` is an asynchronous method; it returns to the Cyberdog text display part immediately, and the stream proceeds to download at its own pace in a separate thread. The stream needs to resolve the address to find the data, establish a connection, and begin downloading the data.

The text display part calls the stream's `GetStreamStatus` method periodically to monitor the progress of the download operation. `GetStreamStatus` returns a set of flags that indicate status and error conditions. In particular, `GetStreamStatus` returns the `kCDDataAvailable` flag when the stream has some data downloaded and ready for the text display part to read. If data is available, the text display part calls the stream's `GetBuffer` method to retrieve a buffer of downloaded data. When the text display part is finished using a buffer, it calls `ReleaseBuffer` to release the buffer back to the stream. When `GetStreamStatus` returns the `kCDDownloadComplete` flag, the text display part deletes the stream object.

The stream methods `GetStreamStatus`, `GetBuffer`, and `ReleaseBuffer` are all synchronous methods; they are designed so that a stream object can always respond immediately. The stream knows its status without any lengthy computation, and `GetBuffer` and `ReleaseBuffer` operate on data the stream has already downloaded.

Cyberdog Item Opening Process

This section discusses the opening process of a Cyberdog item and how various Cyberdog objects play a role in that process. It begins with a description of how Cyberdog items are manipulated and stored. Then it discusses the opening process, including a description of the roles played by the Cyberdog item, Cyberdog display part, opener part, navigator, and download part. Finally, it describes various scenarios for implementing a Cyberdog item's `Open` method and a Cyberdog display part's `OpenCyberItem` method.

Manipulating and Storing Cyberdog Items

In order to understand the opening process of a Cyberdog item, it is useful to first understand the different ways in which a Cyberdog item is represented and how those representations are manipulated and stored.

When displayed as an icon in a window, such as the log, a notebook, or a web page, a Cyberdog item is an object in memory; it is not an OpenDoc part. A user can open a Cyberdog item that is in memory by clicking on its icon. This action results in a call to the Cyberdog item's `Open` method.

Cyberdog items implement their opening behavior; in other words, they know how to open themselves. In the simplest cases, `Open` creates a Cyberdog display part and calls its `OpenCyberItem` method. `OpenCyberItem` initiates a download of the data referenced by the Cyberdog item and displays the display part. For more information on the objects involved in the opening process, see "Object Roles in the Opening Process" (page 72).

When the user drags a Cyberdog item object (from a notebook, for example), the Cyberdog item is stored in the storage unit of the OpenDoc drag-and-drop object as kind `kCyberItemKind`. The destination of the drop determines what happens.

- If the destination of the drop is the desktop or a Finder window, the Cyberdog item is stored as an OpenDoc part whose part kind is `kCyberItemKind`. If the user clicks on that part, OpenDoc creates an opener part (which binds to parts of kind `kCyberItemKind`) to open the part.

- If the destination of the drop is a container that does not manipulate data of kind `kCyberItemKind`, the container creates an embedded part, clones the content of the drag-and-drop storage unit into its draft, and embeds the new part at an appropriate location in its content. Because the kind of the storage unit is `kCyberItemKind`, OpenDoc creates an opener part to display the part.

- If the destination of the drop is a container that does manipulate data of kind `kCyberItemKind`, the container can incorporate the data. For example, the container might display the Cyberdog item as an icon instead of displaying the content the item references.

Copying and pasting of Cyberdog items are handled in a similar fashion.

Object Roles in the Opening Process

"A Cyberdog Example" (page 66) shows how to open a Cyberdog item that references content stored on a Gopher server. Because that Cyberdog item references text, it creates a Cyberdog text display part. The text display part downloads the data and displays it. That example represents the simplest case of opening a Cyberdog item: the Cyberdog item knows the type of the data it references and the text display part opens itself immediately.

The primary responsibility for opening a Cyberdog item is shared between the Cyberdog item being opened (the Cyberdog item's `Open` method) and the display part that will display the data referenced by the Cyberdog item (the display part's `OpenCyberItem` method). However, opening a Cyberdog item is more complex in these situations:

- The Cyberdog item cannot identify the type of the data it references and thus cannot create a display part immediately.

- The Cyberdog item can identify the type of data it references, but cannot create a Cyberdog display part capable of downloading and displaying that type of data.

- The Cyberdog display part cannot open until all the data it is to display has been downloaded. For example, the Cyberdog QuickTime display part does not open until all of its data has been downloaded.

- The Cyberdog display part is embedded in a navigator.

The Cyberdog item and the Cyberdog display part may rely on other objects, such as an opener part, a navigator, or a download part, in these more complex opening scenarios.

Role of the Cyberdog Item

A Cyberdog item's `Open` method is responsible for

- **resolving,** or determining the type of data it refers to

- creating a Cyberdog display part appropriate for the data type in the appropriate document

- calling the display part's `OpenCyberItem` method

Some Cyberdog items (Gopher items, for example) are resolved inherently; they always refer to a single, known type of data. If you are developing a Cyberdog item that is resolved inherently, your Cyberdog item's `Open` method can be synchronous.

Some other Cyberdog items (HTTP items, for example) cannot be resolved without communicating with the server on which the data they reference resides. If you are developing a Cyberdog item that is not resolved inherently, your Cyberdog item's `Open` method must be asynchronous.

Role of the Display Part

When a Cyberdog item calls a Cyberdog display part's `OpenCyberItem` method, the display part is responsible for the following:

- It must perform tasks to prepare for displaying the data referenced by its Cyberdog item, such as creating a stream and opening it to initiate the download operation.

- It must call its inherited `OpenCyberItem` method, which displays the display part.

Some display parts (the Cyberdog HTML display part, for example) display data as it is downloaded; they do not wait to display until all the data has been downloaded. If you want your display part to display before the data referenced by its Cyberdog item has been completely downloaded, the display part's `OpenCyberItem` method can be synchronous.

Some other display parts (the Cyberdog QuickTime display part, for example) do not display until all of the data they are to display has been downloaded. If you do not want your display part to display until the data referenced by its Cyberdog item has been completely downloaded, the display part's `OpenCyberItem` method must be asynchronous.

In addition, a Cyberdog display part decides whether it is to be embedded in a navigator. If your display part is to be embedded in a navigator, you need to modify your `OpenCyberItem` method to obtain a navigator and call its `GoToCyberItem` method.

Role of the Opener Part

The primary purpose of the opener part is to bridge the gap between a Cyberdog item stored in an OpenDoc document and the Cyberdog display part that displays the content referenced by the Cyberdog item. To bridge this gap, the opener part does the following:

- It binds to parts of kind `kCyberItemKind`.

- It serves as a placeholder in a document until the appropriate display part can be opened. The opener part replaces itself in a document, putting the resulting display part in its stead.

A secondary purpose of the opener part is to display progress to the user during an asynchronous operation. A Cyberdog item or Cyberdog display part that initiates an asynchronous operation can attach a progress broadcaster to the opener part and use the opener part to display progress.

An **initial opener part** is an opener part created by OpenDoc to bind to a part of kind `kCyberItemKind`. In this situation, the initial opener part is passed as a parameter to the Cyberdog item's `Open` method. However, before the Cyberdog item can use the initial opener part, the item must first **obtain** it from the Cyberdog session by calling the session object's `ObtainOpener` method; this method returns an **obtained opener part.**

You should always use the opener part returned by `ObtainOpener` and should not assume that it is the same as the initial opener part that you passed in. Once you have obtained an opener part, you should use the opener part's methods to manipulate it. For example, you should not call an obtained opener part's `Open` method or place the opener part in an embedded frame. You can call

ObtainOpener without worrying about whether it has already been called during the opening of a given Cyberdog item; the method can be called more than once.

Binding to Stored Cyberdog Items

When a Cyberdog item is stored in a storage unit (for example, when it is stored on the desktop as a reference) its part kind is kCyberItemKind. If the user later clicks on the Cyberdog item's reference icon on the desktop, OpenDoc attempts to create a part for the storage unit. Because the storage unit contains data of kind kCyberItemKind, OpenDoc creates an opener part.

The opener part reads the Cyberdog item from the storage unit by calling CyberSession::CreateCyberItemFromSU. The opener part waits until it is displayed in a frame and then calls the Cyberdog item's Open method, passing itself as the initial opener part.

Acting as a Placeholder for Display Parts

If either the Cyberdog item's Open method or the Cyberdog display part's OpenCyberItem method is asynchronous, the method must obtain an opener part by calling CyberSession::ObtainOpener and attach to the opener part a progress broadcaster representing the asynchronous operation. If either Open or OpenCyberItem is passed an opener part as a parameter, the method can try to obtain that opener part by passing it as a parameter to ObtainOpener. However, ObtainOpener may return a different opener part than the one passed to it.

The opener part opens in its own window or in an embedded frame and displays progress during the opening process. The opener part is responsible for ensuring that a Cyberdog display part is created in the appropriate document and displayed in the right place on the screen.

- Your Cyberdog item's Open method must call CyberSession::CreateCyberPart to create a display part. This method creates the display part in either an OpenDoc document or the session document, depending on which document contains the opener part.

- Unless your display part is to be embedded in a navigator, your part's OpenCyberItem method must call its inherited method to display the part. The inherited OpenCyberItem method checks whether an opener part is being used. If so, the inherited method calls the opener part's OpenPart method; OpenPart ensures that the display part is displayed in the right place. If not, the inherited method calls the display part's Open method.

Role of the Navigator

A navigator is a special type of opener part; `CyberNavigatorExtension` is a subclass of `CyberOpenerPartExtension`. As an opener part, a navigator can be a placeholder in a document during the opening process and can display progress. Unlike other opener parts, a navigator does not replace itself in a document, putting the resulting display part in its stead. Rather, the display part is embedded in the navigator. Also, a navigator does not bind to parts of kind `kCyberItemKind`.

The calling Cyberdog item may pass a navigator as a parameter to a Cyberdog display part's `OpenCyberItem` method. However, it is up to the display part to decide whether it will be embedded in a navigator.

A display part that wants to be embedded in a navigator must obtain a navigator by calling `ObtainOpener`, passing `kNavigatorKind` as the part kind of the opener part. The display part should always use the navigator returned by `ObtainOpener`. If a navigator was passed into the `OpenCyberItem` method, the display part can try to obtain that navigator by passing it as a parameter to `ObtainOpener`. However, `ObtainOpener` may not return the same navigator that the display part passed to it. For example, if the user has disabled the Browse in Place menu item in the Navigate menu, `ObtainOpener` returns a new navigator.

Once the display part has obtained a navigator, the display part should call the navigator's `GoToCyberItem` method, which displays the display part in the navigator.

Role of the Download Part

A Cyberdog item calls `CyberSession::CreateCyberPart` to create an appropriate Cyberdog display part for the data type referenced by the item. If no Cyberdog display part editor is available for that data type, `CreateCyberPart` cannot create a Cyberdog display part. If so, the Cyberdog item can use a download part to download the data referenced by the item, save it to a file, and attempt to open the file in some other way.

To create a download part, the Cyberdog item calls `CyberSession::CreatePartInCyberDocument`, passing `kDownloadPartKind` as the part kind to be created. The Cyberdog item calls the resulting download part's `OpenCyberItem` method, which takes these actions:

■ It obtains an opener part by calling `CyberSession::ObtainOpener`, passing `kOpenerPartKind` as the opener part kind.

- It downloads the data referenced by the Cyberdog item and saves it to a file.

- It calls the opener part's `OpenFile` method. `OpenFile` tries to find a part editor (a non-Cyberdog part editor) that can open files of this type; if it cannot, it asks the Finder to open the file.

Implementing the Opening Methods

Responsibility for opening a Cyberdog item is divided between the `Open` method of the Cyberdog item being opened and the `OpenCyberItem` method of the display part that will display the data referenced by the Cyberdog item.

Implementing a Cyberdog Item's Open Method

The Cyberdog item's `Open` method is responsible for determining the type of data the item references, creating an appropriate display part for that type of data, and calling the display part's `OpenCyberItem` method.

If you are developing your own Cyberdog item, you must subclass the `CyberItem` class and override your subclass's `Open` method to implement the item's opening behavior.

Open as a Synchronous Method

If a Cyberdog item is inherently resolved, its `Open` method can be asynchronous. Before returning, `Open` calls the Cyberdog display part's `OpenCyberItem` method, which displays the display part. In this case, the `Open` method should perform the following steps:

1. If the parameter set contains either an initial or an obtained opener part, retrieve it. For example, the parameter set may contain an opener part if the Cyberdog item is being opened from a storage unit, as discussed in "Binding to Stored Cyberdog Items" (page 75).

```
if (params)
    if (!params->GetParameter (ev, kCDInitialOpenerPartKey,
        &openerPart))
    params->GetParameter (ev, kCDObtainedOpenerPartKey, &openerPart);
```

2. Call `CyberSession::GetISOTypeFromMIMEType` to translate the MIME type of the data referenced by the Cyberdog item to a part kind.

```
ODValueType kind = cyberSession (ev)->GetISOTypeFromMIMEType (ev,
    someMIMEType);
```

3. Call `CyberSession::CreateCyberPart` to create the part, passing the part kind and the opener part, if any. `CreateCyberPart` determines whether to create the new part in the session document or in another OpenDoc document by checking which document the opener part is contained in.

```
ODPart* part = cyberSession->CreateCyberPart (ev, openerPart,
    kind, kODNULL);
```

4. If `CreateCyberPart` cannot create a Cyberdog display part for the type of data referenced by the Cyberdog item and the referenced data can be downloaded, call `CyberSession::CreatePartInCyberDocument` to create a download part.

```
if (!part && this->IsDownloadable (ev))
    part = cyberSession->CreatePartInCyberDocument (ev,
        kDownloadPartKind, kODNULL);
```

5. Call the display part's (or the download part's) `OpenCyberItem` method.

```
CyberPartExtension* CyberPartExt = part->GetExtension (ev,
    kCyberPartExtension);
CyberPartExt->OpenCyberItem (ev, this, openerPart, params);
CyberPartExt->Release (ev);
```

Open as an Asynchronous Method

If the Cyberdog item is not inherently resolved, its `Open` method must be asynchronous. In this case, the Cyberdog item must obtain an opener part to act as a placeholder and to display progress until an appropriate Cyberdog display part can be created. The Cyberdog item defers the call to `OpenCyberItem` until the display part is created. In this case, `Open` should perform the following steps:

1. Determine whether the Cyberdog item has been resolved by calling its `isResolved` method. If the Cyberdog item is resolved, perform steps 1 to 5 described in "Open as a Synchronous Method" (page 77).

2. If the Cyberdog item has not been resolved, retrieve an initial or obtained opener part, if any, from the parameter set. For example, the parameter set may contain an opener part if the Cyberdog item is being opened from a storage unit, as discussed in "Binding to Stored Cyberdog Items" (page 75).

```
if (params)
    if (!params->GetParameter (ev, kCDInitialOpenerPartKey,
        &openerPart))
        params->GetParameter (ev, kCDObtainedOpenerPartKey,
            &openerPart);
```

3. Call the `CyberSession::ObtainOpener` method to obtain an opener part, passing the opener part retrieved from the parameter set, if any. You should acquire the parameter set before passing it to `ObtainOpener`. If no parameter set was passed to the `Open` method, you should create one before calling `ObtainOpener`.

```
openerPart = cyberSession->ObtainOpener (ev, openerPart,
    kODNULL, this, params);
```

4. Call the Cyberdog item's `Resolve` method, passing a pointer to a notification function that `Resolve` can call when the Cyberdog item is resolved.

```
this->Resolve (ev, MyCyberItemResolved, params, openerPart);
```

Your Cyberdog item's `Resolve` method should initiate whatever process is necessary for its resolution, such as creating and opening a Cyberdog stream. To display progress during the resolution process, the `Resolve` method should attach a progress broadcaster to the opener part and call the broadcaster's accessor methods to update its progress settings. When the `Resolve` method has finished trying to resolve the Cyberdog item, it should call the notification function.

Note
Do not call the resolution notification function at interrupt time. ◆

Your resolution notification function should check the error code parameter to determine whether the Cyberdog item was resolved successfully. If the Cyberdog item is resolved, the resolution notification function should perform steps 1 to 5 described in "Open as a Synchronous Method" (page 77). The resolution notification function should release the parameter set.

Implementing a Display Part's OpenCyberItem Method

The Cyberdog display part's `OpenCyberItem` method is responsible for downloading and displaying the data referenced by the Cyberdog item. If you are developing your own Cyberdog display part, you must subclass `CyberPartExtension` and override your subclass's `OpenCyberItem` method.

OpenCyberItem as a Synchronous Method

A Cyberdog display part's `OpenCyberItem` method can be synchronous if the display part can be displayed before all of the data it is to display has been downloaded. In this case, `OpenCyberItem` should perform the following steps:

1. Call the Cyberdog item's `CreateCyberStream` method to retrieve a stream for downloading the data, and call the stream's `Open` method to initiate the download operation.

   ```
   fMyStream = fMyItem->CreateCyberStream (ev);
   fMyStream->Open (ev);
   ```

2. Retrieve the Cyberdog item's parent item, if any, from the parameter set, and call `CyberSession::AddCyberItemToLog` to add the Cyberdog item to the log.

   ```
   CyberItem* parent = kODNULL;
   if (params)
       params->GetParameter (ev, kCDParentItemKey, &parent);
   GetCyberSession (ev)->AddCyberItemToLog (ev, parent, fMyItem);
   ```

3. Call the inherited `OpenCyberItem` method, which displays the display part.

   ```
   inherited::OpenCyberItem (item, openerPart, params);
   ```

OpenCyberItem as an Asynchronous Method

If a Cyberdog display part cannot be displayed until all the content referenced by its Cyberdog item has been downloaded, the display part's `OpenCyberItem` method must be asynchronous. `OpenCyberItem` does not call its inherited method; calling the inherited method is deferred until the data has been downloaded.

In this case, `OpenCyberItem` should perform the following steps:

1. Retrieve the Cyberdog item's parent item, if any, from the parameter set, and call `CyberSession::AddCyberItemToLog` to add the Cyberdog item to the log.

```
CyberItem* parent = kODNULL;
if (params)
    params->GetParameter (ev, kCDParentItemKey, &parent);
GetCyberSession (ev)->AddCyberItemToLog (ev, parent, fMyItem);
```

2. Call the `CyberSession::ObtainOpener` method to obtain an opener part, which will be used to display progress until the display part can be displayed. You must acquire the parameter set before passing it to `ObtainOpener`. If no parameter set was passed to the `Open` method, you should create one before calling `ObtainOpener`.

```
openerPart = cyberSession->ObtainOpener (ev, openerPart,
    kODNULL, this, params);
```

3. Call a method that initiates whatever asynchronous process is necessary for the data to be displayed, such as creating and opening a Cyberdog stream. To display progress while the data is downloaded, the method should attach a progress broadcaster to the opener part and call the broadcaster's accessor methods to update its progress settings. When the method is finished downloading the data, it should call the inherited `OpenCyberItem` method.

Embedding a Display Part in a Navigator

A Cyberdog display part determines whether to embed itself in a navigator. If so, the display part must call `ObtainOpener` to obtain a navigator. In this case, `OpenCyberItem` performs the following steps:

1. Call the Cyberdog item's `CreateCyberStream` method to retrieve a stream for downloading the data, and call the stream's `Open` method to initiate the download operation.

```
fMyStream = fMyItem->CreateCyberStream (ev);
fMyStream->Open (ev);
```

2. Retrieve the Cyberdog item's parent item, if any, from the parameter set, and call `CyberSession::AddCyberItemToLog` to add the Cyberdog item to the log.

```
CyberItem* parent = kODNULL;
if (params)
    params->GetParameter (ev, kCDParentItemKey, &parent);
GetCyberSession (ev)->AddCyberItemToLog (ev, parent, fMyItem);
```

3. Call the display part's `SetCyberItem` method to store a reference to the Cyberdog item. This method is called by the inherited `OpenCyberItem` method; however, in this case, the inherited `OpenCyberItem` method is not called.

```
SetCyberItem (item, params);
```

4. Call the `CyberSession::ObtainOpener` method, passing `kNavigatorKind` as the opener part kind, to obtain a navigator. You must acquire the parameter set before passing it to `ObtainOpener`. If no parameter set was passed to the `Open` method, you should create one before calling `ObtainOpener`.

```
ODPart* navPart = GetCyberSession()->ObtainOpener (ev, openerPart,
    kNavigatorKind, item, params);
```

5. Instead of calling the display part's `OpenCyberItem` method, call the navigator's `GoToCyberItem` method, which displays the display part in the navigator.

```
TempNavigatorExtension navigatorExt (navPart,
    kCyberNavigatorExtension);
navigatorExt->GoToCyberItem (ev, item, this->GetODPart(), params);
```

6. Release the parameter set.

```
params->Release (ev);
```

Note

The previous scenario assumes that `OpenCyberItem` is synchronous. However, a display part whose `OpenCyberItem` method is asynchronous can also be embedded in a navigator. ◆

Programming in Cyberdog

Each of the chapters in Part Two introduces a sample program that demonstrates ways to use the Cyberdog API and outlines common techniques for using the API.

- Chapter 3, "Adding Cyberdog Features to an OpenDoc Part," uses a button example to show how to create and use Cyberdog items. The chapter also shows how to set up Cyberdog's menus, including the Cyberdog Preferences menu item.

- Chapter 4, "Creating a Cyberdog Display Part," demonstrates how to implement a Cyberdog display part, the part's Cyberdog part extension subclass, and the name-mapping resource. It also shows how to use these techniques with a display part:

  - using streams to download data
  - supporting the Document menu
  - locating a window that displays a Cyberdog item
  - positioning and closing windows

- Chapter 5, "Embedding a Cyberdog Display Part in a Navigator," outlines how to embed a Cyberdog display part in a Cyberdog navigator, how to open a Cyberdog item from an embedded display part, and how to use a progress broadcaster. It also shows additional techniques for supporting an embedded part's menus.

PART TWO

Adding Cyberdog Features to an OpenDoc Part

Contents

3

This chapter describes the steps required to create and use a Cyberdog item, Cyberdog menus, and the Cyberdog Preferences dialog box in any OpenDoc part. This chapter shows you how to

- initialize and release Cyberdog objects

- create a Cyberdog item from URL text

- read a Cyberdog item from a storage unit

- write a Cyberdog item to a storage unit

- open a Cyberdog item

- handle drag and drop of a Cyberdog item

- set up Cyberdog menus

- implement the Cyberdog Preferences menu item

The examples shown in this chapter are based on the CybTxtBtn sample code on the *Cyberdog Programmer's Kit* CD.

About the Sample Cyberdog Button

The sample Cyberdog button is an OpenDoc part based on SamplePart, an OpenDoc sample program that is described in the *OpenDoc Cookbook*. The button part demonstrates the use of the Cyberdog item (CyberItem) and Cyberdog service menu (CyberServiceMenu) classes. It also uses the Cyberdog session class (CyberSession) to open the Preferences dialog box.

The button part contains a Cyberdog item, which is opened when the user clicks in the part. The part displays the name of the item. The user can replace the item by dropping another item or text on the part. If text is dropped, the button part assumes the text is a URL and uses the text to create a Cyberdog item. The button part also displays Cyberdog menus.

Figure 3-1 shows an example of the Cyberdog part in its own document window.

Figure 3-1   A Cyberdog item in the button part

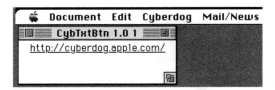

The button part initially contains an item for the http://cyberdog.apple.com/ URL. When the user clicks in the part, the part opens the Cyberdog item associated with the URL.

The button part can be embedded in another part. Figure 3-2 shows the button part embedded in a graphics part.

Figure 3-2   The button part embedded in a graphics part

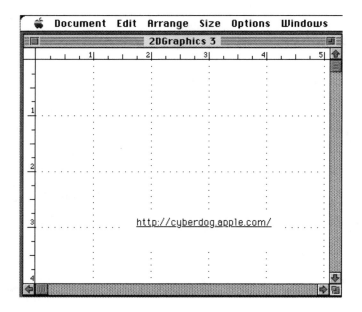

A Cyberdog item representing an e-mail address has been dropped on the button shown in Figure 3-3. The name of the mail item is Cyberdog Feature Suggestions; its URL is `features@cyberdog.apple.com`. The item could have been dragged, for example, out of the Cyberdog notebook or dragged from another e-mail message. When the user clicks in the button part, the mail item opens. The item displays the New Message dialog box as the first step in the sequence of sending mail. After the user chooses the format of the message, the mail service creates an empty message and places the item in the To: field.

Figure 3-3   A Cyberdog item for locating a mail address

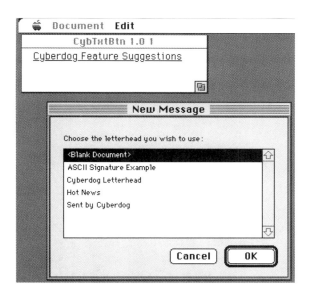

The following sections show you how to create and use Cyberdog items in an OpenDoc part subclass, `CybTxtBtn`, as well as how to support Cyberdog menus and the Cyberdog Preferences dialog box.

Modifying Your Part's Class Definition

To add Cyberdog features to your OpenDoc part class, you need to modify several methods and define new methods and fields. The button part example assumes that you are modifying the `SamplePart` class. This example shows only the steps necessary to modify the class to support Cyberdog items, the Cyberdog menus, and the Cyberdog Preferences command. Listing 3-1 shows the definitions of the methods and fields that you must either add or modify.

Listing 3-1 The `CybTxtBtn` class definition

```
class CybTxtBtn {
public:
    // Modified to initialize Cyberdog-related fields
    CybTxtBtn();
    virtual ~CybTxtBtn();

    // Modified to create a Cyberdog item
    void          InitPart(Environment* ev, ODStorageUnit* storageUnit,
                          ODPart* partWrapper);

    // Modified to allow drag and drop of Cyberdog items or text
    ODDragResult   DragEnter(Environment* ev,
                          ODDragItemIterator* dragInfo,
                          ODFacet* facet, ODPoint* where);
    ODDropResult   Drop  (Environment* ev,
                          ODDragItemIterator* dragInfo,
                          ODFacet* facet, ODPoint* where);

    // Modified to remove the Cyberdog service menu object
    void   ReleaseAll(Environment* ev);

    // Added to handle menus
    void CreateMenus(Environment* ev);
    void CheckMenus(Environment *ev, ODFrame* frame);
    ...
```

```
protected:
    // Added to initialize Cyberdog
    void    Initialize(Environment* ev, ODStorageUnit* storageUnit);

    // Modified to handle reading and writing of Cyberdog items
    void    InternalizeContent( Environment* ev,
                                ODStorageUnit* storageUnit);
    void    ExternalizeContent( Environment* ev,
                                ODStorageUnit* storageUnit,
                                ODDraftKey key, ODFrame* scopeFrame);

    // Modified to open a Cyberdog item
    ODBoolean   HandleMouseEvent(Environment* ev, ODEventData* event,
                                ODFacet* facet, ODEventInfo* eventInfo);

    // Modified to handle Cyberdog menus and the Preferences command
    ODBoolean   HandleMenuEvent(Environment* ev, ODEventData* event,
                                ODFrame* frame);
    void    PartActivated(Environment* ev, ODFrame* frame);
    void    FocusLost    (Environment* ev,ODTypeToken focus,
                        ODFrame* ownerFrame);
    void    AdjustMenus (Environment* ev, ODFrame* frame);
    ...
private:
    // Added or modified to support Cyberdog
    CyberItem* fCyberItem;                  // Reference to Cyberdog item
    CyberServiceMenu* fCyberServiceMenu;    // Reference to the Cyberdog
                                            // service menu object
    ODMenuBar* fMenuBar;                    // Reference to the menu bar
    ...
}
```

The constructor, destructor, and `Initialize` and `ReleaseAll` methods handle initialization and release or deletion of the Cyberdog objects used in this example. They are described in "Initializing and Releasing Cyberdog Objects" (page 94).

The `InitPart` method handles creating the initial Cyberdog item associated with the button part. The `InternalizeContent` and `ExternalizeContent` methods read and write Cyberdog items to and from a storage unit. They are described in "Reading and Writing Cyberdog Items" (page 98).

The `DragEnter` and `Drop` methods handle drag and drop of text or Cyberdog items on the button part. They are described in "Supporting Drag and Drop of Cyberdog Items" (page 102). The `HandleMouseEvent` opens the Cyberdog item when the user clicks in the part. It is described in "Opening a Cyberdog Item" (page 100).

The `CreateMenus`, `CheckMenus`, `HandleMenuEvent`, `PartActivated`, `FocusLost`, and `AdjustMenus` methods handle manipulation of Cyberdog service menus. The `HandleMenuEvent` method also initiates the display of the Cyberdog Preferences dialog box. For information about setting up Cyberdog menus, see "Displaying Cyberdog Menus" (page 105). For information about implementing the Cyberdog Preferences command, see "Implementing the Cyberdog Preferences Command" (page 109).

The `fCyberItem` field holds a reference to the current Cyberdog item associated with the part. The `fCyberServiceMenu` field holds a reference to the Cyberdog service menu object. The `fMenuBar` field refers to the part's menu bar. Initially, these fields are set to `kODNULL`.

Initializing and Releasing Cyberdog Objects

When it is created or destroyed, your part must take several actions to support Cyberdog and its menus. When your part is created, it must call the `InitCyberdog` function to initialize Cyberdog. It should also set up Cyberdog's menus. Before your part is released or destroyed, it must delete the Cyberdog service menu object and release the Cyberdog item, if it exists.

In the button part, the initialization is performed by the `InitPart` method, shown in Listing 3-5 (page 97), and the `InitPartFromStorage` method (not shown). These methods call the `Initialize` method (Listing 3-2) to actually perform the required initialization. The `Initialize` method obtains the OpenDoc session and calls the `InitCyberdog` function to initialize Cyberdog. It calls the `CreateMenus` method to create the menus; for more information, see "Displaying Cyberdog Menus" (page 105).

Note
In this example, a Cyberdog item is created initially by the `InitPart` method. For information about creating Cyberdog items, see "Creating a Cyberdog Item From a URL" (page 97). ◆

Listing 3-2   Initializing the button part

```
void CybTxtBtn::Initialize( Environment* ev, ODStorageUnit* storageUnit)
{
    ...
    // Initialize Cyberdog.
    ODSession* session = ODGetSession(ev,fSelf);
    OSErr err = InitCyberdog(ev, session);
    ...
    CreateMenus(ev);
    ...}
```

When a part is destroyed, its `ReleaseAll` method is called. This method is a
good place to delete the Cyberdog item and the Cyberdog service menu object
and to release the menu bar associated with the menu object. Listing 3-3 shows
how the button part handles these actions.

Listing 3-3   The button part's `ReleaseAll` method

```
void CybTxtBtn::ReleaseAll( Environment* ev )
{
    TRY
        if (fCyberServiceMenu != kODNULL)
        {
            delete fCyberServiceMenu;
            fCyberServiceMenu = kODNULL;
        }
        if (fMenuBar != kODNULL)
        {
            fMenuBar->Release(ev);
            fMenuBar = kODNULL;
        }
        if (fCyberItem != kODNULL)
        {
            fCyberItem->Release(ev);
            fCyberItem = kODNULL;
        }
        ...
```

```
CATCH_ALL
    RERAISE;
ENDTRY
}
```

The destructor for your part class should release any objects that the part still references. You should release the Cyberdog item. Releasing the item decrements its reference count and causes it to be deleted. Listing 3-4 shows the destructor for the `CybTxtBtn` part class.

Listing 3-4   The `CybTxtBtn` destructor

```
CybTxtBtn::~CybTxtBtn()
{
    Environment* ev = somGetGlobalEnvironment();
    if (fCyberItem != kODNULL)
    {
        TRY
            fCyberItem->Release(ev);
        CATCH_ALL
        ENDTRY

        fCyberItem = kODNULL;

    }
}
```

Manipulating a Cyberdog Item

To use a Cyberdog item, your part must be able to create and open one. If you want a Cyberdog item to persist between sessions, you must support reading and writing Cyberdog items. To support data interchange between Cyberdog items, your part should support drag and drop.

As described in the subsequent sections, the button part manipulates Cyberdog items in the following ways:

- It creates a Cyberdog item from a URL.

- It reads a Cyberdog item from a storage unit and writes an item to the unit.

- It opens a Cyberdog item.

- It handles drag and drop of a Cyberdog item.

Creating a Cyberdog Item From a URL

To create a Cyberdog item from a URL, you must first obtain a reference to the Cyberdog session by calling the GetCyberSession function. You then can create a Cyberdog item from the URL text by calling the Cyberdog session's CreateCyberItemFromURL method. Optionally, you can set the default name of the Cyberdog item.

Listing 3-5 shows how the button part creates a Cyberdog item when the part is first opened. The default URL text, which is stored in the part's resource fork, is used to create the item and to set the item's display name.

Listing 3-5   The button part's InitPart method

```
void CybTxtBtn::InitPart( Environment* ev,
                          ODStorageUnit* storageUnit,
                          ODPart* partWrapper )
{
    TRY
        fSelf = partWrapper;
        fReadOnlyStorage = kODFalse;

        // Call the common initialization code to initialize Cyberdog.
        this->Initialize(ev, storageUnit);

        // Use CUsingLibraryResources to access part's resource fork.
        {
            CUsingLibraryResources fil;
            Str255  defaultURL;
```

```
                // Get the default string from the resource fork.
                ::GetIndString( defaultURL, kMenuStringResID,
                                        kDefaultContent1ID);

            if (defaultURL[0] == 0)
                DebugStr("\p InitPart -- couldn't get strirc.");
            else
            {
                // Convert the default URL Pascal string to a C string.
                char cStr[255];
                ODBlockMove(&defaultURL[1], cStr, defaultURL[0]);
                cStr[ defaultURL[0] ] = 0;

                // Create a Cyberdog item from the URL.
                fCyberItem = GetCyberSession(ev)->CreateCyberItemFromURL
                                                (ev, (char*)cStr);

                // Make the default name equivalent to the URL.
                // Assume all URLs are smRoman font.
                if (fCyberItem)
                    fCyberItem->SetDefaultName(ev, defaultURL, smRoman);
            }
        }
        // Allow the state and content info to be written to storage.
        this->SetDirty(ev);

    CATCH_ALL
        RERAISE;
    ENDTRY
}
```

Note
The default font for displaying URLs is smRoman. ◆

Reading and Writing Cyberdog Items

To read a Cyberdog item from a storage unit, you must obtain a reference to the Cyberdog session by calling the GetCyberSession function. You then can call the session's CreateCyberItemFromSU method. Optionally, you can call the Cyberdog item's GetStringProperty method to retrieve the string associated with the item's display name, as indicated by the kCDDefaultName constant.

Listing 3-6 shows the button part's `InternalizeContent` method, which replaces the current Cyberdog item, if one exists, with one that has just been created from the storage unit. (The `InternalizeContent` method is called by the `InitPartFromStorage` method.)

Listing 3-6   The button part's `InternalizeContent` method

```
void CybTxtBtn::InternalizeContent (Environment* ev,
                                    ODStorageUnit* storageUnit)
{
    if (ODSUExistsThenFocus(ev, storageUnit, kODPropContents,
                                             kCybTxtBtnKind))
    {
        CyberItem* ci = kODNULL;

        // Retrieve the Cyberdog item from the storage unit.
        ci = GetCyberSession(ev)->CreateCyberItemFromSU(ev, storageUnit);

        // Replace the current Cyberdog item with the one in the
        // storage unit.
        if (ci != kODNULL)
        {
            if (fCyberItem != kODNULL)
                fCyberItem->Release(ev);
            fCyberItem = ci;
        }
    }
}
```

To write a Cyberdog item to a storage unit, you can call the item's `StreamToStorageUnit` method. Listing 3-7 shows the button part's `ExternalizeContent` method, which takes this action. (The `InternalizeContent` method is called by the `Externalize` method and other methods that write to storage units.)

Listing 3-7   The button part's `ExternalizeContent` method

```
void CybTxtBtn::ExternalizeContent( Environment* ev,
                                    ODStorageUnit* storageUnit,
                                    ODDraftKey /*key*/,
                                    ODFrame* /*scopeFrame*/ )
{
    // Focus on content property and get the current size of the data.
    ODSUForceFocus(ev, storageUnit, kODPropContents, kCybTxtBtnKind);
    ODULong oldSize = storageUnit->GetSize(ev);

    // Flatten an item to a buffer and then write the
    // buffer out to the specified ODStorageUnit.
    fCyberItem->StreamToStorageUnit(ev, storageUnit);

    ODULong newSize = storageUnit->GetOffset(ev);
    if (newSize < oldSize)
        storageUnit->DeleteValue(ev, oldSize - newSize);
}
```

Once you write the Cyberdog item to storage in this fashion, you must call the Cyberdog session's `CreateCyberItemFromSU` method to re-create the item in the storage unit (see Listing 3-6).

Note
Whenever you store data in an OpenDoc storage unit, you must modify all methods that work with storage and change them to support your kind of data. In this example, the `kCybTxtBtnKind` constant specifies the kind of data associated with the Cyberdog item. It is defined as follows:

```
#define kCybTxtBtnKind kODISOPrefix "Apple:Kind:CybTxtBtn"
```

Opening a Cyberdog Item

You call the Cyberdog item's `Open` method to open a Cyberdog item. What it means to open a Cyberdog item depends on the kind of data at the location referenced by the Cyberdog item. For example, if the Cyberdog item represents a URL for HTML-formatted data, calling the item's `Open` method causes the data to be downloaded and displayed in a Cyberdog display part. If the Cyberdog item represents an e-mail address, calling the item's Open method results in actions to send mail.

The Open method takes, as a parameter, a ParameterSet object that specifies various options for opening the Cyberdog item. The value can be nil, meaning that no additional options are used. For information about the ParameterSet class, see the ParameterSet class (page 387).

Listing 3-8 shows a portion of the button part's HandleMouseEvent method from which the Cyberdog item's Open method is called. The HandleMouseEvent method is called when the user clicks in the button part. (The HandleMouseEvent method is called from the HandleEvent method.)

Listing 3-8   Opening the Cyberdog item

```
ODBoolean CybTxtBtn::HandleMouseEvent( Environment* ev,
                                       ODEventData* event,
                                       ODFacet* facet,
                                       ODEventInfo* eventInfo )
{
    if ( facet != kODNULL )
    {
        if ( event->what == kODEvtMouseUp )
        {
            ...
        }
        else if ( event->what == kODEvtMouseDown )
        {
            if (fCyberItem == kODNULL)
                SysBeep(1);
            else
                fCyberItem->Open(ev, nil);
        }
    }
    else
    {
        SysBeep(1);
    }
    return kODTrue;
}
```

Supporting Drag and Drop of Cyberdog Items

To support drag and drop, you must implement the OpenDoc drag-and-drop protocol, which is explained in *OpenDoc Programmer's Guide*. It involves overriding the DragEnter, DragWithin, DragLeave, and Drop methods. To support drag and drop of Cyberdog items, you must modify two methods:

- Modify the DragEnter method so that a Cyberdog item can be dragged onto the part.

- Modify the Drop method so that the part accepts the dropped item.

In this example, the button part accepts drags of Cyberdog items and of text. Text is used to create a Cyberdog item representing a URL.

Listing 3-9 shows the DragEnter method, which checks for Cyberdog items and for text. The kCyberItemKind constant, which is passed to the storage unit's Exists method, identifies a Cyberdog item.

Listing 3-9   The button part's DragEnter method

```
ODDragResult CybTxtBtn::DragEnter(Environment* ev,
                                  ODDragItemIterator* dragInfo,
                                  ODFacet* facet, ODPoint* where)
{
    ODUnused(facet);
    ODUnused(where);

    ODStorageUnit dragSU;
    ODValueType textType = ODGetSession(ev,fSelf)->GetTranslation(ev)->
                      GetISOTypeFromPlatformType(ev, 'TEXT',
                                                 kODPlatformDataType);

    fAcceptThisDrag = kODFalse;
    fActiveFrameHilitedForDrop = kODFalse;

    // Accept the drag if it is a Cyberdog item or text
    for (dragSU = dragInfo->First(ev);
         dragSU != kODNULL;
         dragSU = dragInfo->Next(ev))
```

```
    {
        if (dragSU->Exists(ev, kODPropContents, kCyberItemKind, 0))
            fAcceptThisDrag = kODTrue;
        else if (dragSU->Exists(ev, kODPropContents, textType, 0))
            fAcceptThisDrag = kODTrue;
    }
    return fAcceptThisDrag;
}
```

The Drop method handles dropping of data allowed by the DragEnter method.
Specifically, the method should create a Cyberdog item from the specified kind
of data. You create a Cyberdog item from an item dropped into your part's
storage unit by calling the Cyberdog session's CreateCyberItemFromSU method.
In the call to CreateCyberItemFromSU, you specify the drag storage unit as a
parameter. If your part supports drag and drop of text, you can create a Cyberdog
item by calling the Cyberdog session's CreateCyberItemFromURL method.

Listing 3-10 shows how the button part creates a Cyberdog item when Cyberdog
item data or text is dropped on the part. If a Cyberdog item already exists, it is
released, and a reference to the newly created Cyberdog item is saved in the
fCyberItem field. The draft is marked as dirty so that its state will be saved, and
the facet is invalidated so that it will be redrawn.

Listing 3-10   The button part's Drop method

```
ODDropResult CybTxtBtn::Drop(Environment* ev,
                            ODDragItemIterator* dragInfo,
                            ODFacet* facet, ODPoint* where)
{
    ODStorageUnit*  dragSU;
    CyberItem*      ci = kODNULL;
    CyberSession*   cyberSession = GetCyberSession(ev);
    ScriptCode      script= smRoman;
    ODValueType     textType = ODGetSession(ev,fSelf)->
                    GetTranslation(ev)->GetISOTypeFromPlatformType(ev,
                                        'TEXT', kODPlatformDataType);

    for (dragSU = dragInfo->First(ev);
         dragSU != kODNULL;
         dragSU = dragInfo->Next(ev))
```

```
{
    // A Cyberdog item is dropped.
    if (dragSU->Exists(ev, kODPropContents, kCyberItemKind, 0))
    {
        // Focus on the Cyberdog item data in the drag storage unit.
        dragSU->Focus(ev, kODPropContents, kODPosUndefined,
                            kCyberItemKind, 0, kODPosUndefined);

        // Retrieve the Cyberdog item from the drag storage unit.
        ci = cyberSession->CreateCyberItemFromSU(ev, dragSU);
    }

    // The drop is not a Cyberdog item; deal with it as text.
    else if (dragSU->Exists(ev, kODPropContents, textType, 0))
    {
        Size textSize = 0;
        ODPtr theText = kODNULL;

        // Get the text from the drag storage unit.
        dragSU->Focus(ev, kODPropContents, kODPosUndefined,
                            textType, 0, kODPosUndefined);

        // Get the text length and enough memory for the text.
        textSize = (long) dragSU->GetSize(ev);
        theText = ODNewPtrClear(textSize + 1);
        if (theText)
        {
            // Read the text.
            StorageUnitGetValue(dragSU, ev, textSize,
                                        (ODValue)theText);

            // Create a Cyberdog item for the text.
            ci = cyberSession->CreateCyberItemFromURL(ev,
                                            (char*)theText);
            if (ci != kODNULL)
            {
                // Convert the text to a Pascal string.
                Str255 pStr;
                Size maxSize = 255;
                textSize = (textSize > maxSize) ? maxSize : textSize;
                ODBlockMove(theText, &pStr[1], textSize);
```

```
                    pStr[0] = textSize;

                    // Set the Cyberdog item's default name.
                    ci->SetDefaultName(ev, pStr, script);
                }
                ODDisposePtr(theText);
            }
        }
        // Replace the current Cyberdog item with the one from the drop.
        if (ci != kODNULL)
        {
            if (fCyberItem != kODNULL)
                fCyberItem->Release(ev);
            fCyberItem = ci;

            // Successful; save the state and invalidate the display.
            this->SetDirty(ev);
            facet->Invalidate(ev, kODNULL, kODNULL);
            return kODDropCopy;
        }
    }
    // Not successful
    return kODDropFail;
}
```

Displaying Cyberdog Menus

A Cyberdog service menu object handles the display of the Cyberdog menu and the Mail/News menu. It also allows services, such as FTP and Gopher, to install their menus as well. Collectively, these menus are called the Cyberdog service menus. You set up these menus by creating a CyberServiceMenu object and calling its ICyberServiceMenu method. When your part is destroyed, you can delete the service menu object. See Listing 3-3 (page 95).

Listing 3-11 shows the button part's CreateMenus method, which creates and initializes the Cyberdog service menu object and adds it to the menu bar.

Listing 3-11   Creating Cyberdog's menus

```
void CybTxtBtn::CreateMenus(Environment* ev)
{
    ODSession* session = ODGetSession(ev,fSelf);

    // Copy the base menu bar.
    fMenuBar = session->GetWindowState(ev)->CopyBaseMenuBar(ev);

    // Extend it with Cyberdog's menus.
    fCyberServiceMenu = new CyberServiceMenu;
    if (fCyberServiceMenu)
        fCyberServiceMenu->ICyberServiceMenu(ev, fMenuBar,
                                             fSelf, kBaseResourceID);

}
```

In the call to the ICyberServiceMenu method, the kBaseResourceID constant specifies the first value to use for Cyberdog menu commands. The value you choose must allow Cyberdog menus to fall within the range supported by OpenDoc. In this example, the kBaseResourceID constant is defined as follows:

```
#define    kBaseResourceID    20001
```

For more information about the Cyberdog command numbers, see the CyberServiceMenu class (page 339).

You must anticipate changes in the menu bar between activations of your part. You should re-create the menu bar each time your part is activated or its menus are adjusted. Listing 3-12 shows the button part's CheckMenus method, which re-creates the menu bar.

Listing 3-12   Re-creating the menu bar

```
void CybTxtBtn::CheckMenus(Environment* ev, ODFrame* frame)
{
    if (fMenuBar->IsValid(ev) == kODFalse)
    {
        // Release the old menu bar and the CyberServiceMenu object.
        if (fCyberServiceMenu)
```

```
{
    delete fCyberServiceMenu;
    fCyberServiceMenu = kODNULL;
}

ODReleaseObject(ev, fMenuBar);
fMenuBar = kODNULL;

// Recreate the menus.
CreateMenus(ev);

// If the part has the menu focus, inform the newly created
// CyberServiceMenu object and display the newly created menu bar.
if (frame != kODNULL)
{
    ODBoolean hasMenuFocus;
    ODArbitrator* arbitrator
                = ODGetSession(ev,fSelf)->GetArbitrator(ev);
    TempODFrame menuOwner
     = arbitrator->AcquireFocusOwner(ev, gGlobals->fMenuFocus);
    hasMenuFocus = ODObjectsAreEqual(ev, frame, menuOwner);

    if (hasMenuFocus)
    {
        if (fCyberServiceMenu)
            fCyberServiceMenu->MenuFocusAcquired(ev, frame);
        // Display the menu bar.
        fMenuBar->Display(ev);
    }
}
}
```

When your part has the menu focus, you must call the service menu object's
MenuFocusAcquired method to activate Cyberdog's menus. Listing 3-13 shows
the button part's PartActivated method, which calls the service menu's
MenuFocusAcquired method.

Listing 3-13   Acquiring the Cyberdog service menu's focus

```
void CybTxtBtn::PartActivated(Environment* ev,
                                ODFrame* frame )
{
    CheckMenus(ev, kODNULL);

    fCyberServiceMenu->MenuFocusAcquired(ev, frame);
    fMenuBar->Display(ev);
    ...
}
```

When your part is no longer active, you must call the service menu's
MenuFocusLost method to deactivate Cyberdog's menus. Listing 3-14 shows the
button part's FocusLost method, which calls the MenuFocusLost method.

Listing 3-14   The button part's FocusLost method

```
void CybTxtBtn::FocusLost(Environment* ev, ODTypeToken focus,
                                        ODFrame* ownerFrame )
{
    if ( focus == gGlobals->fSelectionFocus )
    {
    ...
    }
    else if( focus == gGlobals->fMenuFocus )
    {
        // Tell the CyberServiceMenu object that the menu focus is lost.
        if (fCyberServiceMenu)
            fCyberServiceMenu->MenuFocusLost(ev, ownerFrame);
    }
}
```

You must also allow menus to adjust their items and allow the menu items to
handle menu events.

■ You call the Cyberdog service menu object's Adjust method, which allows
service menus to enable or disable their menu items. See Listing 3-15
(page 109).

■ You call the Cyberdog service menu object's `DoCommand` method, which allows services to handle their commands. See Listing 3-16 (page 111).

In this example, these methods are called by the button part's `AdjustMenus` and `HandleMenuEvents` methods, respectively, as shown in the following section. The `AdjustMenus` method also deletes and re-creates the Cyberdog service menu object when a root part's menus are adjusted.

Implementing the Cyberdog Preferences Command

The Cyberdog Preferences command displays the Cyberdog Preferences dialog box. When your part is activated, its `AdjustMenus` method is called to set up its menus. You can modify this method to enable the Cyberdog Preferences menu item. To enable the Cyberdog Preferences menu item, you must take these actions:

■ Set the menu item string and enable a command for the preferences.

■ Call the Cyberdog service menu's `Adjust` method.

Listing 3-15 shows the button part's `AdjustMenus` method.

Listing 3-15   The button part's `AdjustMenus` method

```
void CybTxtBtn::AdjustMenus( Environment* ev,
                             ODFrame* frame )
{
    if (frame->IsRoot(ev))
    {
        // A root part must validate the menu bar before displaying it
        // because a part can swap the base menu bar at any time.
        CheckMenus(ev, kODNULL);
    }
    // After copying the base menu bar, install your part's menus.
    ...
    TRY

        ...
        ODArbitrator* arbitrator
                    = ODGetSession(ev,fSelf)->GetArbitrator(ev);
```

```
TempODFrame menuOwner
    = arbitrator->AcquireFocusOwner(ev, gGlobals->fMenuFocus);
if ( ODObjectsAreEqual(ev, frame, menuOwner) )
{
    Str63 text;
    ...
    ODGetIndString(text, kMenuStringResID, kDefaultContent2ID);
    // Create an IText object to pass into the menu bar.
    TempODIText prefItem(CreateIText(gGlobals->fEditorsScript,
                         gGlobals->fEditorsLanguage,
                         (StringPtr)&text));
    // Change the text of the "Preferences" menu item.
    fMenuBar->SetItemString(ev, kODCommandPreferences, prefItem);
    fMenuBar->EnableCommand(ev, kODCommandPreferences, kODTrue);
}
// Allow Cyberdog services to enable or disable their menu items.
if(fCyberServiceMenu)
    fCyberServiceMenu->Adjust(ev, frame);
CATCH_ALL
ENDTRY
}
```

Note

In this example, the part's standard Preferences menu
item, specified by `kODCommandPreferences`, is replaced by
the Cyberdog Preferences menu item. ◆

When a menu event occurs, you should call the Cyberdog service menu's
`DoCommand` method to allow a Cyberdog service to handle the event. If the
Cyberdog Preferences menu item is selected, you must call the Cyberdog
session's `ShowPreferencesDialog` method to display the Cyberdog Preferences
dialog box. Listing 3-16 shows the button part's `HandleMenuEvent` method.

Listing 3-16   The button part's `HandleMenuEvent` method

```
ODBoolean CybTxtBtn::HandleMenuEvent(Environment* ev,
                                     ODEventData* event,
                                     ODFrame* frame )
{
    ODULong menuResult = event->message;
    ODUShort menu = HiWord(menuResult);
    ODUShort item = LoWord(menuResult);
    ODBoolean handled = kODTrue;
    ODULong commandID;

    commandID = fMenuBar->GetCommand(ev, menu, item);

    // Give Cyberdog the first chance to handle the command.
    if (fCyberServiceMenu)
        handled = fCyberServiceMenu->DoCommand(ev, commandID, frame);

    if (handled == kODFalse)
    {
        switch (commandID)
        {
            ...
            // The Cyberdog Preferences command was sent.
            // Show the Cyberdog Preferences dialog box.
            case kODCommandPreferences:
                CyberSession* cyberSession = GetCyberSession(ev);
                cyberSession->ShowPreferencesDialog(ev);
                handled = kODTrue;
            break;
            ...
            default:
                handled =  kODFalse;
        }
    }
    return handled;
}
```

Creating a Cyberdog Display Part

Contents

This chapter outlines the steps you take to create an editor for a Cyberdog display part. A Cyberdog display part is an OpenDoc part that can retrieve and display data from an Internet location specified by a Cyberdog item; for example, the contents of an HTTP or Gopher site. Specifically, a Cyberdog display part class is a subclass of ODPart that has a Cyberdog part extension.

You create a Cyberdog display part editor much as you create an editor for any OpenDoc part; for example, you specify how data is rendered and stored, and you specify its resources. However, creating a Cyberdog display part editor involves a few additional steps, as follows:

- Implement a Cyberdog part extension subclass to allow Cyberdog to communicate with your part editor.

- Implement the OpenDoc extension protocol in your part editor.

- Use window-position hints when your part is opened.

- Replace OpenDoc's Document menu with Cyberdog's Document menu.

- Access data referenced by a Cyberdog item; for example, by using a Cyberdog stream to download data for display.

- Allow Cyberdog to participate in closing your part's windows.

- Support Cyberdog's service menus, as described in "Displaying Cyberdog Menus" (page 105).

- Modify your part's name-mapping ('nmap') resource to support the Cyberdog part kind of data.

This chapter illustrates these steps using a sample Cyberdog display part, CybTxtViewer, which downloads and displays text. Cyberdog already provides a real display part for text; your display part would likely display other kinds of data or display text data some other way.

Implementing Your Cyberdog Part Extension

A Cyberdog display part is associated with a Cyberdog part extension. An extension is an OpenDoc object that provides additional capabilities or behaviors. The Cyberdog part extension allows Cyberdog to send messages to your display part. This extension defines methods that implement Cyberdog behaviors, such as opening the location represented by a Cyberdog item.

You create a Cyberdog part extension subclass from the `CyberPartExtension`
class. The `CyberPartExtension` class is an indirect subclass of the `ODExtension`
OpenDoc class. The `CyberPartExtension` class is a SOM class. This chapter
shows you how to define a `CyberPartExtension` subclass and override
its methods.

To implement a Cyberdog part extension, you typically take these actions:

■ Override the `somInit` method if you use additional fields.

■ Override the `OpenCyberItem` method to open your display part in the way
you specify. Cyberdog calls this method to notify a part that it is being
opened by a Cyberdog item rather than some other way, such as being
restored from disk.

■ Override the `GetCyberItemWindow` method if you want your display part's
window to be selected when the same Cyberdog item is redisplayed.
Cyberdog calls this method to locate a window that is already displaying the
Cyberdog item. For example, if the user double-clicks a Cyberdog item in
the notebook and then repeats the action, your override of the
`GetCyberItemWindow` method can return the window in which the item is
currently displayed. If you do not override this method, the item appears in
a new window each time it is displayed.

You may also wish to provide a way for your SOM part extension object to
obtain a reference to the C++ display part object. This technique is used in the
text-viewer example.

Listing 4-1 shows the SOM class definition of the text viewer's part
extension subclass.

Listing 4-1   The text-viewer sample's part extension class definition

```
module Apple {
    interface som_CybTxtViewerCyberExt : CyberPartExtension
    {
        void       SetBasePart(in somToken basePart);
        somToken   GetBasePart();

    #ifdef __SOMIDL__
        implementation
        {
        functionprefix = som_CybTxtViewerCyberExt__;
```

```
        override:
            somInit,
            OpenCyberItem,
            GetCyberItemWindow,
            BaseRemoved;

        releaseorder:
            SetBasePart,
            GetBasePart;

        majorversion = 1; minorversion = 0;

    #ifdef __PRIVATE__
        somToken      fBasePart;
    #endif
        };
    #endif
    };
};
```

The BaseRemoved, SetBasePart, and GetBasePart methods and the fBasePart field are used to associate a SOM part extension object with a C++ display part object, as described in the following section.

Associating a Part Extension With a Display Part

You may find it convenient to implement the tasks performed by SOM methods in methods of a C++ class. For example, the text viewer uses a straightforward technique to associate a Cyberdog part extension subclass, which is a SOM class, with the C++ implementation of a Cyberdog display part class, CybTxtViewer. The CybTxtViewer C++ class implements the text-viewer part's behavior.

The SOM class contains a field, fBasePart, which points to the associated C++ object. The SOM class provides the SetBasePart and GetBasePart methods, which respectively set and retrieve the value of this field. When it creates the part extension object, the text-viewer part calls the extension's SetBasePart method to associate the C++ display part object with the extension. See Listing 4-13 (page 128).

Listing 4-2 shows an override of the `somInit` method, which initializes the `fBasePart` field to `kODNULL`. Note that the `somInit` method's inherited method is also invoked.

Listing 4-2   The `somInit` method of the text viewer's part extension

```
SOM_Scope void  SOMLINK som_CybTxtViewerCyberExt__somInit
                              (Apple_som_CybTxtViewerCyberExt *somSelf)
{
    ...
    Apple_som_CybTxtViewerCyberExt_parent_CyberPartExtension_somInit
                                                            (somSelf);
    somThis->fBasePart = kODNULL;
}
```

The `SetBasePart` method sets the `fBasePart` field with the contents of the `basePart` parameter, as follows:

```
somThis->fBasePart = basePart;
```

The `GetBasePart` method retrieves the contents of the `fBasePart` field.

```
return somThis->fBasePart;
```

The extension class overrides the `ODExtension::BaseRemoved` method to reset the `fBasePart` field to `kODNULL` when the associated C++ object no longer exists, as shown in Listing 4-3. The inherited `BaseRemoved` method is then called.

Listing 4-3   The `BaseRemoved` method of the text viewer's part extension

```
SOM_Scope void  SOMLINK som_CybTxtViewerCyberExt__BaseRemoved
                              (Apple_som_CybTxtViewerCyberExt *somSelf,
                               Environment *ev)
{
...
SOM_TRY
    somThis->fBasePart = kODNULL;
    Apple_som_CybTxtViewerCyberExt_parent_CyberPartExtension_BaseRemoved
                                                            (somSelf,ev);
```

```
SOM_CATCH_ALL
SOM_ENDTRY
}
```

Overriding Cyberdog Part Extension Methods

To implement a Cyberdog part extension class, you typically override the
`OpenCyberItem` method. You must override the `somInit` method if you define
fields. See Listing 4-2 (page 118). You override the `GetCyberItemWindow` method
if you want your display part's window to be selected when the same
Cyberdog item is redisplayed.

In the text viewer example, the methods defined in the SOM part extension
subclass pass control to the corresponding methods in the C++ text-viewer part
class. Listing 4-4 shows an override of the `OpenCyberItem` method that calls its
inherited `OpenCyberItem` method and then calls the text-viewer part's
`OpenCyberItem` method.

Listing 4-4   The `OpenCyberItem` method of the text viewer's part extension

```
SOM_Scope void  SOMLINK som_CybTxtViewerCyberExt__OpenCyberItem(
                        Apple_som_CybTxtViewerCyberExt *somSelf,
                        Environment *ev,
                        CyberItem* item,
                        ODPart* openerPart,
                        ParameterSet* openParams)
{
...
SOM_TRY
Apple_som_CybTxtViewerCyberExt_parent_CyberPartExtension_OpenCyberItem
                        (somSelf,ev,item,openerPart,openParams);
    CybTxtViewer* realPart = (CybTxtViewer*) somThis->fBasePart;
    if (realPart)
        realPart->OpenCyberItem(ev, item, openerPart, openParams);
SOM_CATCH_ALL
SOM_ENDTRY
}
```

Listing 4-5 shows an override of the GetCyberItemWindow method that calls the text-viewer part's GetCyberItemWindow method.

Listing 4-5   The GetCyberItemWindow method of the part extension

```
SOM_Scope ODWindow*  SOMLINK som_CybTxtViewerCyberExt__GetCyberItemWindow
        (Apple_som_CybTxtViewerCyberExt *somSelf,
         Environment *ev,
         CyberItem* item)
{
    ...
    ODWindow* result;
    ODVolatile(result);

    SOM_TRY
        CybTxtViewer* realPart = (CybTxtViewer*) somThis->fBasePart;
        if (realPart)
            return realPart->GetCyberItemWindow(ev, item);
    SOM_CATCH_ALL
        result = kODNULL;
    SOM_ENDTRY
    return result;
}
```

Implementing Your Cyberdog Display Part Class

This section describes the steps you take to implement a Cyberdog display part class. You take the following steps to create your display part class:

■ Define your Cyberdog part class.

■ Set up the OpenDoc extension protocol to use your Cyberdog part extension subclass.

■ Handle release of the part extension object.

■ Initialize objects created in your display part class.

- Use Cyberdog's Document menu.

- Use window-position hints.

- Handle downloading of data.

- Determine the window in which to display the Cyberdog item.

- Handle closing of the display part's window.

The following sections describe the steps in more detail, using the text-viewer part, `CybTxtViewer`. The text-viewer part is based on the OpenDoc sample program, `SamplePart`. These sections assume that you are working with an `ODPart` subclass that has already been defined and whose methods have been overridden for some purpose, such as to display text. The chapter does not show, for example, how to implement drawing. For an example of defining an OpenDoc part subclass from the `ODPart` class, see the *OpenDoc Cookbook*. For more general information about programming with OpenDoc, see the *OpenDoc Programmer's Guide*.

Modifying Your ODPart Subclass

You can start with your existing subclass of `ODPart` and modify it to support the Cyberdog part extension and to handle events that affect Cyberdog-related operations. To modify your part class so that it becomes a Cyberdog display part class, you should modify the class definition to include

- a pointer to the Cyberdog part extension object

- methods that initialize the Cyberdog display part object and its part extension object

- methods that set up the Cyberdog part extension

- methods that handle releasing the extension when the part is closed

Listing 4-6 shows the portion of the part class definition that defines both the new fields and methods and also the methods whose implementation must be modified.

Listing 4-6   The `CybTxtViewer` class definition

```
class CybTxtViewer {
public:
    CybTxtViewer();
    virtual ~CybTxtViewer();
    ...
    // Modified to implement the Cyberdog part extension
    ODBoolean HasExtension(Environment* ev, ODType name);
    ODExtension* AcquireExtension(Environment* ev, ODType name);
    void ReleaseExtension(Environment* ev, ODExtension* extension);

    // Modified or added to release the part extension
    void ReleaseAll(Environment* ev);
    void ReleaseCyberPartExtension(Environment* ev);

    // Modified to handle closing windows
    ODBoolean    HandleEvent     (Environment* ev, ODEventData* event,
                                  ODFrame* frame, ODFacet* facet,
                                  ODEventInfo* eventInfo);
    ODBoolean    HandleMenuEvent (Environment* ev, ODEventData* event,
                                  ODFrame* frame);

    // Modified to download a Cyberdog item's data
    void OpenCyberItem          (Environment *ev,
                                  CyberItem* item,
                                  ODPart* openerPart,
                                  ParameterSet* openParams);
    void PollStream(Environment* ev);

    // Modified to reuse a Cyberdog item's window
    ODWindow* GetCyberItemWindow(Environment *ev, CyberItem* item);

    // Modified or added to support window-position hints
    ODID    Open(Environment* ev, ODFrame* frame);
    ODWindow* CreateWindow (Environment* ev, ODFrame* frame,
                              ODType frameType,
                              WindowProperties* windowProperties,
                              WindowPtr behindThisWindow = (WindowPtr) -1);
    WindowPtr GetBehindWindow(Environment* ev);
```

```
WindowProperties* GetDefaultWindowProperties(Environment* ev,
                    ODFrame* frame,
                    Rect* windowRect,
                    CDWindowPositionHint* windowPositionHint = nil);

    // Modified to support Cyberdog's Document menu
    void CreateMenus(Environment* ev);
    void CheckMenus(Environment *ev, ODFrame* frame);

protected:
    // Added to initialize Cyberdog and a part extension
    void    Initialize(Environment* ev);

private:
    // A reference to the Cyberdog part extension
    CyberSample_som_CybTxtViewerCyberExt*    fCybTxtViewerCyberExt;

    Handle      fDocMenu;    // Cyberdog's Document menu
    CyberStream* fStream;    // Cyberdog stream

    // The following fields are used with downloading:
    char* fChars;
    ODULong fCharsLength;
    ODULong fCharsAllocLength;
    }
```

Listing 4-6 defines several fields that maintain references to the Cyberdog part extension (CyberSample_som_CybTxtViewerCyberExt), the Cyberdog Document menu (fDocMenu), and the Cyberdog stream (fStream) used to download the data. Other fields are used to manage the downloading operation. The constructor and the Initialize method handle initialization of these fields, which are discussed in "Creating and Destroying the Display Part Object" (page 127).

The HasExtension, AcquireExtension, and ReleaseExtension methods implement the OpenDoc extension protocol. They are discussed in "Implementing the OpenDoc Extension Protocol" (page 124). The ReleaseAll and ReleaseCyberPartExtension methods handle the release of the extension when the part is deleted. These methods are discussed in "Releasing the Part Extension" (page 126).

The `HandleEvent` method handles polling and the closing of the text-viewer part's window. The `HandleMenuEvent` method also handles the closing of the text-viewer part's window. The methods `OpenCyberItem` and `PollStream` initiate downloading from the stream and manage the stream, respectively. For information about setting up a Cyberdog stream, see "Creating a Stream for Downloading" (page 135). For information about using a Cyberdog stream, see "Downloading From the Stream" (page 136). For information about closing the display part's window, see "Closing Your Display Part's Window" (page 140).

The `Open` and `CreateWindow` methods use window-position hints. These hints are manipulated by the `GetBehindWindow` and `GetDefaultWindowProperties` methods. For more information about using window-position hints, see "Using Window-Position Hints" (page 130).

The `CreateMenus` and `CheckMenus` methods allow Cyberdog's Document menu to be displayed. For more information about Cyberdog's Document menu, see "Supporting Cyberdog's Document Menu" (page 129).

Implementing the OpenDoc Extension Protocol

To implement the extension protocol between your Cyberdog display part and your Cyberdog part extension, you override three `ODPart` methods in your part class:

- Override the `HasExtension` method to return `kODTrue` if the part has an extension with the name `kCyberPartExtension`.

- Override the `AcquireExtension` method to return a reference to your Cyberdog part extension object.

- Override the `ReleaseExtension` method to delete the Cyberdog part extension.

These are the same methods that you override to associate an extension with any OpenDoc part. For more information about extending an OpenDoc part, see the *OpenDoc Programmer's Guide*.

Listing 4-7 shows the `HasExtension` method for the text-viewer part. It returns `kODTrue` if the extension is `kCyberPartExtension`; otherwise, it returns `kODFalse`.

_____

Listing 4-7   The text-viewer part's `HasExtension` method

```
ODBoolean CybTxtViewer::HasExtension(Environment* ev, ODType name)
{
    ODBoolean    result = kODFalse;

    if (strcmp(name, kCyberPartExtension) == 0)
        result = kODTrue;
    return result;
}
```

Listing 4-8 shows the `AcquireExtension` method for the text-viewer part. It sets the `fCybTxtViewerCyberExt` field and acquires a reference to the extension.

_____

Listing 4-8   The text-viewer part's `AcquireExtension` method

```
ODExtension* CybTxtViewer::AcquireExtension(Environment* ev, ODType name)
{
    ODExtension* extension = kODNULL;

    if (strcmp(name, kCyberPartExtension) == 0)
    {
        if (fCybTxtViewerCyberExt)
        {
            extension = (ODExtension*) fCybTxtViewerCyberExt;
            extension->Acquire(ev);
        }
    }
    return extension;
}
```

Listing 4-9 shows the `ReleaseExtension` method for the text-viewer part. It deletes the reference to the extension, if it exists, and sets the `fCybTxtViewerCyberExt` field to `kODNULL`.

Listing 4-9   The text-viewer part's `ReleaseExtension` method

```
void CybTxtViewer::ReleaseExtension(Environment* ev,
                                    ODExtension* extension)
{
    if (extension == (ODExtension*) fCybTxtViewerCyberExt)
    {
        delete fCybTxtViewerCyberExt;
        fCybTxtViewerCyberExt = kODNULL;
    }
}
```

Releasing the Part Extension

When your display part is closed, OpenDoc calls the part's `ReleaseAll` method to release all resources that continue to be referenced by the part. You must make sure that your part's `ReleaseAll` method releases your Cyberdog part extension object. If your part is the only one that currently references the extension, you can delete the object; otherwise, you should release the part extension and call the extension's `BaseRemoved` method to notify the extension that the part no longer exists.

Listing 4-10 shows only the portion of the text-viewer part's override of the `ReleaseAll` method that relates to releasing the part extension. The `ReleaseAll` method calls the `ReleaseCyberPartExtension` method to do the actual work of releasing the part extension. It also deletes the stream if it exists.

Listing 4-10   The text-viewer part's `ReleaseAll` method

```
void CybTxtViewer::ReleaseAll( Environment* ev )
{
    ...
    ReleaseCyberPartExtension(ev);
    if (fStream)
    {
        delete fStream;
        fStream = kODNULL;
    }
}
```

The `ReleaseCyberPartExtension` method is defined by the `CybTxtViewer` class, not by the `ODPart` class. It exists to separate the work associated with releasing the Cyberdog part extension from the other work being performed (but not shown) in the `ReleaseAll` method.

Listing 4-11 shows the `ReleaseCyberPartExtension` method. It calls the part extension's `Release` method, which decrements the part extension's reference count. If the extension is in use by another part and has not been deleted as a result of calling `Release`, the `BaseRemoved` method is called and the `fCybTxtViewerCyberExt` field is set to `kODNULL`.

Listing 4-11   Releasing the text viewer's Cyberdog part extension

```
void CybTxtViewer::ReleaseCyberPartExtension(Environment* ev)
{
    if (fCybTxtViewerCyberExt)
    {
        fCybTxtViewerCyberExt->Release(ev);

        // The part extension may not exist at this point.
        if(fCybTxtViewerCyberExt)
        {
            fCybTxtViewerCyberExt->BaseRemoved(ev);
            fCybTxtViewerCyberExt = kODNULL;
        }
    }
}
```

Creating and Destroying the Display Part Object

When a display part object is created, you must initialize its fields. Then the part must take these actions:

- Call the `InitCyberdog` function to initialize Cyberdog.
- Create an object from your Cyberdog part extension subclass. The part must then take these two actions:
    - Call its `ICyberPartExtension` method to initialize the extension.
    - Establish a reference to your display part object in the Cyberdog part extension.
- Replace the OpenDoc Document menu with Cyberdog's Document menu.

The constructor must set its fields to safe values, as shown in Listing 4-12.

Listing 4-12 The `CybTxtViewer` constructor

```
CybTxtViewer::CybTxtViewer()
{
    ...
    fCybTxtViewerCyberExt = kODNULL;
    fStream = kODNULL;
    fDocMenu = kODNULL;
    fCharsLength = 0;
    fCharsAllocLength = 0;
    fChars = kODNULL;
}
```

You perform initialization in your `InitPart` and `InitPartFromStorage` methods. Listing 4-13 shows the text-viewer part's `Initialize` method, which is called from both the `InitPart` and `InitPartFromStorage` methods (not shown). It initializes Cyberdog, and creates and initializes the part extension.

Listing 4-13 Initializing the Cyberdog environment

```
void CybTxtViewer::Initialize( Environment* ev )
{
    ...
    // Initialize Cyberdog.
    ODSession* session = ODGetSession(ev,fSelf);
    OSErr err = InitCyberdog(ev, session);
    ...
    // Create and initialize the Cyberdog part extension.
    fCybTxtViewerCyberExt = new Apple_som_CybTxtViewerCyberExt;
    if(fCybTxtViewerCyberExt != kODNULL)
    {
        fCybTxtViewerCyberExt->ICyberPartExtension(ev, fSelf);
        fCybTxtViewerCyberExt->SetBasePart(ev, this);
    }
    ...
}
```

The destructor must delete any data that has been left in memory and may also need to delete a stream if the display part was terminated while a download operation was in progress. It also must delete the Cyberdog Document menu. Listing 4-14 shows the destructor for the text-viewer part.

Listing 4-14   The `CybTxtViewer` destructor

```
CybTxtViewer::~CybTxtViewer()
{
    // Delete downloaded data.
    if (fChars)
        ODDisposePtr(fChars);

    // Delete the stream.
    if (fStream)
        delete fStream;

    // Delete the Cyberdog document menu.
    if (fDocMenu != nil)
        DisposeHandle(fDocMenu);
}
```

Supporting Cyberdog's Document Menu

Your display part must replace OpenDoc's Document menu with Cyberdog's Document menu. You call the Cyberdog session's `InstallCyberDocumentMenu` method to install Cyberdog's Document menu. The Document menu is replaced only if the display part is in the Cyberdog session document.

For example, the text-viewer part calls the `InstallCyberDocumentMenu` method from its `CreateMenus` method whenever menus need to be created.

```
fDocMenu = GetCyberSession(ev)->InstallCyberDocumentMenu
                                        (ev, fSelf, fMenuBar);
```

For information about creating menus, see "Displaying Cyberdog Menus" (page 105).

When menus need to be re-created, or when the part is destroyed, you should dispose of the Document menu. The text-viewer part's destructor disposes of

the Document menu's handle before the part re-creates menus in its
`CheckMenus` method.

```
if (fDocMenu != nil)
{
    DisposeHandle(fDocMenu);
    fDocMenu = nil;
    }
```

IMPORTANT

Do not forget to install the Cyberdog Document menu. The
OpenDoc Document menu contains items that are not
applicable to a Cyberdog session document, such as the
Delete menu item, whose use would have undesirable
consequences. ▲

Using Window-Position Hints

A window-position hint provides information to your display part about
where to open its window. It specifies that the window should be in front of
your part's window and gives the coordinates of your part's window.

A window-position hint may have been written to the storage unit by an
opener part before your display part is opened. For example, the user may start
an operation involving your part, such as a download operation, and then
activate a different window or open a modal dialog box. When the first
operation ends, your part should use the window-position hint instead of
opening its window in front of the user's active window.

On opening, your Cyberdog display part should use a window-position hint to
place a part's window at the specified position on the screen and behind the
specified window. You must read the `CDWindowPositionHint` data structure from
storage when opening your display part. You then use the hint when you
create the window.

Listing 4-15 shows the text-viewer part's `Open` method, which calls the
`CDGetWindowPositionHint` function to retrieve a window-position hint from the
storage unit. The `Open` method then calls the `GetBehindWindow` method to
determine the window behind which to open the text-viewer's window. It then
calls the `GetDefaultWindowProperties`, which uses the position hint. Finally,
it calls the `CreateWindow` method to create the window using the hint.

Listing 4-15   The text-viewer part's `Open` method

```
ODID CybTxtViewer::Open(Environment* ev, ODFrame* frame)
{
    ODID windowID;
    TempODWindow window(kODNULL);

    WindowProperties* windowProperties = kODNULL;
    ODVolatile(windowProperties);

    WindowPtr behindThisWindow = (WindowPtr)-1;

    TRY
        if ( frame == kODNULL )
        {
            CDWindowPositionHint windowPositionHint;
            CDWindowPositionHint* windowPositionHintPtr;

            // Retreive the window-position hint from the storage unit.
            if (CDGetWindowPositionHint(ev,
                            GetODPart(ev)->GetStorageUnit(ev),
                            &windowPositionHint))
                windowPositionHintPtr = &windowPositionHint; // Found
            else
                windowPositionHintPtr = nil; // No hint in storage unit

            // Deterimine the window layer to open in.
            behindThisWindow = GetBehindWindow (ev,
                                        windowPositionHintPtr);

            // Calculate the bounding rectangle for a new window.
            Rect windowRect = this->CalcPartWindowSize(ev, kODNULL);

            // Get the default settings for a document window.
            windowProperties = this->GetDefaultWindowProperties(ev,
                        kODNULL, &windowRect, windowPositionHintPtr);

            // Create a window and register it with OpenDoc.
            window = this->CreateWindow(ev, kODNULL, kODFrameObject,
                                windowProperties, behindThisWindow);
        }
```

```
...
// Create the window's root facet.
window->Open(ev);
// Make the window visible.
window->Show(ev);
// Activate and select the window if it is in front.
if (behindThisWindow == (WindowPtr)-1)
    window->Select(ev);
...
windowID = (window ? window->GetID(ev) : kODNULLID);
CATCH_ALL
...
RERAISE;
ENDTRY
return windowID;
}
```

Listing 4-16 shows the text-viewer part's `CDGetWindowPositionHint` method, which reads the window-position hint from the storage unit.

Listing 4-16   Reading the window-position hint from storage

```
ODBoolean CDGetWindowPositionHint(Environment* ev,
                                  ODStorageUnit* su,
                                  CDWindowPositionHint *windowPositionHint)
{
    if (ODSUExistsThenFocus(ev, su, kCDWindowPositionHintProperty,
                       kCDWindowPositionHintValue))
    {
        StorageUnitGetValue(su, ev, sizeof(CDWindowPositionHint),
                       (ODValue)windowPositionHint);
        return kODTrue;
    }
    else
        return kODFalse;
}
```

The text-viewer part's `GetBehindWindow` method, shown in Listing 4-17, returns the window behind which the display part will open, which is the window specified in the window-position hint, if available. Otherwise, the method ensures that the window appears behind any modal windows.

Listing 4-17   Using the window-position layer hint

```
WindowPtr CybTxtViewer::GetBehindWindow(Environment* ev,
                              CDWindowPositionHint* windowPositionHint)
{
    WindowPtr window = nil;

    // Get the window indicated in the window-position hint.
    if (windowPositionHint)
    {
        window = windowPositionHint->behindWindow;
    }
    else
    // If no hint, make sure the window goes behind any modal windows.
    {
        // Find last modal window in the window list.
        WindowPtr aWindow = FrontWindow();
        while (aWindow && WindowIsModal(aWindow))
        {
            window = aWindow;
            aWindow = (WindowPtr) GetNextWindow(aWindow);
        }
    }

    if (!window)
        // No hint or modal dialog box; open in front
        window = (WindowPtr) -1;

    return window;
}
```

Listing 4-18 shows the text-viewer part's `GetDefaultWindowProperties` method, which uses the window-position coordinates to position the window.

Listing 4-18   Using the window-position coordinate hint

```
WindowProperties*
CybTxtViewer::GetDefaultWindowProperties(Environment* ev,
                                ODFrame*             sourceFrame,
                                Rect*                windowRect,
                                CDWindowPositionHint* windowPositionHint)
{
    WindowProperties* windowProperties = new WindowProperties;

    TRY
        // Position the window.
        if ( sourceFrame )
            // Use the source frame if one exists.
            this->CalcPartWindowPosition(ev, sourceFrame, windowRect);
        else if ( windowPositionHint )
            // Otherwise, use the window-position hint, if one exists.
            OffsetRect (windowRect,
                        windowPositionHint->windowPosition.h,
                        windowPositionHint->windowPosition.v);
        else
            // If none, place the window at the top left of the desktop.
            OffsetRect(windowRect, kALittleNudge,
                        GetMBarHeight() + kMacWindowTitleBarHeight);
    ...
    CATCH_ALL
        ODDeleteObject(windowProperties);
        RERAISE;
    ENDTRY

    return windowProperties;
}
```

The window layer (`behindThisWindow`) and coordinates (in `windowProperties`) are used when creating the window, as shown in the following call to the `NewCWindow` function from the `CreateWindow` method (not shown):

```
platformWindow = NewCWindow((Ptr)ODNewPtr(sizeof(WindowRecord)),
                            &(windowProperties->boundsRect),
                            windowProperties->title,
                            kODFalse, /* visible */
                            windowProperties->procID,
                            behindThisWindow,
                            windowProperties->hasCloseBox,
                            windowProperties->refCon);
```

Creating a Stream for Downloading

When a Cyberdog item is opened, Cyberdog calls your part extension's `OpenCyberItem` method. This is the most convenient place for you to specify tasks that need to be performed in conjunction with opening the Cyberdog item.

In the case of the text-viewer sample, the part extension's `OpenCyberItem` method—see Listing 4-4 (page 119)—calls the text-viewer part's `OpenCyberItem` method to do the work of creating a stream and to use it for downloading data. The text-viewer part's `OpenCyberItem` method also registers the item in the log. Listing 4-19 shows the text-viewer part's method.

Listing 4-19   The `OpenCyberItem` method of the text-viewer part

```
void CybTxtViewer::OpenCyberItem(Environment *ev,
                                 CyberItem* item,
                                 ODPart* openerPart,
                                 ParameterSet* openParams)
{
    // Create a stream for the download operation.
    fStream = item->CreateCyberStream(ev);

    // Open the stream, which starts the download operation.
    fStream->Open(ev);

    // Get the Cyberdog item's parent for the log.
    CyberItem* parent = kODNULL;
```

```
if(openParams)
    openParams->GetParameter(ev, kCDParentItemKey, &parent);

// Add the Cyberdog item to the log.
GetCyberSession(ev)->AddCyberItemToLog(ev, parent, item);
}
```

The method creates the Cyberdog stream by calling the Cyberdog item's
CreateCyberStream method. It then calls the stream's Open method to initiate
downloading. Finally, it calls the session's AddCyberItemToLog method to add
the item to the log.

Downloading From the Stream

When downloading, you must periodically check whether the stream contains
any data and, if so, display the data. You can, for example, check the status of
downloading from the stream during idle time. You should try not to do too
much work during idle time; otherwise, the system will be perceived as
unresponsive. You must balance the work so as to avoid this perception yet
obtain enough data from the stream on each poll to complete the download
operation in a reasonable time. You take these steps to manipulate the stream:

1. Call the stream's GetStreamStatus method to determine whether new data
   has arrived.

2. When data is present, call the stream's GetBuffer method to obtain the data.

3. Copy the data to your display part's storage.

4. Call the stream's ReleaseBuffer method to release the buffer after the data
   has been copied.

5. Repeat steps 1 through 4 until enough data has been copied or until there is
   no more data to download.

6. Draw the data; for example, by notifying OpenDoc that the data needs to be
   drawn or by drawing it yourself.

7. When the download operation is complete, delete the stream.

Listing 4-20 shows the text-viewer part's HandleEvent method. It calls the
PollStream method when a null event is received.

Listing 4-20   The text-viewer part's `HandleEvent` method

```
ODBoolean CybTxtViewer::HandleEvent( Environment*    ev,
                                     ODEventData*    event,
                                     ODFrame*        frame,
                                     ODFacet*        facet,
                                     ODEventInfo*    eventInfo )
{
    ODBoolean   eventHandled = kODFalse;

    switch ( event->what )
    {
        ...
        case kODEvtNull:
            if (fStream)
                PollStream(ev);
            break;
        ...
        default:
            break;
    }
    return eventHandled;
}
```

The `PollStream` method does the work associated with managing the stream. It checks whether any data is available to download from the stream. If so, the `PollStream` method copies the data into a buffer and invalidates the screen so that OpenDoc displays the data when the screen is redrawn. When downloading ends or an error occurs, the stream is deleted. Listing 4-21 shows these actions.

Listing 4-21   Handling downloaded data

```
void CybTxtViewer::PollStream(Environment* ev)
{
    StreamStatus status;
    ODBoolean gotData = kODFalse;
    Size bytesThisPoll = 0;

    if (fStream == kODNULL)
        return;
```

```
while (bytesThisPoll < kBytesPerPoll)
{
    status = fStream->GetStreamStatus(ev);

    // Exit the loop if no data is available.
    if (!(status & kCDDataAvailable))
        break;

    // Data is available. Get the buffer; copy it to the data area.
    char* buffer;
    Size size;

    fStream->GetBuffer(ev, &buffer, &size);
    if (buffer)
    {
        Size newLength = fCharsLength + size;
        if (newLength > fCharsAllocLength)
                                    newLength = fCharsAllocLength;
        if (newLength > fCharsLength)
        {
            ODBlockMove(buffer, fChars+fCharsLength,
                                    newLength - fCharsLength);
            fCharsLength = newLength;
        }
        gotData = kODTrue;
        bytesThisPoll += size;
        fStream->ReleaseBuffer(ev, buffer);
    }
}
// Check status.
status = fStream->GetStreamStatus(ev);

// Downloading is complete or an error occurred.
if ((status & kCDDownloadComplete) ||
    (status & kCDErrorOccurred) ||
    (status & kCDAbortComplete))
{
    delete fStream;
    fStream = kODNULL;
}
if (gotData)
    ForceRedraw(ev);
}
```

During each call to `PollStream`, at most `kBytesPerPoll` (defined as 8,192 bytes) is copied from the stream into the `fchars` data structure. The text-viewer part, not Cyberdog, defines the `kBytesPerPoll` constant.

The `ForceRedraw` method is simply a method that invalidates the area in which the data in the `fchars` structure is to be displayed. OpenDoc redraws the invalidated area in the usual way.

Locating the Cyberdog Item's Window

Cyberdog calls the part extension's `GetCyberItemWindow` method to locate a window that currently displays the specified Cyberdog item. If you do not override this method, the default `GetCyberItemWindow` method returns `kODNULL` and Cyberdog opens a new window in which to display the Cyberdog item's data. Your override can return a window that already displays the Cyberdog item's data. In this case, the window you return will be opened when the Cyberdog item is opened.

In this example, the text-viewer part extension's `GetCyberItemWindow` method calls the text-viewer part's `GetCyberItemWindow` method to do the actual work. See "Overriding Cyberdog Part Extension Methods" (page 119) for information about the part extension's `GetCyberItemWindow` method.

Listing 4-22 shows the text-viewer part's `GetCyberItemWindow` method. The method returns a reference to a window if the window is already displaying the same Cyberdog item. The Cyberdog part extension's `CanShowCyberItem` method specifies whether or not the Cyberdog item is displayed. If the Cyberdog item to be opened is not currently displayed, the method returns `kODNULL`. In response, Cyberdog opens a new window for the item.

Listing 4-22   The `GetCyberItemWindow` method of the text-viewer part

```
ODWindow* CybTxtViewer::GetCyberItemWindow (Environment *ev,
                                            CyberItem* item)
{
    ODWindow* window = kODNULL;

    // Determine whether the part already displays the specified
    // Cyberdog item.
    if ( fCybTxtViewerCyberExt->CanShowCyberItem(ev, item) )
```

```
{
    // Iterate over the list of frames, looking for a root frame.
    // If a root frame is found, return its window.
    if(fDisplayFrames)
    {
        CListIterator fiter(fDisplayFrames);
        for ( CFrameProxy* proxy = (CFrameProxy*) fiter.First();
                fiter.IsNotComplete();
                proxy = (CFrameProxy*) fiter.Next() )
        {
            if ( proxy->FrameIsLoaded(ev) )
            {
                ODFrame* odFrame = proxy->GetFrame(ev);
                if(odFrame->IsRoot(ev))
                {
                    TempODWindow window = odFrame->AcquireWindow(ev);
                    return window;
                }
            }
        }
    }
    return kODNULL;
}
```

Closing Your Display Part's Window

When a user attempts to close a display part's window, your part must intercept this command and allow Cyberdog to close the window. This action is necessary because OpenDoc normally closes the Cyberdog session document when it closes the last open window and, thus, would require a new Cyberdog session document to be created the next time Cyberdog is used. Allowing Cyberdog to close the window avoids creating unnecessary sessions and session documents.

Take these steps to close your part's window:

■ Obtain a reference to the Cyberdog session by calling the GetCyberSession function.

■ Close the window by calling the Cyberdog session's CloseCyberDraftWindow method. The parameter to the CloseCyberDraftWindow method is a pointer to your part.

- Close the window in the normal way if the `CloseCyberDraftWindow` method returns `kODFalse`, indicating that the window was not in the Cyberdog session document.

In the text-viewer part, two methods handle the closing of the part's window. The `HandleEvent` method closes the window after a click in the window's close box. The `HandleMenuEvent` method closes the window in response to a Close command. Both methods close the window in the same way.

Listing 4-23 shows the `HandleEvent` method.

Listing 4-23   The `HandleEvent` method of the text-viewer part

```
ODBoolean CybTxtViewer::HandleEvent( Environment*    ev,
                                     ODEventData*    event,
                                     ODFrame*        frame,
                                     ODFacet*        facet,
                                     ODEventInfo*    eventInfo )
{
    ODBoolean    eventHandled = kODFalse;

    switch ( event->what )
    {
        ...
        case kODEvtWindow:
            if (event->message == inGoAway) {
                eventHandled =
                    GetCyberSession(ev)->CloseCyberDraftWindow(ev, fSelf);
            }
            break;
        ...
        default:
            break;
    }
    return eventHandled;
}
```

Listing 4-24 shows the HandleMenuEvent method, which closes the window in response to a menu event.

Listing 4-24   The HandleMenuEvent method of the text-viewer part

```
ODBoolean CybTxtViewer::HandleMenuEvent( Environment*    ev,
                                         ODEventData*    event,
                                         ODFrame*        frame )
{
    ODULong    menuResult    = event->message;
    ODUShort   menu          = HiWord(menuResult);
    ODUShort   item          = LoWord(menuResult);
    ODBoolean  handled = kODTrue;
    ODULong commandID;
...

    switch (commandID) )
    {
        ...
        case kODCommandClose:
            handled
                = GetCyberSession(ev)->CloseCyberDraftWindow(ev, fSelf);
            break;
        ...
        default:
            handled =   kODFalse;
    }

    return handled;
}
```

Modifying Your Name-Mapping Resource

The name-mapping ('nmap') resource specifies the kinds of data that your part editor supports. Cyberdog prefers to use ISO strings based on MIME types for its part kinds. You must include the kCyberPartKind in your part editor's name-mapping resource in addition to any kinds of data your part editor supports.

Listing 4-25 shows the name-mapping resource for the text-viewer part. The text-viewer part supports text-application and plain-text data in addition to the Cyberdog part kind.

Listing 4-25   The kODNameMappings resource

```
resource kODNameMappings (kEditorKindMapId) {
    kODEditorKinds,
    {   /* array Types: 2 elements */
        /* [1] */
        kCybTxtViewerID,
        kODIsAnISOStringList
        {
            {   /* array ClassIDs: 3 elements */
                /* [3] */
                kTextPlainKind,
                kApplicationTextKind,
                kCyberPartKind
            }
        }
    }
};
```

Embedding a Cyberdog Display Part in a Navigator

Contents

This chapter outlines the steps required to embed a Cyberdog display part in a Cyberdog navigator. A Cyberdog navigator is an OpenDoc container part that has an associated Cyberdog navigator extension. When embedded in a Cyberdog navigator, the display part appears as the content area in the navigator's frame. From the navigator, the user can issue navigation commands, such as "next" and "previous."

You develop a Cyberdog display part that you want to embed in a navigator much as you develop any Cyberdog display part. You should be familiar with the steps required to build a Cyberdog display part, which are described in the previous chapter, "Creating a Cyberdog Display Part" (page 115). When developing an embedded display part, you typically need to provide support for several operations:

- opening an embedded display part in a navigator when the part is opened by a Cyberdog item

- opening a Cyberdog item from a display part embedded in a navigator

- using a progress broadcaster to update the status bar area of a navigator

- enabling a navigator's Save a Copy, Page Setup, and Print commands from an embedded display part

This chapter shows how to implement these operations. This chapter assumes that you are working with a sample Cyberdog display part class, such as the one described in "Implementing Your Cyberdog Display Part Class" (page 120). The examples in the following sections use an embedded text-viewer display part class called `CybTxtNavViewer`.

Modifying Your Cyberdog Display Part Class

To embed a display part in a navigator, you can start with your existing Cyberdog display part class and modify it slightly. Listing 5-1 shows the portion of the embedded text-viewer part's class definition that defines the new fields and methods and also the methods you must modify to support embedding, to support progress broadcasters, and to enable the navigator's Save a Copy, Page Setup, and Print commands. To enable the navigator's Save a Copy, Page Setup, and Print commands, you must also override the `HandleCommand` method of the associated part extension class.

Listing 5-1   The `CybTxtNavViewer` class definition

```
class CybTxtNavViewer {
public:
    CybTxtViewer();
    virtual ~CybTxtViewer();
    ...
    // Modified to embed a display part
    void OpenCyberItem(Environment *ev, CyberItem* item,
                                   ODPart* openerPart,
                                   ParameterSet* openParams);

    // Modified to enable Document menu items
    ODBoolean HandleCommand(Environment *ev, long commandCreator,
                         long commandID, ODFrame* frame, void* cmdData);

    // Modified to attach or detach progress broadcasters
    void    DisplayFrameAdded(Environment* ev, ODFrame* frame);
    void    DisplayFrameRemoved(Environment* ev, ODFrame* frame);
    void    DisplayFrameClosed(Environment* ev, ODFrame* frame);
    void    DisplayFrameConnected(Environment* ev, ODFrame* frame);

    // Added to find an embedded part's navigator
    ODPart* GetContainingNavigator(Environment* ev);

    // Added to handle parameter set creation
    ParameterSet* AcquireCreateParameterSet(Environment* ev,
                                       ParameterSet* params);

    // Modified to add progress broadcaster capabilities
    void    InitiateDownload(Environment *ev, CyberItem* item,
                           ParameterSet* openParams)
    void PollStream(Environment* ev);

private:
    ...
    CyberProgressBroadcaster* fBroadcaster; // Reference to a progress
                                            // broadcaster object
```

```
// Modified to abort download operations
static void CyberAbortProc( CDAbortProcMessage msgCode,
                            CyberProgressBroadcaster* process,
                            Ptr thisPtr);
static CyberAbortUPP gMyCyberAbortUPP;
}
```

In the embedded text-viewer part sample, the `OpenCyberItem` method embeds the text viewer. For more information see "Opening a Display Part Embedded in a Navigator" (page 150).

The `HandleCommand` method enables some of the navigator's Document menu items. For more information see "Enabling Menu Items From an Embedded Display Part" (page 161).

The `GetContainingNavigator` method returns a reference to the navigator in which the Cyberdog display part is embedded. See Listing 5-5 (page 154). The `AcquireCreateParameterSet` method encapsulates creation of a parameter set object. See Listing 5-3 (page 152).

The `InitiateDownload` method starts the download operation and creates the progress broadcaster object. The `PollStream` method reports progress during a download operation. The `CyberAbortProc` method is associated with the `CyberAbortUPP` callback procedure, which is used to abort a download operation. For more information about how these methods are used, see "Using a Progress Broadcaster" (page 155).

The `fBroadcaster` field is a reference to a progress broadcaster object. It is initialized in the `CybTxtNavViewer` constructor to `kODNULL`. The reference is deleted by the `CybTxtNavViewer` destructor.

Note
The `fCybTxtNavViewerCyberExt` field has exactly the same purpose and use as the `fCybTxtViewerCyberExt` in Chapter 4, "Creating a Cyberdog Display Part," (page 115). ◆

Opening a Display Part Embedded in a Navigator

When a Cyberdog item is opened, the item calls the Cyberdog part extension's `OpenCyberItem` method. The parameter set associated with the call to the `OpenCyberItem` method may specify an opener part; the opener part may be a navigator. Your implementation of the `OpenCyberItem` method must support using the opener part, if it exists. For more information about opener parts, see "Cyberdog Item Opening Process" (page 71).

If you handle embedding in the part extension's `OpenCyberItem` method, your implementation of the `OpenCyberItem` method must take these actions:

- Call your part extension's `SetCyberItem` method to store a reference to the Cyberdog item being opened.
- Obtain a navigator part by calling the Cyberdog session's `ObtainOpener` method, specifying the navigator kind of opener part.
- Acquire the navigator part's Cyberdog navigator part extension.
- Embed your display part by calling the navigator part extension's `GoToCyberItem` method.

To embed your display part in a navigator, you must completely override the `OpenCyberItem` method; do not call its inherited method.

In the embedded text-viewer sample, the part extension's `OpenCyberItem` method calls the embedded text-viewer part's `OpenCyberItem` method. For information about the Cyberdog part extension's `OpenCyberItem` method, see "Overriding Cyberdog Part Extension Methods" (page 119). Listing 5-2 shows how the embedded text-viewer part's `OpenCyberItem` method performs these actions.

Listing 5-2   The `OpenCyberItem` method of the embedded text-viewer part

```
void CybTxtNavViewer::OpenCyberItem(Environment *ev,
                                    CyberItem* item,
                                    ODPart* openerPart,
                                    ParameterSet* openParams)
{
```

```
// Start the download.
this->InitiateDownload(ev, item, openParams);

// Let the extension know which Cyberdog item is being displayed.
fCybTxtNavViewerCyberExt->SetCyberItem(ev, item, openParams);

// Ensure that a parameter set is available for the call to
// the ObtainOpener method.
TempParameterSet acquiredParams
                        = AcquireCreateParameterSet(ev, openParams);

// Obtain a navigator kind of opener part.
ODPart* navPart = GetCyberSession(ev)->ObtainOpener(ev,
                                                openerPart,
                                                kNavigatorKind,
                                                item,
                                                acquiredParams);

// Tell the navigator to go to this part, which causes the part to
// become embedded in the navigator's content area.
TempNavigatorExtension navigatorExt(navPart,
                                kCyberNavigatorExtension);
navigatorExt->GoToCyberItem(ev, item, GetODPart(ev), acquiredParams);
}
```

The call to InitiateDownload starts the download operation and sets up the progress broadcaster. For information about starting a download operation, see "Creating a Stream for Downloading" (page 135). For information about progress broadcasters, see "Using a Progress Broadcaster" (page 155).

When a Cyberdog item calls the OpenCyberItem method, it passes an opener part in the openerPart parameter, if one exists; otherwise, it passes kODNULL. If an opener part is passed in the parameter, the ObtainOpener method uses it if the part matches the specified kind of opener part.

Thus, in Listing 5-2, the call to ObtainOpener specifies a kNavigatorKind opener part. If this kind of part is passed when the Cyberdog item calls the OpenCyberItem method, the ObtainOpener method returns it; otherwise, the method returns a new navigator part.

Note
Even if Cyberdog calls the `OpenCyberItem` method with a
`kNavigatorKind` opener part, the `ObtainOpener` method
might return a new navigator part; for example, if the
Browse in Place preferences are different. ◆

The `ObtainOpener` method requires a parameter set object to be passed in. You
cannot pass `kODNULL`. In Listing 5-2, the `AcquireCreateParameterSet` method
creates a parameter set object if the Cyberdog item calls the `OpenCyberItem`
method and passes `kODNULL` in the `openParams` parameter. Listing 5-3 shows the
`AcquireCreateParameterSet` method.

Listing 5-3   Creating a parameter set object

```
ParameterSet* CybTxtNavViewer::AcquireCreateParameterSet
                                          (Environment* ev,
                                           ParameterSet* params)
{
    if (params)
    {
        params->Acquire(ev);
        return params;
    }
    else
    {
        TempParameterSet newParams = new ParameterSet;
        FailNil(newParams);
        newParams->IParameterSet(ev);
        return newParams.DontRelease();
    }
}
```

Listing 5-2 shows the use of objects created from C++ templates, such as
`TempNavigatorExtension` and `TempOpenerPartExtension`. These templates define
extensions that are based on Cyberdog classes, such as
`CyberNavigatorExtension` and `CyberOpenerPartExtension`, but whose methods
handle existence checks and automatically manage the release of their
corresponding Cyberdog objects. Otherwise, objects created from these
templates behave exactly as their corresponding Cyberdog objects behave.

IMPORTANT

These template classes are not part of the Cyberdog API. They are provided with the sample code on the accompanying CD-ROM "as is" for your convenience. ▲

Opening a New Cyberdog Item in the Same Navigator

Your embedded display part may need to open a Cyberdog item and display it in the same navigator that embeds your part. To handle this situation, you must pass a reference to the navigator when you call the Cyberdog item's Open method. You must choose the navigator in which to open the Cyberdog item and a parameter set to specify the navigator. Specify the parameter's key as kCDInitialOpenerPartKey.

Listing 5-4 shows an example from the embedded text viewer's HandleMenuEvent method.

Listing 5-4   Opening a Cyberdog item from an embedded display part

```
{
    TempParameterSet params = kODNULL;

    // Create a Cyberdog item.
    char* url = "http://www.cyberdog.apple.com";
    TempCyberItem item
            = GetCyberSession(ev)->CreateCyberItemFromURL(ev, url);

    // Find the navigator in which this part is embedded.
    ODPart* navPart = this->GetContainingNavigator(ev);
    if (navPart)
    {
        // Create and initialize a parameter set object.
        params = new ParameterSet;
        params->IParameterSet(ev);
```

```
        // Add the navigator to the parameter set as the
        // "initial opener part."
        params->PutParameter(ev, kCDInitialOpenerPartKey, navPart, nil);
    }


    // Open the Cyberdog item.
    item->Open(ev, params);
}
```

Listing 5-5 shows the embedded text-viewer part's GetContainingNavigator method. The method iterates over its display frames and calls the Cyberdog session's AcquireContainingNavigatorPart method to determine if the frame is in a navigator. If so, the GetContainingNavigator method returns a reference to the navigator.

Listing 5-5   The GetContainingNavigator method of the embedded text-viewer part

```
ODPart* CybTxtNavViewer::GetContainingNavigator(Environment* ev)
{
    ODPart* navPart = kODNULL;
    CyberSession* cyberSession = GetCyberSession(ev);
    CListIterator fiter(fDisplayFrames);
    CFrameProxy* proxy;

    while ((proxy = (CFrameProxy*) fiter.Next()) != nil)
    {
        navPart = cyberSession->AcquireContainingNavigatorPart
                                        (ev, proxy->GetFrame(ev));
        if (navPart)
        {
            navPart->Release(ev);
            break;
        }
    }
    return navPart;
}
```

Using a Progress Broadcaster

Your embedded display part can set up a progress broadcaster to send status information to progress receivers. This information might include the amount of data transferred by a download operation or a stream's status. Progress receivers are associated with progress parts, such as Cyberdog navigators and Cyberdog opener parts. Progress parts display the status of time-consuming operations. Thus, the navigator and opener parts support behavior to receive and display progress. The navigator or opener part can use the information received to animate and display the status bar.

To use a progress broadcaster, you must support the following operations:

- Create and initialize a `CyberProgressBroadcaster` object.

- Supply an abort callback function.

- Attach the broadcaster to a navigator.

- Detach the broadcaster.

- Send status messages to the navigator.

The following sections show you how to implement these operations.

Setting Up the Progress Broadcaster

You can set up a progress broadcaster when you initiate any time-consuming operation. To set up a progress broadcaster, you must take the following actions:

- Create a `CyberProgressBroadcaster` object and keep a reference to it.

- Call the `NewCyberAbortProc` utility to create a Cyberdog abort callback function.

- Call the broadcaster object's `ICyberProgressBroadcaster` method to initialize the broadcaster object and associate it with the Cyberdog abort callback function.

- Call the broadcaster object's `SetProgressMode` method to specify whether progress is metered (`kMeteredProgress`) or not (`kUnmeteredProgress`).

The embedded text-viewer part creates a progress broadcaster when it starts a download operation. Listing 5-6 shows the InitiateDownload method, which is called from the OpenCyberItem method.

Listing 5-6   The InitiateDownload method of the embedded text-viewer part

```
void CybTxtNavViewer::InitiateDownload (Environment *ev,
                                        CyberItem* item,
                                        ParameterSet* openParams)
{
    // Start the download and add the item to the log.
    ...

    // Prepare a progress broadcaster to attach to the navigator part.
    if (fBroadcaster == kODNULL)
    {
        fBroadcaster = new CyberProgressBroadcaster;

        if (gMyCyberAbortUPP == nil)
        {
            gMyCyberAbortUPP = NewCyberAbortProc(CyberAbortProc);
        }
        fBroadcaster->ICyberProgressBroadcaster
                                    (ev, gMyCyberAbortUPP, (Ptr) this);
        // Set the progress mode.
        fBroadcaster->SetProgressMode(ev, kUnmeteredProgress);
    }
}
```

Listing 5-6 shows the this pointer being passed as an argument to the ICyberProgressBroadcaster method. The this pointer allows the calling object to be referenced from the abort callback function.

Note
The gMyCyberAbortUPP class variable holds a pointer to the callback function. It is initialized as follows:

```
CyberAbortUPP CybTxtNavViewer::gMyCyberAbortUPP = nil; ◆
```

Implementing the Abort Callback Function

When the user cancels an operation associated with a Cyberdog broadcaster, such as by closing the navigator's window during a download operation, the broadcaster's abort callback function is called. The abort callback function takes the appropriate action to abort the operation. Listing 5-7 shows the embedded text viewer's abort callback function, called `CyberAbortProc`. It aborts the stream.

Listing 5-7   The embedded text viewer's abort callback function

```
void CybTxtNavViewer::CyberAbortProc(CDAbortProcMessage msgCode,
                                     CyberProgressBroadcaster*,
                                     Ptr thisPtr)
{
    CybTxtNavViewer* THIS = (CybTxtNavViewer*)thisPtr;

    switch(msgCode)
    {
        case kAbortMessage:
            if (THIS->fStream)
                THIS->fStream->Abort(somGetGlobalEnvironment());
            break;
        default:
            break;
    }
    return;
}
```

The `PollStream` method deletes the stream and the broadcaster when the download operation is aborted. See Listing 5-10 (page 160).

Attaching the Broadcaster Object

You can attach a Cyberdog broadcaster object to a Cyberdog navigator when your display part appears in a navigator. Your part is notified when a new display frame is created or when a display frame that was previously written out is instantiated from storage. OpenDoc calls the `DisplayFrameAdded` and

`DisplayFrameConnected` methods, respectively, to handle these cases; you can use these methods to attach the broadcaster object.

To attach a progress broadcaster, you must take the following actions:

■ Retrieve the Cyberdog navigator for the embedded display part.

■ Acquire a Cyberdog navigator extension for the navigator.

■ Call the extension's `AttachProgressBroadcaster` method to attach the broadcaster to the Cyberdog navigator.

Listing 5-8 shows how the embedded text-viewer part attaches a progress broadcaster to a Cyberdog navigator. The part calls its `GetContainingNavigator` method to find a frame that is a navigator; see Listing 5-5 (page 154).

Listing 5-8   Adding a progress broadcaster

```
if (fBroadcaster)
{
    ODPart* navPart = this->GetContainingNavigator(ev);
    if (navPart)
    {
        TempNavigatorExtension navExt(navPart, kCyberNavigatorExtension);
        navExt->AttachProgressBroadcaster(ev, fBroadcaster);
    }
}
```

Detaching the Broadcast Object

When your display part is no longer displayed in a navigator, you should detach the progress broadcaster object by calling your part extension's `DetachProgressBroadcaster` method. You may need to detach the broadcaster object when OpenDoc calls the `DisplayFrameRemoved` or the `DisplayFrameClosed` methods.

Listing 5-9 shows the embedded text-viewer part's `DisplayFrameRemoved` method, which detaches the broadcaster.

Listing 5-9   The `DisplayFrameRemoved` method of the embedded text-viewer part

```
void CybTxtNavViewer::DisplayFrameRemoved( Environment* ev,
                                    ODFrame*        frame )
{
    TRY
        // Keep a reference to the navigator; it may be necessary to
        // detach the broadcaster from the navigator.
        ODPart* preNavPart = kODNULL;
        if(fBroadcaster)
            preNavPart = this->GetContainingNavigator(ev);


        // Perform the operations associated with removal.
        ...

        // Detach the broadcaster if the part is no longer displayed
        // in the navigator.
        if (fBroadcaster)
        {
            if (preNavPart && (preNavPart != GetContainingNavigator(ev)))
            {
                TempNavigatorExtension
                        navExt(preNavPart, kCyberNavigatorExtension);
                navExt->DetachProgressBroadcaster(ev, fBroadcaster);
            }
        }
        this->SetDirty(ev);

    CATCH_ALL
    ...
        RERAISE;
    ENDTRY
}
```

Sending Status Messages to the Navigator

You can send messages to a navigator by calling broadcaster methods. Listing 5-10 shows how the embedded text-viewer part sends messages during a polling operation. The PollStream method calls the broadcaster's SetAmountDone method to update the number of characters transferred. It then calls the broadcaster's SetStatusString method to update the status string. The PollStream method calls the stream's GetStatusString method to obtain the content information to display.

Listing 5-10   Sending status messages to the navigator

```
void CybTxtNavViewer::PollStream(Environment* ev)
{
    StreamStatus status;
    ODBoolean gotData = kODFalse;
    Size bytesThisPoll = 0;
    ODULong savedLength = fCharsLength;

    while (bytesThisPoll < kBytesPerPoll)
    {
        status = fStream->GetStreamStatus(ev);
        // Get the data.
        ...
    }

    // Check status after data transfer; it may have changed.
    status = fStream->GetStreamStatus(ev);

    // Animate the Amount Done field of the navigator's status bar.
    if (fCharsLength > savedLength)
        fBroadcaster->SetAmountDone(ev, fCharsLength);

    // Get the status string from the stream and display it in the
    // navigator's status bar.
    if (status & kCDStatusStringChanged)
    {
        Str255 status;
        fStream->GetStatusString(ev, status);
        fBroadcaster->SetStatusString(ev, status);
    }
```

```
// Downloading is complete or an error occurred.
if ((status & kCDDownloadComplete) ||
    (status & kCDErrorOccurred) ||
    (status & kCDAbortComplete))
{
    // Delete the stream.
    delete fStream;
    fStream = kODNULL;

    // Delete the progress broadcaster.
    if (fBroadcaster)
    {
        delete fBroadcaster;
        fBroadcaster = kODNULL;
    }
}
...
}
```

Enabling Menu Items From an Embedded Display Part

A navigator allows an embedded display part to specify whether it wishes to enable several Document menu items. These commands are Save a Copy, Page Setup, and Print. The navigator calls the part extension's `HandleCommand` method for each command. Your part extension's `HandleCommand` method should return `kODTrue` if your embedded display part handles the command or `kODFalse` if it does not. If your part does not handle the command, you must call the part extension's inherited `HandleCommand` method.

The last parameter to the `HandleCommand` method for these commands specifies whether or not the menu item should be enabled. If your `HandleCommand` method returns `kODTrue`, you can set this parameter to `kODTrue` if you want the menu item enabled or `kODFalse` if you want the menu item disabled.

Listing 5-11 shows the embedded text-viewer part extension's `HandleCommand` method. It calls its part's `HandleCommand` method to specify whether it handles commands.

Listing 5-11   The `HandleCommand` method of the embedded text viewer's part extension

```
SOM_Scope ODBoolean  SOMLINK som_CybTxtNavViewerCyberExt__HandleCommand
                            (Apple_som_CybTxtNavViewerCyberExt *somSelf,
                             Environment *ev,
                             long commandCreator,
                             long commandID,
                             ODFrame* frame,
                             void* commandData)
{
    ...
    ODBoolean handled = kODFalse;

    SOM_TRY

        CybTxtNavViewer* realPart
                            = (CybTxtNavViewer*) somThis->fBasePart;
        if (realPart)
            handled = realPart->HandleCommand(ev,
                                        commandCreator,
                                        commandID,
                                        frame,
                                        commandData);

        if(handled == kODFalse)
            handled = Apple_som_CybTxtNavViewerCyberExt_parent
                                    _CyberPartExtension_HandleCommand
                                    (somSelf,ev,
                                     commandCreator,
                                     commandID,
                                     frame,
                                     commandData);

    SOM_CATCH_ALL
        handled = kODFalse;
    SOM_ENDTRY

    return handled;
}
```

Listing 5-12 shows the embedded text-viewer part's `HandleCommand` method. The `commandCreator` parameter is used to qualify the commands to only those issued by the navigator, as specified by `kNavigatorCreator`. The embedded text-viewer part indicates that each of the commands are handled; however, they appear disabled in the menu.

Listing 5-12   The `HandleCommand` method of the embedded text-viewer part

```
ODBoolean CybTxtNavViewer::HandleCommand(Environment*,
                                            long commandCreator,
                                            long commandID,
                                            ODFrame* ,
                                            void* cmdData)
{
    ODBoolean handled = kODFalse;

    switch(commandCreator)
    {
        case kNavigatorCreator:
            {
                // This sample handles all of these commands but
                // leaves them disabled.
                ODBoolean* enableTheMenuCommand = (ODBoolean*)cmdData;
                switch(commandID)
                {
                    case kODCommandPrint:
                    case kODCommandPageSetup:
                    case kODCommandSaveACopy:
                        *enableTheMenuCommand = kODFalse;
                        handled = kODTrue;
                        break;
                }
            }
            break;
    }

    return handled;
}
```

Cyberdog Reference

The chapters in this part describe the Cyberdog programming interface.

- Chapter 6, "Types, Constants, and Global Functions," describes the data types, constants, global functions, and programmer-defined functions you use when writing Cyberdog software.

- Chapter 7, "Classes and Methods," describes the classes and methods of the Cyberdog class library.

PART THREE

Types, Constants, and Global Functions

Contents

This chapter describes all the globally defined Cyberdog data types, constants, global functions, and programmer-defined functions.

Types and Constants

This section describes the Cyberdog data types and constants organized by topic. Under each topic, the scalar types, enumerations, and structures are listed and described. The description of each scalar type identifies constants of that type, if defined.

The following naming conventions can help you understand the purpose of the various Cyberdog identifiers.

- Names of Cyberdog constants begin with the prefix k.

- The names of certain constants include a type prefix after the standard k prefix. For example, constants that begin with kLog are related to the Cyberdog log.

Asynchronous Processes

This section describes types and constants used for monitoring asynchronous processes.

The Asynchronous Process Message

The enumeration CDAbortProcMessage specifies the possible error conditions of an asynchronous process. For Cyberdog version 1.0, there is only one possible error condition. The CyberProgressBroadcaster::Abort method calls MyAbortFunction (page 191), a callback function that you define to implement the abort behavior of a progress broadcaster. A CDAbortProcMessage constant is passed as a parameter to the callback function.

```
enum CDAbortProcMessage
{
    kAbortMessage
};
```

Constants of this type

kAbortMessage   The asynchronous process was terminated.

Progress Modes

The following constants represent possible progress modes for an asynchronous process. You call the accessor methods of a progress broadcaster to get and set the progress mode of an asynchronous process.

kMeteredProgress   Progress toward completion can be quantified. For example, if you know in advance the number of bytes to be downloaded, you can meter the progress of a download operation.

kUnmeteredProgress   Progress toward completion cannot be quantified. For example, if you do not know in advance the number of bytes to be downloaded, you cannot meter the progress of a download operation.

Cyberdog Display Parts

This section describes types and constant used with Cyberdog display parts.

Semantic Events

This section contains semantic events defined by Cyberdog for use by Cyberdog display parts. Semantic events can be passed to a Cyberdog display part's HandleCommand method (page 288).

kCDCmdRefresh   Reconnect to the server and download the data referenced by the display part's Cyberdog item again.

Window Positioning Hint Structure

The CDWindowPositionHint data type represents window-positioning information for a Cyberdog display part. Cyberdog can write a window-positioning hint structure to a Cyberdog display part's storage unit prior to calling the part's Open method to give the display part information about where to open its window.

```
struct CDWindowPositionHint
{
    WindowPtr behindWindow;
    Point windowPosition;
};
```

Field descriptions

behindWindow   A pointer to the window behind which the Cyberdog display part should open. A value of -1 indicates that the display part should open in front.

windowPosition The point where the window should be positioned.

Cyberdog Items

This section describes types and constants used when working with Cyberdog items.

Signature and Version Number

The following constants represent the signature and version number of a Cyberdog item. You include the signature and version number when you flatten a Cyberdog item for storage. See the CyberItem::GetFlatSize method (page 236) for a description of the storage format for Cyberdog items.

kCyberItemSignature   The signature of a Cyberdog item.

kCyberItemVersionNum   The version number of a Cyberdog item.

Cyberdog Item List

The CyberItemList data type defines a collection of CyberItem objects.

```
typedef sequence<CyberItem> CyberItemList;
```

Parameter Keys

A ParameterKey data type is a string used to represent the different types of parameters that can be added to a parameter set. The following constants are parameter keys for parameters that may be used during the opening of a Cyberdog item.

Constants of this type

kCDHeightKey
: The parameter specifies the desired height of the frame that will display the content referenced by the Cyberdog item.

kCDFrameSizeFixed
: The parameter specifies that the size of the frame used to display the content referenced by the Cyberdog item should not be increased.

kCDInitialOpenerPartKey
: The parameter specifies an initial opener part that can be used to open the Cyberdog item.

kCDObtainedOpenerPartKey
: The parameter specifies an obtained opener part that can be used to open the Cyberdog item.

kCDOpenerPartDestDraftKey
: The parameter specifies the draft in which an opener part is embedded. This parameter is used by CyberSession::ObtainOpener (page 368) when creating new opener parts.

kCDParentItemKey
: The parameter specifies the parent Cyberdog item of the Cyberdog item being opened. The parent is passed to the CyberSession::AddCyberItemToLog method (page 349) to establish hierarchical relationships among items in the log.

kCDRefreshKey
: The parameter specifies whether or not the opening of the Cyberdog item is a refresh operation.

kCDSearch4ExistingWindowKey
: The parameter specifies whether or not a window that displays the content referenced by the Cyberdog item should be brought to the front if it exists.

kCDWidthKey
: The parameter specifies the desired width of the frame used to display the content referenced by the Cyberdog item.

Comparison Types

The enumeration `CDCompareType` specifies the possible outcomes of the `CyberItem::Compare` method (page 231), which compares two Cyberdog items according to an order defined by the Cyberdog item developer. For example, a developer implementing a Cyberdog item subclass might order Cyberdog items of the subclass by performing an ASCII comparison of their URL strings.

```
enum CDCompareType {
    kCDCompareLessThan,
    kCDCompareEqual,
    kCDCompareGreaterThan
};
```

Constants of this type

`kCDCompareLessThan`	The receiving Cyberdog item occurs earlier in the order than the other Cyberdog item.
`kCDCompareEqual`	The receiving Cyberdog item and the other Cyberdog item are equal.
`kCDCompareGreaterThan`	The receiving Cyberdog item occurs later in the order than the other Cyberdog item.

Information Types

The enumeration `CDInfoType` specifies the possible representations for a Cyberdog item stored on the desktop or in a Finder window. A constant of this type is passed to the `CyberItem::GetFileInfo` method (page 235) to specify which file creator and file type to retrieve and to the `CyberItem::GetIconSuite` (page 237) method to specify which icon suite to retrieve.

```
enum CDItemInfoType {
    kCDInfoDownload,
    kCDInfoReference,
    kCDInfoPart
};
```

Constants of this type

kCDInfoDownload	The content referenced by a Cyberdog item, downloaded to a file in its native form.
kCDInfoReference	A reference to remotely located content.
kCDInfoPart	The content referenced by a Cyberdog item, stored as a part.

Flags

The following constants represent flags that describe properties of a Cyberdog item. A Cyberdog item's flags are retrieved by calling the CyberItem::GetFlags method (page 236). Each flag has a corresponding mask that can be used to isolate the flag from the value returned by GetFlags.

kCDFlagDontEmbed	Indicates that a display part whose content is referenced by the Cyberdog item should not be embedded in a document.
kCDFlagDontEmbedMask	Mask used to isolate the kCDFlagDontEmbed flag.
kCDFlagDontLog	Indicates that the Cyberdog item should not be added to the log.
kCDFlagDontLogMask	Mask used to isolate the kCDFlagDontLog flag.

String Properties

A CDStringProperty data type is an ODOSType type that represents a **string property,** a string describing some aspect of a Cyberdog item.

Constants of this type

kCDDefaultName	The default display name to be used for the Cyberdog item.
kCDHomeName	The home name to be used for the Cyberdog item. A home name is a shortened version of a display name; home names can be used in place of long newsgroup names. For example, the home name for the display name "rec.arts.movies" might be "movies".
kCDWindowName	The name to be used for the Cyberdog item when it is displayed in its own window.

kCDLogName	The name to be used for the Cyberdog item when it is displayed in the log.
kCDLog2ndCol	Reserved.
kCDNotebookName	The name to be used for the Cyberdog item when it is displayed in a notebook.
kCDNotebook2ndCol	Reserved.
kCDFileName	The filename to be used for the Cyberdog item when it is stored in a file.

Script Code

A ScriptCode data type is a 16-bit value that identifies the script system (Roman, for example) to be used to draw a text string.

Download Part

This section describes types and constants used with Cyberdog download parts.

Download Event

The enumeration CDDownloadEvent specifies the possible outcomes when a download part downloads the data referenced by a Cyberdog item and saves it to disk. These events are passed to the MyDownloadCompleted programmer-defined function (page 193).

```
enum CDDownloadEvent
{
    kCDDownloadSucceeded,
    kCDDownloadFailed,
    kCDDownloadCancelled
};
```

Constants of this type

kCDDownloadSucceeded	The data referenced by the Cyberdog item was successfully downloaded and saved to disk.
kCDDownloadFailed	The attempt to download the data and save it to disk failed.

kCDDownloadCancelled The request to download the data and save it to disk was canceled.

Download Request ID

A CDDownloadRequestID data type is a 32-bit value that represents the ID of a request to download the data referenced by a Cyberdog item and save it to disk. These requests are sent to download parts. To cancel a request, you call the CyberDownloadExtension::CancelRequest method (page 214), passing the ID of the request.

Constants of this type

kCDAllDownloadRequests Cancel all requests to download and save data referenced by Cyberdog items.

Log

This section describes types and constants used with the Cyberdog log.

Log Kinds

The following constants represent different ways that Cyberdog items can be displayed by the Cyberdog log. The Cyberdog log uses these constants in its stored representation.

kLogKindAlphabetical Log entries are listed alphabetically.

kLogKindChronological Log entries are listed chronologically.

kLogKindHierarchical Log entries are listed hierarchically.

Notebook

This section describes types and constants used with Cyberdog notebooks.

Address Field

The enumeration `CDAddressField` specifies possible values that can be passed to the `MyNotebookAddressHandler` programmer-defined function (page 194). These values specify the field of the mail message where the addresses should be placed.

```
enum CDAddressField
{
    kToField = 1,
    kCCField,
    kBCCField
};
```

Constants of this type

`kToField`	Add the address to the "To:" field.
`kCCField`	Add the address to the "CC:" field.
`kBCCField`	Add the address to the "BCC:" field.

Notebook Kinds

The following constants represent the different types of entries in a Cyberdog notebook. These constants are used in the implementation of the Cyberdog notebook.

`kNotebookKindTagCategory`
> The notebook entry is a category.

`kNotebookKindTagCyberItem`
> The notebook entry is a Cyberdog item.

Cyberdog Services

This section describes types and constants used with Cyberdog services.

Service Resource

Figure 6-1 shows the format of the service resource, 'srvc'. You use this resource to specify characteristics of a Cyberdog service. When a Cyberdog session is initialized, it creates a Cyberdog service for each 'srvc' resource in your shared library.

Figure 6-1   'srvc' resource

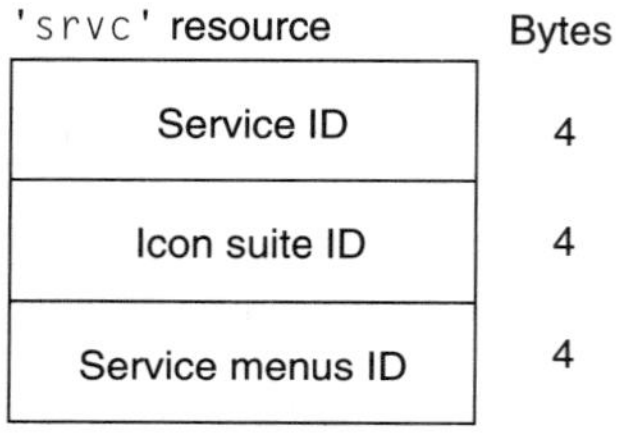

'srvc' resource	Bytes
Service ID	4
Icon suite ID	4
Service menus ID	4

This resource contains the following elements:

■ Service ID. The service ID specifies the resource ID of a 'STR#' resource that contains strings describing the service. The strings in the 'STR#' resource are specified in the following order:

□ SOM class ID of the CyberService subclass. This is required for CyberService subclasses.

□ User-readable name of the service. This is required for CyberService subclasses.

□ URL scheme supported by the service. This is required for SimpleCyberService objects.

□ Part kind of the service's Connect To panel. This is required for SimpleCyberService objects. This is an empty string if the service does not have a Connect To panel.

□ Part kind of the service's Preferences panel. This is required for `SimpleCyberService` objects. This is an empty string if the service does not have a Preferences panel.

□ SOM class ID of the `CyberItem` subclass for which this service will manufacture Cyberdog items. This is required for `SimpleCyberService` objects.

■ Icon suite ID. The icon suite ID specifies the resource ID of the icon suite for the service. This is required for `SimpleCyberService` objects.

■ Service menus ID. The service menus ID specifies the resource ID of a `'STR#'` resource that contains the menu item names for this service. This is required for `SimpleCyberService` objects. This field is set to 0 if the service does not have any menu items.

Proxy Scheme

The `kCyberProxyScheme` constant is a string constant ("cyberproxy:") that represents the URL scheme for a proxy server. A Cyberdog service that wants to provide proxy services must include this scheme in the list of URL schemes that it supports.

Cyberdog Streams

This section describes types and constants used with Cyberdog streams.

Stream Status

The `StreamStatus` data type is a 16-bit value that contains flags describing the status of a Cyberdog stream. They are returned by the `CyberStream::GetStreamStatus` method.

Flag descriptions

`kCDDataAvailable`	The stream has been opened successfully and contains at least one buffer of nonzero length that you can retrieve by calling `CyberStream::GetBuffer` (page 379).

kCDErrorOccurred	An error has occurred. You can call CyberStream::GetStatusString (page 381) to retrieve the error message.
kCDStatusStringChanged	The status string that describes the current status of the stream has changed. You can retrieve the current status string by calling CyberStream::GetStatusString (page 381). When an error occurs, the status string is changed, but the value of the kCDStatusStringChanged flag is not changed.
kCDBuffersAreLow	The stream's supply of buffers is low. You should call CyberStream::ReleaseBuffer (page 386) to release any buffers that you have retrieved from the stream.
kCDDownloadComplete	The download operation is complete.
kCDAbortComplete	The abort operation initiated on the stream is complete.

Data Size

The following constants represent values that can be returned by the CyberStream::GetTotalDataSize method (page 383).

kCDTotalDataSizeUnknown	The number of bytes of data to be downloaded is unknown.
kCDTotalDataSizeUnknowable	The number of bytes of data to be downloaded is unavailable.

Last Modification Time

The following constants represent values that can be returned by the CyberStream::GetLastModTime method (page 380).

kCDLastModTimeUnknown	The time that the data was last modified is unknown.
kCDLastModTimeUnknowable	The time that the data was last modified is unavailable.

Internet Config Keys

This section describes the **Internet Config keys,** string constants used to identify various preference settings stored in Internet Config, which is software used by Cyberdog to store and recall a user's Internet-related preferences. These keys supplement keys that are defined by Internet Config in `ICKeys.h`.

For more information on Internet Config, see the Internet Config documentation located at the FTP site `ftp://redback.cs.uwa.edu.au//Others/PeterLewis/InternetConfig1.2.sit` or search on the Internet for "Internet Config".

General preferences

`kCyberICDefaultScheme`   Reserved.

`kCyberICConnectService`   An `ODType` value specifying the part kind of the Connect To panel to display when the Connect To dialog box is opened.

Security preferences

`kCyberICEnteringSecureSpace`

A Boolean value specifying whether to show a security warning when the user enters a secure space.

`kCyberICLeavingSecureSpace`

A Boolean value specifying whether to show a security warning when the user leaves a secure space.

`kCyberICMixedSecureDocument`

A Boolean value specifying whether to show a security warning when the user receives a document that contains both secure and nonsecure content.

`kCyberICNonSecureForm`   A Boolean value specifying whether to show a security warning when the user submits a form using an nonsecure connection.

FTP preferences

`kCyberICFTPPrefShowHiddenFiles`

A Boolean value specifying whether to show UNIX hidden (".") files.

`kCyberICFTPPrefUniqueNameOnUpload`

A Boolean value specifying whether unique names should be created for files that are uploaded with nonunique names.

kCyberICFTPPrefUsePassive

> A Boolean value specifying whether to use FTP passive mode when communicating with FTP servers.

Log preferences

kCyberICLogSize

> A 32-bit value specifying the maximum number of items in the log.

Mail preferences

kCyberICDistributionForPostedArticles

> A string specifying the distribution for posted articles.

kCyberICMailDefaultMailboxFolder

> A file specification specifying the default folder for creating new mailbox trays.

kCyberICMailPrefShowButtonsInEnvelope

> A Boolean value specifying whether buttons should be shown on the mail envelope.

kCyberICMailPrefCloseLetterWindow

> A Boolean value specifying whether the letter window should be closed after a message is sent.

kCyberICMailPrefWarnWhenUnsaved

> A Boolean value specifying whether the user should be warned if a sent message has not been saved.

kCyberICMailLeaveMailInOutTrayChoice

> A Boolean value specifying whether to leave mail in the user's out tray permanently.

kCyberICMailLeaveMailInOutTrayDays

> A 16-bit value specifying the number of days that mail should be kept in the user's out tray.

kCyberICMailPrefExpandEnvelopeNew

> A Boolean value specifying whether the envelope should be expanded when a letter is created.

kCyberICMailPrefExpandEnvelopeOpen

> A Boolean value specifying whether the envelope should be expanded when a letter is opened.

kCyberICMailPrefPrintEnvelope

> A Boolean value specifying whether the envelope should be printed when a letter is printed.

Notebook preferences

`kCyberICNotebookFile`   A file specification specifying the name and location of the default notebook.

Telnet preferences

`kCyberICTelnetPrefTerminalEmulation`

A string specifying the type of terminal emulation to be used.

`kCyberICTelnetPrefTerminalToolName`

A string specifying the terminal emulation tool to be used.

`kCyberICTelnetPrefTerminalToolConfig`

Text specifying the terminal configuration.

Web preferences

`kCyberICWebPrefHeadlineFont`

An Internet Config font record specifying the font to be used for headlines.

`kCyberICWebPrefTextFont`   An Internet Config font record specifying the font to be used for proportional text.

`kCyberICWebPrefTypewriterFont`

An Internet Config font record specifying the font to be used for nonproportional text.

`kCyberICWebPrefReadColor`

An RGB color value specifying the color to be used for links that have been read.

`kCyberICWebPrefUnreadColor`

An RGB color value specifying the color to be used for links that have not been read.

`kCyberICWebPrefUnderlineLinks`

A Boolean specifying whether links should be underlined.

Navigator preferences

`kCyberICNavigatorPrefShowControlBanner`

A Boolean specifying whether the navigator's control banner should be shown.

kCyberICNavigatorPrefShowLocationBanner

> A Boolean specifying whether the navigator's location banner should be shown.

kCyberICNavigatorPrefTunnel

> A Boolean specifying whether the same navigator should be used to display all Cyberdog display parts.

Part Kinds

This section describes data type and part kind constants used in Cyberdog.

Media Types and Part Kinds

Table 6-1 contains constants used to represent Cyberdog items and their downloaded content.

- MIME media types are strings ('text/html' for example) used in MIME transmissions to indicate the type of the data being transmitted.

- When the user drags a Cyberdog item to the Finder or to a document as an OpenDoc part, Cyberdog assigns a part kind (an ISO string) to the part according to the type of data it contains.

- When the user drags a Cyberdog item to the Finder as a reference, Cyberdog assigns a reference kind (an ISO string) to the reference according to the type of data to which it refers.

The following additional constant represents the ISO prefix for part kinds.

kMIMEPrefix

> The ISO prefix prepended to a MIME media type to create a part kind.

Table 6-1   MIME media types, part kinds, and reference kinds

MIME media type	Part kind	Reference kind	MIME media type string
kApplicationAppleFile	kApplicationAppleFileKind	kApplicationAppleFileRefKind	'application/applefile'
kApplicationCompress	kApplicationCompressKind	kApplicationCompressRefKind	'application/x-compress'
kApplicationMacBinary	kApplicationMacBinaryKind	kApplicationMacBinaryRefKind	'application/macbinary'
kApplicationMacBinhex40	kApplicationMacBinhex40Kind	kApplicationMacBinhex40RefKind	'application/mac-binhex-40'
kApplicationOctetStream	kApplicationOctetStreamKind	kApplicationOctetStreamRefKind	'application/octet-stream'
kApplicationPostscript	kApplicationPostscriptKind	kApplicationPostscriptRefKind	'application/postscript'
kApplicationText	kApplicationTextKind	kApplicationTextRefKind	'application/text'
kAudioAIFF	kAudioAIFFKind	kAudioAIFFRefKind	'audio/x-aiff'
kAudioBasic	kAudioBasicKind	kAudioBasicRefKind	'audio/basic'
kAudioWAV	kAudioWAVKind	kAudioWAVRefKind	'audio/x-wav'
kImageGIF	kImageGIFKind	kImageGIFRefKind	'image/gif'
kImageJPEG	kImageJPEGKind	kImageJPEGRefKind	'image/jpeg'
kImagePICT	kImagePICTKind	kImagePICTRefKind	'image/x-pict'
kImageTIFF	kImageTIFFKind	kImageTIFFRefKind	'image/tiff'
kImageXBM	kImageXBMKind	kImageXBMRefKind	'image/x-xbitmap'
kImageXPM	kImageXPMKind	kImageXPMRefKind	'image/x-xpixmap'
kMessageExternalBody	kMessageExternalBodyKind	kMessageExternalBodyRefKind	'message/external-body'
kMessagePartial	kMessagePartialKind	kMessagePartialRefKind	'message/partial'
kMessageRFC822	kMessageRFC822Kind	kMessageRFC822RefKind	'message/rfc822'
kMultipartAlternative	kMultipartAlternativeKind	kMultipartAlternativeRefKind	'multipart/alternative'
kMultipartDigest	kMultipartDigestKind	kMultipartDigestRefKind	'multipart/digest'
kMultipartMixed	kMultipartMixedKind	kMultipartMixedRefKind	'multipart/mixed'
kMultipartParallel	kMultipartParallelKind	kMultipartParallelRefKind	'multipart/parallel'
kTextEnriched	kTextEnrichedKind	kTextEnrichedRefKind	'text/enriched'

continued

Table 6-1   MIME media types, part kinds, and reference kinds (continued)

MIME media type	Part kind	Reference kind	MIME media type string
kTextHTML	kTextHTMLKind	kTextHTMLRefKind	'text/html'
kTextPlain	kTextPlainKind	kTextPlainRefKind	'text/plain'
kVideoAVI	kVideoAVIKind	kVideoAVIRefKind	'video/avi'
kVideoMPEG	kVideoMPEGKind	kVideoMPEGRefKind	'video/mpeg'
kVideoQuickTime	kVideoQuickTimeKind	kVideoQuickTimeRefKind	'video/quicktime'

Cyberdog Kinds

The following string constants represent part kinds of Cyberdog components.

kCyberItemGroupKind   An ISO string that represents the part kind of a collection of Cyberdog items.

kCyberItemKind   An ISO string that represents the part kind of a Cyberdog item. The opener part editor binds to parts of kind kCyberItemKind.

kCyberPartKind   An ISO string that represents parts that are extended with an object of a subclass of CyberPartExtension. A Cyberdog display part should include this part kind in its name-mapping resource ('nmap') so that Cyberdog can tell that the display part is a Cyberdog display part.

kConnectDialogKind   An ISO string that represents the part kind of the Cyberdog Connect To dialog box.

kDownloadPartKind   An ISO string that represents the part kind of the Cyberdog download part.

kLogKind   An ISO string that represents the part kind of the Cyberdog log.

kLogManagerKind   An ISO string that represents the part kind of the Cyberdog log manager.

kNavigatorKind   An ISO string that represents the part kind of the Cyberdog navigator.

kNotebookKind   An ISO string that represents the part kind of the Cyberdog notebook.

kNotebookManagerKind	An ISO string that represents the part kind of the Cyberdog notebook manager.
kOpenerPartKind	An ISO string that represents the part kind of the opener part.
kPrefsDialogKind	An ISO string that represents the part kind of the Cyberdog Preferences dialog box.
kTelnetPartKind	An ISO string that represents the part kind of the Cyberdog Telnet part.

Cyberdog File Creator

The following constants represent creators used by Cyberdog.

kCyberdogCreator	Creator used internally by Cyberdog.
kNavigatorCreator	Creator used to qualify commands sent by a navigator to its embedded display part's HandleCommand method.

Class IDs

This section describes ISO string constants used to refer to Cyberdog classes. You use an extension's class ID when you call an object's HasExtension and AcquireExtension methods.

kCyberConnectExtension	The CyberConnectExtension class.
kCyberContainerExtension	The CyberContainerExtension class.
kCyberDownloadExtension	The CyberDownloadExtension class.
kCyberFormExtension	The CyberFormExtension class.
kCyberItemPromptExtension	The CyberItemPromptExtension class.
kCyberLogExtension	The CyberLogExtension class.
kCyberNavigatorExtension	The CyberNavigatorExtension class.
kCyberNotebookExtension	The CyberNotebookExtension class.

kCyberOpenerPartExtension

The `CyberOpenerPartExtension` class.

kCyberPartExtension   The `CyberPartExtension` class.

kCyberPrefsExtension   The `CyberPrefsExtension` class.

kCyberProgressPartExtension

The `CyberProgressPartExtension` class.

kSimpleCyberServiceClassName

The `SimpleCyberService` class.

Exceptions

The following constants represent exceptions that can be raised by Cyberdog methods and functions.

kCyberErrorsBase   The base Cyberdog error constant. All Cyberdog exceptions are defined as offsets from `kCyberErrorsBase`.

kCDErrInvalidObject   The object whose method was called is invalid. This exception is thrown by objects whose internal state has been corrupted.

kCDErrInvalidURL   The specified URL is invalid. This exception is thrown by `CyberSession::CreateCyberItemFromURL` (page 353).

kCDErrServerBusy   The server is unable to process requests at this time.

kCDErrAuthentication   The server does not recognize the user name or password.

kCDErrItemUnavailable   The mail message or news group posting is no longer available.

kCDErrParamAlreadyExists

An attempt was made to add a parameter with a duplicate parameter key to a parameter set.

kCDErrNoInternetConfig   The Internet Config extension is not installed.

kCDErrCyberSessionAlreadyExists

An attempt was made to create and initialize a Cyberdog session object when one already exists.

kCDErrInvalidServiceResource

The contents of the `'srvc'` resource are invalid.

`kCDErrNoFileRepresentation`

> The Cyberdog item is not downloadable. `CyberItem::GetFileInfo` (page 235) throws this exception when it is called with the `kCDInfoDownload` constant and the Cyberdog item does not reference downloadable data.

`kCDErrPasswordRetriesExceeded`

> The number of password retries was exceeded.

`kCDErrMacTCPorOTMissing` The required networking software (MacTCP or Open Transport) is not installed.

`kCDErrItemNotResolved` The Cyberdog item is not resolved.

Global Functions

This section presents summary descriptions of the Cyberdog global functions grouped according to purpose, followed by detailed descriptions.

Initialization and Cleanup

`InitCyberdog`   Creates and initializes Cyberdog and the global session object.

Accessing the Cyberdog Session

`GetCyberSession`   Retrieves the global session object.

GetCyberSession

Retrieves the global session object.

```
pascal CyberSession* GetCyberSession (Environment* ev);
```

`ev`   A pointer to the SOM environment parameter used to pass exceptions.

return value   A pointer to the global `CyberSession` object or `kODNULL` if the `CyberSession` object has not yet been created.

DISCUSSION

You can call this function when you need to retrieve the global session object. You can also retrieve the global session object by calling `CyberExtension::GetCyberSession` method.

SEE ALSO

The `CyberExtension::GetCyberSession` method (page 219).

InitCyberdog

Creates and initializes Cyberdog and the global session object.

```
pascal OSErr InitCyberdog (Environment* ev, ODSession* session);
```

ev   A pointer to the SOM environment parameter used to pass exceptions.

session   A pointer to the `ODSession` object to associate with the `CyberSession` object.

return value   An error code.

DISCUSSION

Any part that calls Cyberdog methods should call this function during its initialization to initialize Cyberdog and create the global session object. An `ODSession` object must exist before a Cyberdog session object can be created. This function returns the error code `noErr` if the initialization was successful. You can also create the global session object by calling the `CyberExtension::CreateCyberSession` method.

SEE ALSO

The `CyberExtension::CreateCyberSession` method (page 219).

Programmer-Defined Functions

This section describes programmer-defined functions that you may need to provide when developing Cyberdog components.

MyAbortFunction

Implements the abort behavior for a progress broadcaster.

```
void MyAbortFunction (CDAbortProcMessage msgCode,
                      CyberProgressBroadcaster* broadcaster,
                      Ptr userDataPtr);
```

msgCode   A message code indicating that the progress broadcaster is being aborted.

broadcaster   A pointer to the progress broadcaster object that is being aborted.

userDataPtr   A pointer to data that may be useful when aborting the progress broadcaster.

DISCUSSION

The purpose of your abort function is to implement any behavior that you want to perform when a progress broadcaster's Abort method is called. The Abort method calls the abort function, which you register when you call CyberProgressBroadcaster::ICyberProgressBroadcaster. This mechanism allows you to customize the abort behavior of a progress broadcaster object without having to subclass CyberProgressBroadcaster.

The userDataPtr parameter contains a pointer to data that may be useful when aborting the progress broadcaster. For example, this parameter might point to a display part whose progress broadcaster should be deleted.

SEE ALSO

The CyberProgressBroadcaster::Abort method (page 300).
The CyberProgressBroadcaster::ICyberProgressBroadcaster method (page 306).

MyCyberItemResolved

Responds to notification that the Cyberdog item resolution process is complete.

```
void MyCyberItemResolved (OSErr err,
                    CyberItem* item,
                    Ptr userDataPtr);
```

err   An error code that indicates whether the Cyberdog item was resolved successfully.

item   A pointer to the Cyberdog item.

userDataPtr   A pointer to data that may be useful when a Cyberdog item is resolved.

DISCUSSION

This notification function is called when the Resolve method of a CyberItem subclass has finished trying to resolve a Cyberdog item. You register your notification function when you call the Resolve method. The value of the err parameter is noErr if the Cyberdog item was resolved successfully.

The userDataPtr parameter contains a pointer to data that may be useful when responding to notification that a Cyberdog item has been resolved. For example, this parameter might point to a method to be called if the Cyberdog item was resolved successfully.

SEE ALSO

The CyberItem::Resolve method (page 242).

MyDownloadCompleted

Responds to notification that a request to download data referenced by a Cyberdog item and save it to disk has been completed.

```
void MyDownloadCompleted (Environment* ev,
                    CyberItem* item,
                    CDDownloadEvent eventCode,
                    FSSpec* destFile,
                    Ptr userDataPtr);
```

ev   A pointer to the SOM environment parameter used to pass exceptions.

item   A pointer to the Cyberdog item whose data was to be downloaded.

eventCode   A code that indicates whether the data referenced by the Cyberdog item was downloaded and saved to disk successfully.

destFile   A pointer to the file specification where the data referenced by the Cyberdog item was stored.

userDataPtr   A pointer to data that may be useful when a download operation has completed.

DISCUSSION

The download part calls your download notification function when it has finished trying to download the content referenced by a Cyberdog item and save it to disk. You register your download notification function when you call the PostDownloadRequest method. Your notification function can test the eventCode parameter to determine whether the download operation succeeded, failed, or was canceled.

The userDataPtr parameter contains a pointer to data that may be useful when responding to notification that a download request has been completed. For example, this parameter might point to a C++ class that defines a method to be called if the Cyberdog item is downloaded successfully.

SEE ALSO

The CDDownloadEvent type (page 175).
The CyberDownloadExtension::PostDownloadRequest method (page 215).

MyMenuDataDestructor

Deallocates the data in a Cyberdog service menu.

```
void MyMenuDataDestructor (void* menuData);
```

menuData   A pointer to data associated with the Cyberdog service menu.

DISCUSSION

A service's AppendCyberMenuCommands method should return the menu data associated with the service and a destructor function for the menu data. Cyberdog calls the menu data destructor when the Cyberdog service menu object is deleted; your menu data destructor function should deallocate the data pointed to by the menuData parameter.

SEE ALSO

The CyberService::AppendCyberMenuCommands method (page 330).

MyNotebookAddressHandler

Handles addresses the user selects in the address browser.

```
void MyNotebookAddressHandler (CDAddressField whichField,
                    void* cyberItemsList,
                    Ptr userDataPtr);
```

whichField   A constant that indicates the address field in which the
                  specified addresses should be placed.

cyberItemsList
                  A pointer to a list of Cyberdog items to be used as mail addresses.

userDataPtr   A pointer to data that may be useful when handling mail addresses.

DISCUSSION

The purpose of your notebook address function is to handle address selections specified by the user in the address browser. Mail developers call the CyberNotebookExtension::PromptForAddresses method to display the address browser; that method registers a notebook address function. Cyberdog calls the notebook address function each time the user selects one or more addresses and clicks a button in the address browser.

For example, if the user selects two addresses from the address list and clicks the "CC:" button, Cyberdog calls the notebook address function, passing it the two Cyberdog items that the user selected and a constant indicating that the addresses should be added to the "CC:" address field of the mail message.

The userDataPtr parameter contains a pointer to data that may be useful when handling mail addresses. For example, this parameter might point to a data structure that represents the mail message for which the addresses are intended.

SEE ALSO

The CDAddressField type (page 177).
The CyberNotebookExtension::PromptForAddresses method (page 267).

MyParamDestructor

Destroys a parameter.

```
void MyParamDestructor (Environment* ev,
                void* param);
```

ev   A pointer to the SOM environment parameter used to pass exceptions.

param   A pointer to the parameter to be destroyed.

Types, Constants, and Global Functions

DISCUSSION

Your parameter destructor function should destroy a parameter when it is removed from a parameter set. You add a parameter and an associated destructor function to a parameter set by calling the `ParameterSet::PutParameter` method. Your destructor function is called either when you call the `ParameterSet::RemoveParameter` method to remove the parameter from the parameter set or when the parameter set is destroyed.

SEE ALSO

The `ParameterSet::PutParameter` method (page 393).
The `ParameterSet::RemoveParameter` method (page 395).

CHAPTER 7

Classes and Methods

Contents

Classes and Methods

Contents

7 Classes and Methods

Classes and Methods

This chapter describes the Cyberdog public classes and methods. The Cyberdog class library provides a complete set of classes and methods that you can use to create Cyberdog display parts, services, and supporting parts.

The discussion of each method notes any special instructions for overriding the method. If no special overriding instructions are noted for a method, you may override the method and your override may call its inherited method.

CyberConnectExtension

Superclasses CyberPanelExtension → CyberExtension → ODExtension → ODRefCntObject → ODObject

Subclasses none

The `CyberConnectExtension` class defines extra behaviors for parts that will be embedded as panels in the Connect To dialog box.

Description

A Connect To panel allows the user to enter all the information necessary to specify a Cyberdog item for a particular service. For example, a Connect To panel to specify a Cyberdog item for an FTP site would allow the user to specify the host computer, the path, and so on.

`CyberConnectExtension` is an abstract superclass you can subclass and implement to create a custom Connect To panel. Typically, you need to create your own Connect To panel only if you add a new service to Cyberdog.

Methods

The `CyberConnectExtension` class has a single method, `CreateCyberItem`. A detailed description of the method follows.

`CreateCyberItem`   Creates a Cyberdog item from information specified in this Connect To panel.

CreateCyberItem

Creates a Cyberdog item from information specified in this Connect To panel.

`CyberItem CreateCyberItem ();`

return value   The newly created `CyberItem` object.

DISCUSSION

Your implementation of this method should return the Cyberdog item the user specified in this Connect To panel. This method is called by the `CyberItemPromptExtension::PromptForCyberItem` method when the user clicks the OK button in the Connect To dialog box.

If you subclass `CyberConnectExtension`, you must override this method. Your override must not call its inherited method; that is, your override method must implement this method's functionality completely.

SEE ALSO

The `CyberItemPromptExtension::PromptForCyberItem` method (page 249).

CyberContainerExtension

Superclasses   `CyberExtension` → `ODExtension` → `ODRefCntObject` → `ODObject`

Subclasses   none

The `CyberContainerExtension` class defines extra behaviors for parts that will act as dialog box containers and embed other parts as panels.

Description

The `CyberContainerExtension` class is an abstract class you can subclass to create an extension that allows a part to behave as a dialog box that embeds other parts as panels. For example, the Cyberdog Connect To and Preferences dialog boxes use embedded panels. The panels to be embedded are parts that are extended by subclasses of the `CyberPanelExtension` class (page 277).

Note
The Cyberdog Connect To dialog box has an additional extension, subclassed from `CyberItemPromptExtension`, which provides the Cyberdog item specified by the user in the Connect To dialog box. ◆

The Cyberdog Connect To and Preferences dialog boxes are fully implemented. If you add a new service to Cyberdog, you need to subclass the panel extension classes `CyberConnectExtension` and `CyberPrefsExtension` to handle the connection information and preferences for the new service. However, you do not need to subclass `CyberContainerExtension` unless you want to create your own custom dialog box container for panel parts.

Methods

This section presents summary descriptions of the `CyberContainerExtension` methods grouped according to purpose, followed by detailed descriptions.

Enabling Buttons

EnableOKButton   Enables or disables the OK button in this dialog
                           box container.

Closing

FlashCancelButton   Highlights the Cancel button in this dialog box container
                           and closes the container.

FlashOKButton   Highlights the OK button in this dialog box container
                           and closes the container.

Acquiring and Losing Focus

TabIn   Notifies this dialog box container that it has received the
                           keyboard focus.

EnableOKButton

Enables or disables the OK button in this dialog box container.

```
void EnableOKButton (in ODBoolean enabled);
```

enabled   kODTrue if the OK button should be enabled; kODFalse if the OK
                   button should be disabled.

DISCUSSION

You call this method from an embedded panel to notify the dialog box to
enable or disable its OK button.

If you subclass CyberContainerExtension, you must override this method. Your
override must not call its inherited method; that is, your override method must
implement this method's functionality completely.

SEE ALSO

The FlashCancelButton method (page 210).
The FlashOKButton method (page 210).

7

Classes and Methods

FlashCancelButton

Highlights the Cancel button in this dialog box container and closes the container.

```
void FlashCancelButton ();
```

DISCUSSION

You call this method from an embedded panel to request the dialog box to highlight its Cancel button and then close. This method is called for you by an embedded panel's `FlashCancelButton` method when the user presses the Escape key while the embedded panel is active.

If you subclass `CyberContainerExtension`, you must override this method. Your override must not call its inherited method; that is, your override method must implement this method's functionality completely.

SEE ALSO

The `FlashOKButton` method (page 210).
The `CyberPanelExtension::FlashCancelButton` method (page 279).

FlashOKButton

Highlights the OK button in this dialog box container and closes the container.

```
void FlashOKButton ();
```

DISCUSSION

You call this method from an embedded panel to request the dialog box to highlight its OK button and then close. This method is called for you by an embedded panel's `FlashOKButton` method when the user presses the Return or Enter key while the embedded panel is active.

If you subclass `CyberContainerExtension`, you must override this method. Your override must not call its inherited method; that is, your override method must implement this method's functionality completely.

The `FlashCancelButton` method (page 210).
The `CyberPanelExtension::FlashOKButton` method (page 279).

TabIn

Notifies this dialog box container that it has received the keyboard focus.

```
void TabIn (in ODBoolean reverse);
```

reverse   `kODTrue` if reverse tab order should be used; otherwise, `kODFalse`.

DISCUSSION

You call this method from an embedded panel to notify the dialog box that it has regained the keyboard focus. This method is called for you by an embedded panel's `TabOut` method when the user presses the Tab key while the embedded panel is active.

If you subclass `CyberContainerExtension`, you must override this method. Your override must not call its inherited method; that is, your override method must implement this method's functionality completely.

SEE ALSO

The `CyberPanelExtension::TabOut` method (page 281).

CyberDownloadExtension

| *Superclasses* | CyberExtension → ODExtension → ODRefCntObject → ODObject |

Superclasses   CyberExtension → ODExtension → ODRefCntObject → ODObject

Subclasses   none

The CyberDownloadExtension class defines extra behaviors for a part that is to be used as a download part.

Description

The CyberDownloadExtension class is an extension that allows a part to be used as a download part, which downloads content referenced by a Cyberdog item to disk. A Cyberdog download part has two extensions: a CyberDownloadExtension subclass extension and a CyberPartExtension subclass extension.

CyberDownloadExtension is an abstract superclass that you must subclass and implement to create your own custom download part. Cyberdog provides a fully implemented download part; to use this download part, you do not need to subclass this class.

The download part is used in several situations, such as the following:

- When the user drags a Cyberdog item from a display part (a Gopher display part, for example) and drops it in the Finder. In this case, the display part can create a download part and call its CyberDownloadExtension methods to download to disk the data referenced by the Cyberdog item. Optionally, the download part can display progress using its own window.

- When the user opens a Cyberdog item (by clicking an HTML link, for example). In this case, if the Cyberdog item cannot find a Cyberdog display part editor to bind to, the Cyberdog item can create a download part and call the download part's OpenCyberItem method. The download part downloads the data to disk, obtains an opener part, and calls the opener part's OpenFile method to open the file created during the download. The download part displays progress in the opener part.

- When the user selects several Cyberdog items and then chooses the Get Items from Server command from either the Gopher or FTP menu. In this case, Cyberdog creates a single download part to download and save to disk the content referenced by all the selected Cyberdog items.

The `CyberDownloadExtension` interface provides two different methods for queuing requests to download the content referenced by a Cyberdog item and save it to a file: `DownloadCyberItem` and `PostDownloadRequest`. Both methods add a request to download data to the download part's queue. You initiate pending download requests by calling `StartDownloads`.

The `DownloadCyberItem` method is the simplest method to use; when you call it, you pass the Cyberdog item and the specification of the destination file. The `PostDownloadRequest` method allows you to register a function that Cyberdog can call to notify you when the download is complete. In addition, the `PostDownloadRequest` method allows you to specify whether you want the downloaded file to be decompressed before it is saved.

The download part requests and uses a Cyberdog item's associated stream to download the Cyberdog item. When the download part is finished processing its download requests, it destroys itself.

Methods

This section presents summary descriptions of the `CyberDownloadExtension` methods grouped according to purpose, followed by detailed descriptions.

Requesting a Download

`CancelRequest`	Cancels a request to download data to disk.
`DownloadCyberItem`	Requests the download of data referenced by a Cyberdog item to disk.
`PostDownloadRequest`	Requests the download of data referenced by Cyberdog item to disk and registers a completion notification function.

Initiating a Download Request

`StartDownloads`	Initiates the download requests queued for a download part.

CancelRequest

Cancels a request to download data to disk.

```
void CancelRequest (in CDDownloadRequestID id);
```

id The unique ID of the request to be cancelled, or
kCDAllDownloadRequests to cancel all of the requests in the
download part's queue.

DISCUSSION

This method cancels a request that was made previously by calling either the
DownloadCyberItem method or the PostDownloadRequest method.

If you subclass CyberDownloadExtension, you must override this method. Your
override must not call its inherited method; that is, your override method must
implement this method's functionality completely.

SEE ALSO

The DownloadCyberItem method (page 214).
The PostDownloadRequest method (page 215).

DownloadCyberItem

Requests the download of data referenced by a Cyberdog item to disk.

```
CDDownloadRequestID DownloadCyberItem (in CyberItem item,
                    in FSSpecPtr spec);
```

item The CyberItem object that specifies the data to be downloaded
to disk.

spec A pointer to a file specification that specifies the file in which to
save the data.

return value An ID that uniquely identifies the download request.

DISCUSSION

This method adds a Cyberdog item to this download part's queue. If nil is specified for the spec parameter, the download part decides where to save the data. To cancel a download request, you call the CancelRequest method, passing the ID returned by this method.

If you wish to receive notification when a download is complete, you should request the download by calling PostDownloadRequest instead of this method.

If you subclass CyberDownloadExtension, you must override this method. Your override must not call its inherited method; that is, your override method must implement this method's functionality completely.

SEE ALSO

The CancelRequest method (page 214).
The PostDownloadRequest method (page 215).

PostDownloadRequest

Requests the download of data referenced by a Cyberdog item to disk and registers a completion notification function.

```
CDDownloadRequestID PostDownloadRequest (in CyberItem item,
                    in FSSpecPtr destSpec,
                    in ODBoolean decomp,
                    in DownloadCompletionUPP completionProc,
                    in Ptr completionProcData);
```

item
: The CyberItem object that specifies the data to be downloaded to disk.

destSpec
: A pointer to a file specification that specifies the file in which to save the data.

decomp
: kODTrue if the download part should attempt to decompress the downloaded data before saving it to the file; otherwise, kODFalse.

completionProc
: A pointer to a programmer-defined function that Cyberdog calls when the data has been downloaded to disk.

`completionProcData`
>	A pointer to data that is passed to the callback function specified by `completionProc`.

return value	An ID that uniquely identifies the download request.

DISCUSSION

This method adds a Cyberdog item to this download part's queue. If `nil` is specified for the `destSpec` parameter, the download part decides where to save the data. To cancel a download request, you call the `CancelRequest` method, passing the ID returned by this method.

This method is similar to `DownloadCyberItem` except that it allows you to control whether the downloaded data is decompressed and to specify a callback function called by Cyberdog when the download operation is complete. The data pointed to by the `completionProc` parameter is passed to the callback function.

The following type is used for download completion functions. The callback function takes five parameters: an environment parameter, a pointer to a Cyberdog item, an event code that describes the results of the download, a pointer to a file specification, and a pointer to some data.

```
typedef void (* DownloadCompletionProcPtr) (
            Environment* ev,
            CyberItem* item,
            CDDownloadEvent eventCode,
            FSSpec* destFile,
            Ptr userDataPtr);
```

The `MyDownloadCompleted` programmer-defined function (page 193) illustrates the form of a download completion function.

If you subclass `CyberDownloadExtension`, you must override this method. Your override must not call its inherited method; that is, your override method must implement this method's functionality completely.

SEE ALSO

The `DownloadCyberItem` method (page 214).

StartDownloads

Initiates the download requests queued for a download part.

```
void StartDownloads (in ODBoolean openWindow);
```

openWindow   kODTrue if the method should open a window to display
              progress; otherwise, kODFalse.

DISCUSSION

You call this method to begin processing a download part's queue of download-to-disk requests. You add a request to the download part's queue by calling either DownloadCyberItem or PostDownloadRequest.

If you specify kODTrue for the openWindow parameter, the download part displays a modeless dialog box that shows the progress of the download operations.

If you subclass CyberDownloadExtension, you must override this method. Your override must not call its inherited method; that is, your override method must implement this method's functionality completely.

SEE ALSO

The DownloadCyberItem method (page 214).
The PostDownloadRequest method (page 215).

CyberExtension

Superclasses	ODExtension → ODRefCntObject → ODObject
Subclasses	CyberContainerExtension, CyberDownloadExtension, CyberFormExtension, CyberItemPromptExtension, CyberLogExtension, CyberNotebookExtension, CyberPanelExtension, CyberPartExtension, CyberProgressPartExtension

The CyberExtension class is the abstract superclass for all Cyberdog-related extensions.

Description

The CyberExtension class provides methods for creating and accessing the global CyberSession object. All Cyberdog extension classes descend from CyberExtension. As a developer, you will probably not need to subclass CyberExtension directly; instead, you should subclass descendants of CyberExtension.

Cyberdog also provides global functions for creating and accessing the global CyberSession object. The InitCyberdog function (page 190) creates and initializes the global session object. The GetCyberSession function (page 189) retrieves the global session object.

Methods

This section presents summary descriptions of the CyberExtension methods, followed by detailed descriptions.

Accessing the Cyberdog Session

CreateCyberSession	Creates and returns a global session object.
GetCyberSession	Retrieves the global session object.

CreateCyberSession

Creates and returns a global session object.

```
CyberSession CreateCyberSession (in ODSession session);
```

session   The `ODSession` object to associate with the `CyberSession` object.

return value   The global `CyberSession` object.

DISCUSSION

You can call this method when you need to create the global session object. If the object already exists, this method simply returns it. You can also call the `InitCyberdog` function to create the global session object.

You can retrieve the global session object by calling either the `GetCyberSession` method or the `GetCyberSession` global function.

If you subclass `CyberExtension`, do not override this method.

SEE ALSO

The `GetCyberSession` function (page 189).
The `InitCyberdog` function (page 190).
The `GetCyberSession` method (page 219).

GetCyberSession

Retrieves the global session object.

```
CyberSession GetCyberSession ();
```

return value   The global `CyberSession` object.

DISCUSSION

You can call this method when you need a reference to the global `CyberSession` object. This method returns `kODNULL` if the `CyberSession` object has not yet been created. You also can call the `GetCyberSession` global function to obtain the reference.

If you subclass `CyberExtension`, do not override this method.

SEE ALSO

The `GetCyberSession` function (page 189).
The `CreateCyberSession` method (page 219).

CyberFormExtension

Superclasses   CyberExtension → ODExtension → ODRefCntObject → ODObject

Subclasses   none

The CyberFormExtension class defines extra behaviors to allow a Cyberdog item to submit HTML forms.

Description

The CyberFormExtension class is an abstract class you can subclass to create an extension that allows a Cyberdog item to submit an HTML form. A Cyberdog HTTP item is extended using the CyberFormExtension subclass. If you develop your own Cyberdog item for referencing data using the HTTP protocol, you must define a subclass of CyberFormExtension and implement your class.

The CyberFormExtension methods allow you to specify form information for a Cyberdog item that can be submitted to the HTTP server. The action of a user clicking a button to submit an HTML form is similar to clicking a link in an HTML document to display another web page. However, the data specified in the form is treated as a request; the HTTP server can use the information specified in the form to dynamically construct the next web page to be displayed.

A form request has three parts:

- The body is the information specified by the user in the form.

- The content type specifies the encoding to be used in the form's body.

- The method specifies how the form is to be processed by the HTTP server. Cyberdog HTTP items support the two most common methods defined by the HTML 2.0 specification, GET and POST.

Methods

This section presents summary descriptions of the `CyberFormExtension` methods grouped according to purpose, followed by detailed descriptions.

Setting Up a Form

`BeginSetup`   Starts a new form.

`EndSetup`   Notifies the Cyberdog item that the form information is complete.

Specifying Form Data

`SetBody`   Sets the data to be included in a form request.

`SetContentType` Sets the content type for a form request.

`SetMethod`   Sets the method for a form request.

BeginSetup

Starts a new form.

```
void BeginSetup ();
```

DISCUSSION

You call this method to notify the Cyberdog item that you are preparing to specify new form data. You should call this method before calling `SetBody`, `SetContentType`, or `SetMethod` to specify form data. This method should clear any data from previous forms.

If you subclass `CyberFormExtension`, you must override this method. Your override must not call its inherited method; that is, your override method must implement this method's functionality completely.

SEE ALSO

The `SetBody` method (page 223).
The `SetContentType` method (page 224).
The `SetMethod` method (page 225).

EndSetup

Notifies the Cyberdog item that the form information is complete.

```
void EndSetup ();
```

DISCUSSION

You call this method to notify the Cyberdog item that the form information is complete. This method should perform any needed processing on the data before you submit the form.

If you subclass CyberFormExtension, you must override this method. Your override must not call its inherited method; that is, your override method must implement this method's functionality completely.

SEE ALSO

The BeginSetup method (page 222).

SetBody

Sets the data to be included in a form request.

```
void SetBody (in char* body);
```

body   A pointer to a buffer that contains the data.

DISCUSSION

This method sets the data that should be included in the form request. For HTML forms, this data is the information the user specified in the form.

If you subclass CyberFormExtension, you must override this method. Your override must not call its inherited method; that is, your override method must implement this method's functionality completely.

SEE ALSO

The SetContentType method (page 224).
The SetMethod method (page 225).

SetContentType

Sets the content type for a form request.

```
void SetContentType (in char* contentType);
```

contentType   A pointer to a buffer that contains the content type.

DISCUSSION

This method sets the content type for a form request. The content type corresponds to the form's ENCTYPE attribute; this attribute specifies the format of the submitted data in case the protocol does not impose a format itself. The content type specifies the encoding of the form body.

For HTML forms to be processed using the POST method, the content type should be the MIME type of the form body. The default content type is "application/x-www-form-urlencoded".

The ENCTYPE attribute and the POST method are defined by the HTML 2.0 specification.

If you subclass CyberFormExtension, you must override this method. Your override must not call its inherited method; that is, your override method must implement this method's functionality completely.

SEE ALSO

The SetBody method (page 223).
The SetMethod method (page 225).

SetMethod

Sets the method for a form request.

```
void SetMethod (in char* method);
```

method   A pointer to a buffer that contains the method name.

DISCUSSION

This method sets the method the HTTP server should use to process the form. Cyberdog HTTP items support the two most common methods defined by the HTML 2.0 specification, GET and POST.

If you subclass CyberFormExtension, you must override this method. Your override must not call its inherited method; that is, your override method must implement this method's functionality completely.

SEE ALSO

The SetBody method (page 223).
The SetContentType method (page 224).

CyberItem

Superclasses	ODRefCntObject → ODObject
Subclasses	none

An object of the CyberItem class is a portable reference to data located on a network.

Description

A Cyberdog item is a reference to a remote location. Usually, a Cyberdog item refers to remotely located data. However, a Cyberdog item may simply describe a location; for example, an e-mail address is represented using a Cyberdog item. A Cyberdog item does not store actual data. Instead, it stores enough information about the location and network protocol of the data so that it can be retrieved when it is needed.

The CyberItem class is an abstract superclass that you can subclass and implement to reference data using a particular network protocol. The subclass encapsulates the specifics of addressing data using that protocol.

The type of Cyberdog item used in a particular situation depends on the location of the data you want to access, not the type of the data. For example, Cyberdog uses an FTPItem object (FTPItem is an implemented subclass of CyberItem supplied with Cyberdog) to reference data stored on an FTP server, whether the data is text, image, or audio. Cyberdog includes Cyberdog item subclasses to support common services, such as HTTP, Gopher, and FTP. You can use any of the existing Cyberdog item subclasses or create a new subclass to support a new service.

A CyberItem subclass usually has a companion CyberStream subclass (page 376). A Cyberdog stream downloads the data referenced by a Cyberdog item. For example, a WebItem object references data located on an HTTP server. A companion WebStream object interacts with the HTTP server to download the data.

A Cyberdog item is resolved if it can identify the kind of data to which it refers. When a Cyberdog item is opened, if it is resolved, the item creates a display part appropriate for displaying the type of data that the Cyberdog item references. Usually, the Cyberdog display part calls the Cyberdog item's `CreateCyberStream` method to retrieve a stream object initialized to download the Cyberdog item's data. The display part interacts with the stream object to download and display the data.

Some types of Cyberdog items (HTTP items, for example), do not inherently know the kind of data they refer to. Such Cyberdog items must override and implement the `Resolve` method to initiate whatever action is necessary to resolve the Cyberdog item.

Cyberdog items are not changeable. Once a Cyberdog item has been initialized, you should not change its attributes.

Cyberdog items are persistent and can be stored in storage units. If you are developing a Cyberdog item, you should store your Cyberdog items as kind `kCyberItemKind`.

There are two methods for storing a Cyberdog item in a storage unit. `ExternalizeContent` writes a Cyberdog item to a storage unit in multiple representations, in decreasing order of fidelity. You call this method to store a Cyberdog item for data interchange operations such as drag and drop.

`StreamToStorageUnit` flattens a Cyberdog item in the format shown in Table 7-1, writes it to a data buffer and then writes the buffer to a storage unit. You can use `StreamToStorageUnit` to store Cyberdog items that will not be used for data interchange. For example, a notebook calls `StreamToStorageUnit` to store its Cyberdog items.

You read Cyberdog items stored using either `ExternalizeContent` or `StreamToStorageUnit` by calling the `CyberSession::CreateCyberItemFromSU` method.

Table 7-1   Format of a flattened Cyberdog item

Length	Data item
4 bytes	The total length of flattened item, including length
2 bytes	The Cyberdog item signature (kCyberItemSignature)
2 bytes	The Cyberdog item version (kCyberItemVersionNum)
4 bytes	The length of the class ID
n bytes	The class ID
2 bytes	The script code for the display name
4 bytes	The length of the display name
n bytes	The display name
4 bytes	The length of the URL
n bytes	The URL
4 bytes	The length of private data required for this class
n bytes	The private data

Gopher and FTP Cyberdog items are capable of accessing data located on a proxy server. When a Gopher or FTP Cyberdog item is opened, it checks the user's preferences to see whether proxy server access is enabled. If so, the Cyberdog item calls CyberSession::CreateProxyItemFromURL (page 356) to create a proxy Cyberdog item capable of connecting to and accessing data through a proxy server.

Methods

This section presents summary descriptions of the CyberItem methods grouped according to purpose, followed by detailed descriptions.

Initialization and Cleanup

ICyberItem	Initializes this Cyberdog item.
SetUpFromURL	Initializes this Cyberdog item from a URL.

Opening Cyberdog Items

CreateCyberStream	Retrieves a Cyberdog stream that can be used to download the data referenced by this Cyberdog item.
Open	Initiates the opening of this Cyberdog item.

Testing and Resolving Cyberdog Items

Compare	Compares this Cyberdog item with another Cyberdog item for equality.
IsDownloadable	Tests whether the data referenced by this Cyberdog item is a file that can be downloaded.
IsResolved	Tests whether this Cyberdog item is resolved.
IsSecure	Tests whether this Cyberdog item references a secure site.
Resolve	Attempts to resolve this Cyberdog item.

Accessing Cyberdog Item Information

GetContentKind	Retrieves the part kind of the data referenced by this Cyberdog item.
GetFileInfo	Retrieves the file creator and file type of the data referenced by this Cyberdog item.
GetFlags	Retrieves flags for this Cyberdog item.
GetIconSuite	Retrieves an icon suite for this Cyberdog item.
GetStringProperty	Retrieves a string property for this Cyberdog item.
GetURL	Retrieves this Cyberdog item's URL.
SetDefaultName	Sets the default display name for this Cyberdog item.

Displaying Cyberdog Item Information

ShowInfoPart	Displays the Item Info window for this Cyberdog item.
ShowSecurityInfo	Displays the Security Info window for this Cyberdog item.

Copying and Storing Cyberdog Items

Clone	Returns a copy of this Cyberdog item.
ExternalizeContent	Writes this Cyberdog item to storage in multiple representations.
Flatten	Flattens this Cyberdog item and writes it to a buffer.

GetFlatSize	Retrieves the length of this Cyberdog item's flattened representation.
StreamToStorageUnit	Writes this Cyberdog item to a storage unit.
Unflatten	Reads this Cyberdog item from a buffer.

Clone

Returns a copy of this Cyberdog item.

```
CyberItem Clone ();
```

return value   The copy of the CyberItem object.

DISCUSSION

This method should return a deep copy of this Cyberdog item; that is, any objects referenced by this Cyberdog item should also be copied. This method should always set the reference count of the copy to 1. This method should return a clone of the Cyberdog item, even if the object has not been initialized by calling ICyberItem.

If you call the Compare method to compare the cloned Cyberdog item returned by this method with the original Cyberdog item, the result of the comparison should be kCDCompareEqual.

If you subclass CyberItem, you must override this method. Your override must not call its inherited method; that is, your override method must implement this method's functionality completely.

SEE ALSO

The Compare method (page 231).
The ICyberItem method (page 239).

Compare

Compares this Cyberdog item with another Cyberdog item for equality.

```
CDCompareType Compare (in CyberItem compare);
```

compare   The `CyberItem` object to compare.

return value The results of the comparison. Valid return values are
                `kCICompareLessThan`, `kCICompareEqual`, and
                `kCICompareGreaterThan`.

DISCUSSION

This method should compare this Cyberdog item with another Cyberdog item object for equality. The superclass implementation performs an ASCII comparison of the SOM class IDs of the two Cyberdog items. In some cases, that is sufficient to distinguish between them.

Therefore, the `Compare` method in a `CyberItem` subclass should first call its inherited `Compare` method. If the inherited `Compare` method indicates that the `CyberItem` objects are equal, then the comparison object is of the same class as the receiver. In this case, the subclass implementation should perform the additional computation necessary to establish a consistent ordering among the items.

The ordering of Cyberdog items in a Cyberdog item subclass is specified by the Cyberdog item developer. For example, a developer implementing a Cyberdog item subclass might order Cyberdog items of the subclass by performing an ASCII comparison of their URL strings.

This method should define a complete ordering among all Cyberdog items of the subclass. For example, for any two Cyberdog items A and B, `A->Compare(B)` must return a result consistent with the result of `B->Compare(A)`. The ordering of Cyberdog items in a subclass should not be affected by other operations on Cyberdog items, such as opening, resolving, cloning, flattening, and unflattening.

If you subclass `CyberItem`, you must override this method. Your override must call its inherited method.

CreateCyberStream

Creates a Cyberdog stream that can be used to download the data referenced by this Cyberdog item.

```
CyberStream CreateCyberStream ();
```

return value   The `CyberStream` object if one is created; otherwise, `kODNULL`.

DISCUSSION

Typically, this method is called by a Cyberdog display part that needs to download and display the content referenced by this Cyberdog item. This method may also be called by a download part, which uses the stream to download and save to disk the content referenced by a Cyberdog item. The superclass implementation returns `kODNULL`.

This method should initialize the Cyberdog stream with information about the location of the data. Because `CreateCyberStream` is synchronous, the item and the stream should be structured so that the `CyberStream` object is created quickly.

Typically, a Cyberdog item can return a stream if the data referenced by the Cyberdog item resides in a file. However, in some cases, a Cyberdog item might refer to a connection rather than a file. For example, a Cyberdog item might reference a Telnet connection or a mailbox on a server. In such cases, the Cyberdog item may not return a stream.

The display part should dispose of the stream object when the download operation is complete.

If you subclass `CyberItem` and override this method, your override must not call its inherited method; that is, your override method must implement this method's functionality completely.

ExternalizeContent

Writes this Cyberdog item to storage in multiple representations.

```
void ExternalizeContent (in ODStorageUnit su);
```

su   The ODStorageUnit object in which to store the CyberItem object.

DISCUSSION

This method should write this Cyberdog item to a storage unit in multiple formats, in decreasing order of fidelity. By convention, Cyberdog items are written in at least two formats: the Cyberdog item kind (kCyberItemKind) and the URL text. This method is called when a Cyberdog item must be written to a storage unit, such as when a Cyberdog item is dragged.

You read a Cyberdog item that has been written to a storage unit by calling the CyberSession::CreateCyberItemFromSU method.

If you subclass CyberItem, you must override this method. Your override must not call its inherited method; that is, your override method must implement this method's functionality completely.

SEE ALSO

The CyberSession::CreateCyberItemFromSU method (page 352).

Flatten

Flattens this Cyberdog item and writes it to a buffer.

```
long Flatten (in Ptr buffer, in long length);
```

buffer   A pointer to a data buffer. On return, the buffer contains the flattened CyberItem object.

length   The length of buffer.

return value   The number of bytes written to the buffer.

DISCUSSION

This method should convert this Cyberdog item to a flat representation and write it to a buffer. The format of a flattened Cyberdog item is described in Table 7-1 (page 228). The superclass implementation returns 0. This method is called by the StreamToStorageUnit method.

If you subclass CyberItem, you must override this method. Your override must not call its inherited method; that is, your override method must implement this method's functionality completely.

SEE ALSO

The GetFlatSize method (page 236).
The StreamToStorageUnit method (page 246).
The Unflatten method (page 247).

GetContentKind

Retrieves the part kind of the data referenced by this Cyberdog item.

```
ODTypeToken GetContentKind ();
```

return value   The part kind of the data referenced by the CyberItem object.

DISCUSSION

If this Cyberdog item references downloadable data, this method should return the part kind of the data that is provided by the corresponding Cyberdog stream. Otherwise, this method should return the constant kODNullTypeToken. The superclass implementation returns kODNULLTypeToken.

This method should call the ODSession::GetTokenizer method of OpenDoc to translate the Cyberdog item's part kind into an ODTypeToken. This method should throw the kCDErrItemNotResolved exception if the Cyberdog item is not resolved.

If you subclass CyberItem and override this method, your override must not call its inherited method; that is, your override method must implement this method's functionality completely.

GetFileInfo

Retrieves the file creator and file type of the data referenced by this Cyberdog item.

```
void GetFileInfo (in CDItemInfoType infoType,
                  out ODOSType flCreator,
                  out ODOSType flType);
```

infoType   The type of file for which information should be returned. Possible values are kCDInfoReference, kCDInfoPart, or kCDInfoDownload.

flCreator   The file creator.

flType   The file type.

DISCUSSION

This method should return a file creator and a file type of the specified form—reference, part, or downloaded file—for a Cyberdog item in the Finder. The superclass implementation returns 0 for the file creator and the file type.

This method throws the kCDErrItemNotResolved exception if the Cyberdog item is not resolved.

If you subclass CyberItem, you must override this method. Your override must not call its inherited method; that is, your override method must implement this method's functionality completely.

SEE ALSO

The CDItemInfoType type (page 173).

Classes and Methods

GetFlags

Retrieves flags for this Cyberdog item.

```
long GetFlags ();
```

return value   A set of flags, expressed as a 32-bit integer.

DISCUSSION

This method should return a set of flags giving information about a Cyberdog item. For Cyberdog version 1.0, two flags are defined: `kCDFlagDontLog` and `kCDFlagDontEmbed`. The superclass implementation returns 0.

SEE ALSO

The `kCDFlagDontEmbed` constant (page 174).
The `kCDFlagDontLog` constant (page 174).

GetFlatSize

Retrieves the length of this Cyberdog item's flattened representation.

```
long GetFlatSize ();
```

return value   The length, in bytes, of the flattened `CyberItem` object.

DISCUSSION

This method should return the size of this Cyberdog item when it is converted to its flattened representation. You can call this method to retrieve the size information in order to allocate a buffer before calling the `Flatten` method. The superclass implementation returns 0.

If you subclass `CyberItem`, you must override this method. Your override must not call its inherited method; that is, your override method must implement this method's functionality completely.

SEE ALSO

The `Flatten` method (page 233).

GetIconSuite

Retrieves an icon suite for this Cyberdog item.

```
Handle GetIconSuite (in CDItemInfoType infoType);
```

`infoType`   The type of icon to retrieve. Possible values are
                    `kCDInfoDownload`, `kCDInfoPart`, or `kCDInfoReference`.

return value   The handle to the icon.

DISCUSSION

This method should return a handle for an icon suite that can be used to display the Cyberdog item. This method should return the Cyberdog item reference icons, the OpenDoc part icons, or the icons for the file type of the downloaded data, depending on the value of the `infoType` parameter. The Cyberdog item owns the handle returned by this method; the caller should not alter its contents.

The superclass implementation calls `GetFileInfo` to retrieve a file type and file creator and uses that information to retrieve an icon suite.

SEE ALSO

The `CDItemInfoType` type (page 173).
The `GetFileInfo` method (page 235).

GetStringProperty

Retrieves a string property for this Cyberdog item.

```
void GetStringProperty (in CDStringProperty property,
                        in StringPtr theString,
                        out ScriptCode script);
```

property   The string property to be retrieved.

theString   A pointer to a string buffer. On return, the buffer contains the
               requested string.

script   The script code of the returned string.

DISCUSSION

Each Cyberdog item has a set of strings that describe its properties. This method
should return one of those strings, depending on the value of the property
parameter. The default name property is the most important of these; it is the
name of the Cyberdog item that is displayed to the user.

If you subclass CyberItem, you must override this method. Your override must
not call its inherited method; that is, your override method must implement
this method's functionality completely.

SEE ALSO

The CDStringProperty type (page 174).
The SetDefaultName method (page 243).

GetURL

Retrieves this Cyberdog item's URL.

```
char* GetURL ();
```

return value   A pointer to a null-terminated string that contains the CyberItem
                  object's URL.

DISCUSSION

This method should return a pointer to this Cyberdog item's URL. The Cyberdog item owns the pointer returned by this method; the caller should not modify or delete the string.

If you subclass CyberItem, you must override this method. Your override must not call its inherited method; that is, your override method must implement this method's functionality completely.

ICyberItem

Initializes this Cyberdog item.

```
void ICyberItem ();
```

DISCUSSION

The superclass implementation of this method calls InitRefCntObject.

If you subclass CyberItem and override this method, your override must call its inherited method.

IsDownloadable

Tests whether the data referenced by this Cyberdog item is a file that can be downloaded.

```
ODBoolean IsDownloadable ();
```

return value   kODTrue if the data is a downloadable file; otherwise, kODFalse.

DISCUSSION

This method should return kODTrue if this Cyberdog item is capable of providing a stream object via the CreateCyberStream method and a file creator and file type via the GetFileInfo method. The superclass implementation returns kODFalse.

This method throws the `kCDErrItemNotResolved` exception if the Cyberdog item is not resolved.

If you subclass `CyberItem` and override this method, your override must not call its inherited method; that is, your override must implement this method's functionality completely.

SEE ALSO

The `CreateCyberStream` method (page 232).
The `GetFileInfo` method (page 235).

IsResolved

Tests whether this Cyberdog item is resolved.

```
ODBoolean IsResolved ();
```

return value   `kODTrue` if the Cyberdog item is resolved; otherwise, `kODFalse`.

DISCUSSION

For some protocols such as HTTP, a Cyberdog item must interact with the network before it can determine the type of data it references. This method should return `kODTrue` if this Cyberdog item has determined the type of data it references. The superclass implementation of the `IsResolved` method returns `kODTrue`.

If `IsResolved` returns `kODFalse`, the Cyberdog item may not be able to determine the information required for the methods `IsDownloadable`, `IsSecure`, `GetFileInfo`, and `GetContentKind`.

SEE ALSO

The `GetContentKind` method (page 234).
The `GetFileInfo` method (page 235).
The `IsDownloadable` method (page 239).
The `IsSecure` method (page 241).
The `Resolve` method (page 242).

IsSecure

Tests whether this Cyberdog item references a secure site.

```
ODBoolean IsSecure ();
```

return value   kODTrue if the Cyberdog item references a secure site; otherwise, kODFalse.

DISCUSSION

If this Cyberdog item is opened embedded in a navigator, the navigator can call this method to determine whether to display security information to the user. The superclass implementation of this method returns kODFalse. If you are developing a Cyberdog item, you should override this method if your Cyberdog items may access data using a secure network protocol.

This method throws the kCDErrItemNoteResolved exception if the Cyberdog item is not resolved.

If you subclass CyberItem and override this method, your override must not call its inherited method; that is, your override method must implement this method's functionality completely.

SEE ALSO

The ShowSecurityInfo method (page 245).

Open

Initiates the opening of this Cyberdog item.

```
void Open (in ParameterSet theParams);
```

theParams   The ParameterSet object associated with the opening process.

DISCUSSION

What happens when `Open` is called depends on the implementation in the `CyberItem` subclass. Typically, the Cyberdog item creates a new display part to display the data and calls that part's `OpenCyberItem` method.

The parameter set contains pointers to objects that may be used during the opening process. For example, the parameter set might contain the parent Cyberdog item whose content contains the Cyberdog item being opened. If so, when the Cyberdog item calls `CyberSession::AddCyberItemToLog` to add itself to the log, it can pass the parent Cyberdog item as a parameter.

If you subclass `CyberItem`, you must override this method. Your override must not call its inherited method; that is, your override method must implement this method's functionality completely.

SEE ALSO

The `ParameterSet` class (page 387).

Resolve

Attempts to resolve this Cyberdog item.

```
void Resolve        (in CyberResolveCompletionUPP completionProc,
                     in void* userData,
                     in ODPart progressPart);
```

completionProc
    A pointer to a programmer-defined function that should be called when the resolution process is complete.

userData   A pointer to data that is passed to the callback function.

progressPart A part used to display progress during the resolution process.

DISCUSSION

This method should initiate the resolution process for this Cyberdog item. Resolving a Cyberdog item may be a lengthy operation; therefore, this method is asynchronous. If the Cyberdog item is not resolved, `Resolve` begins whatever asynchronous computation is necessary to resolve it and returns to the caller immediately. The method calls the callback function when the resolution is complete. The superclass implementation of the Resolve method calls the callback function immediately.

If you are implementing a Cyberdog item subclass whose objects cannot always identify the kind of data they refer to, you must override this method.

The following type is used for the resolution notification function. The function takes three parameters: an error code, a pointer to a Cyberdog item, and a pointer to some data. The function returns no value.

```
typedef void (* CyberResolveCompletionProcPtr) (OSErr err,
              CyberItem* item,
              Ptr userDataPtr);
```

The MyCyberItemResolved programmer-defined function (page 192) illustrates the form of a resolution notification function.

SEE ALSO

The IsResolved method (page 240).
The Open method (page 241).

SetDefaultName

Sets the default display name for this Cyberdog item.

```
void SetDefaultName (in StringPtr defaultName,
                     in ScriptCode script);
```

defaultName   A pointer to a string buffer containing the new default name.

script   The script code of the default name string.

DISCUSSION

The default display name is used to refer to a Cyberdog item in the user interface. This method should make its own copy of the name string.

7

Classes and Methods

A Cyberdog item may call this method itself during the opening process once it determines what its display name should be. Cyberdog also calls this method to rename Cyberdog items in the notebook.

Once initialized, a Cyberdog item should not be changed. If you need to change the default display name of a Cyberdog item, you should clone the Cyberdog item, call this method to change the name of the clone, and then replace the original item with the clone.

If you subclass `CyberItem`, you must override this method. Your override must not call its inherited method; that is, your override method must implement this method's functionality completely.

SEE ALSO

The `GetStringProperty` method (page 238).

SetUpFromURL

Initializes this Cyberdog item from a URL.

```
void SetUpFromURL    (in char* url,
                      in StringPtr defaultName,
                      in ScriptCode defaultNameScript);
```

url   A pointer to the URL to be parsed and incorporated into this `CyberItem` object.

defaultName   A pointer to the default display name for the `CyberItem` object.

defaultNameScript
                The script code of the name specified by `defaultName`.

DISCUSSION

If the value of the `defaultName` parameter is `kODNULL`, the method should manufacture an appropriate default display name based on the URL.

You can retrieve a Cyberdog item's default display name by calling `GetStringProperty`, passing `kCDDefaultName` for the string property parameter.

If you subclass `CyberItem`, you must override this method. Your override method must not call its inherited method; that is, your override method must implement this method's functionality completely.

SEE ALSO

The `CDStringProperty` type (page 174).
The `GetStringProperty` method (page 238).

ShowInfoPart

Displays the Item Info window for this Cyberdog item.

```
void ShowInfoPart ();
```

DISCUSSION

This method should display the Item Info window for this Cyberdog item. The superclass implementation creates and opens a default Item Info window that displays the Cyberdog item's default display name and URL.

ShowSecurityInfo

Displays the Security Info window for this Cyberdog item.

```
void ShowSecurityInfo ();
```

DISCUSSION

If a Cyberdog item is secure, this method should display a Security Info window for the item.

If you subclass `CyberItem` and override this method, your override must not call its inherited method; that is, your override method must implement this method's functionality completely.

7

Classes and Methods

SEE ALSO

The IsSecure method (page 241).

StreamToStorageUnit

Writes this Cyberdog item to a storage unit.

```
void StreamToStorageUnit (in ODStorageUnit su);
```

su   The ODStorageUnit object in which the Cyberdog item is to
                      be written.

DISCUSSION

This method calls Flatten to flatten this Cyberdog item to a byte stream and
then writes the stream to the specified storage unit. This method is called to
write a Cyberdog item to a storage unit in a single format. You can call this
method to store a Cyberdog item when the stored Cyberdog item will not be
used for data interchange. For example, this method is called by the notebook
to store the contents of the notebook to a storage unit.

This method assumes that the specified storage unit is focused on the correct
storage unit property and value. To read a Cyberdog item saved using
StreamToStorageUnit, you should call the CyberSession::CreateCyberItemFromSU
method.

If you subclass CyberItem, do not override this method.

SEE ALSO

The Flatten method (page 233).
The CyberSession::CreateCyberItemFromSU method (page 352).

Unflatten

Reads this flattened Cyberdog item from a buffer.

```
long Unflatten (in Ptr buffer);
```

buffer   A pointer to a data buffer containing the flattened
            CyberItem object.

return value   The number of bytes read from the buffer.

DISCUSSION

This method should restore a Cyberdog item to its saved state from a flat representation stored in a buffer. The superclass implementation returns 0. This method is called by the CyberSession::CreateCyberItemFromSU method. The format of a flattened Cyberdog item is described in Table 7-1 (page 228).

If you subclass CyberItem, you must override this method. Your override must not call its inherited method; that is, your override method must implement this method's functionality completely.

SEE ALSO

The Flatten method (page 233).
The GetFlatSize method (page 236).
The CyberSession::CreateCyberItemFromSU method (page 352).

CyberItemPromptExtension

Superclasses　CyberExtension → OODExtension → ODRefCntObject → ODObject

Subclasses　none

CyberItemPromptExtension defines extra behaviors for parts that are to be used as a Connect To dialog box.

Description

The CyberItemPromptExtension class is an abstract class that you can subclass to create an extension for a Connect To dialog box. The subclass provides an interface for displaying the dialog box and retrieving the Cyberdog item the user specified in the dialog box.

The Connect To dialog box also requires an extension that is subclassed from the CyberContainerExtension class (page 208). The CyberContainerExtension extension allows the part to behave as a dialog box and embed panels. The embedded panels in the Connect To dialog box are parts with extensions subclassed from CyberConnectExtension (page 206).

Methods

The CyberItemPromptExtension class has a single method, PromptForCyberItem. A detailed description of the method follows.

PromptForCyberItem　　Displays the Connect To dialog box and returns the Cyberdog item specified by the user.

PromptForCyberItem

Displays the Connect To dialog box and returns the Cyberdog item specified by the user.

```
CyberItem PromptForCyberItem (in Str255 windowTitle);
```

windowTitle   The title to be used for the Connect To dialog box.

return value   A `CyberItem` object if the user specified one; otherwise, `kODNULL`.

DISCUSSION

This method displays the Connect To dialog box with the specified title. The dialog box allows the user to select from any services installed in the system and to specify a Cyberdog item in the corresponding Connect To panel. This method calls the `CyberConnectExtension::CreateCyberItem` method to retrieve the Cyberdog item specified by the user in the Connect To panel and then returns that item.

You should not call this method directly; to prompt the user for a Cyberdog item, you should call `CyberSession::PromptForCyberItem`, which calls this method.

If you subclass `CyberItemPromptExtension`, you must override this method. Your override must not call its inherited method; that is, your override method must implement this method's functionality completely.

SEE ALSO

The `CyberConnectExtension::CreateCyberItem` method (page 206).
The `CyberSession::PromptForCyberItem` method (page 369).

CyberLogExtension

Superclasses	CyberExtension → ODExtension → ODRefCntObject → ODObject
Subclasses	none

The CyberLogExtension class defines extra behaviors for a part to be used as a log.

Description

The CyberLogExtension class defines an extension that allows a part to be used as a log. The CyberLogExtension class is an abstract superclass that you must subclass and implement to create your own custom log. However, Cyberdog provides a fully implemented log; to use the Cyberdog log, you do not need to subclass this class.

The Cyberdog log implementation is divided between two parts: a log manager and a log part. The Cyberdog log manager (kLogManagerKind) is composed of an object of an ODPart subclass extended with a subclass of CyberLogExtension. The log manager does not provide a user interface. The log user interface is provided by the log part (kLogKind), an object of an ODPart subclass.

You never need to call CyberLogExtension methods directly; the CyberSession class provides the methods you should use to interact with the log.

Methods

This section presents summary descriptions of the CyberLogExtension methods grouped according to purpose, followed by detailed descriptions.

Initialization and Cleanup

Cleanup	Shuts down this log.

Managing the Log Finger

ClearLogFinger	Clears the log finger from a Cyberdog item.
SetLogFinger	Sets the log finger to a particular Cyberdog item.

Adding Items to the Log

AddCyberItemToLog	Adds a Cyberdog item to the log.
ContainsCyberItem	Tests whether a particular Cyberdog item is in the log.

Displaying the Log

IsLogWindowShown	Tests whether the log window is currently displayed.
ShowLogWindow	Displays the log window.

AddCyberItemToLog

Adds a Cyberdog item to the log.

```
void AddCyberItemToLog (in CyberItem parent,
                        in CyberItem child);
```

parent	The CyberItem object's parent if one exists; otherwise, kODNULL.
child	The CyberItem object to be added.

DISCUSSION

This method should add a Cyberdog item to the log. You should not call this method directly; to add a Cyberdog item to the log, you should call CyberSession::AddCyberItemToLog, which calls this method.

If you subclass CyberLogExtension, you must override this method. Your override must not call its inherited method; that is, your override method must implement this method's functionality completely.

SEE ALSO

The CyberSession::AddCyberItemToLog method (page 349).

Cleanup

Shuts down this log.

```
void Cleanup ();
```

DISCUSSION

The global Cyberdog session object calls this method before terminating Cyberdog to give the log the opportunity to deallocate its structures.

If you subclass CyberLogExtension, you must override this method. Your override must not call its inherited method; that is, your override method must implement this method's functionality completely.

ClearLogFinger

Clears the log finger from a Cyberdog item.

```
void ClearLogFinger (in CyberItem item);
```

item   The CyberItem object to be cleared.

DISCUSSION

This method should remove the finger from the specified Cyberdog item in the log. If the log finger does not point to the specified Cyberdog item, the method should do nothing. You should not call this method directly; to clear the log finger, you should call CyberSession::ClearLogFinger, which calls this method.

If you subclass CyberLogExtension, you must override this method. Your override must call its inherited method.

SEE ALSO

The SetLogFinger method (page 254).
The CyberSession::ClearLogFinger method (page 351).

ContainsCyberItem

Tests whether a particular Cyberdog item is in the log.

```
ODBoolean ContainsCyberItem (in CyberItem item);
```

item   The `CyberItem` object for this operation.

return value   `kODTrue` if the log contains an equivalent Cyberdog item;
                    otherwise, `kODFalse`.

DISCUSSION

This method should determine whether a particular Cyberdog item is in the
log; it should call the `CyberItem::Compare` method to determine whether two
`CyberItem` objects are equivalent.

You should not call this method directly; to determine whether a Cyberdog
item is in the log, you should call `CyberSession::LogContainsCyberItem`, which
calls this method.

If you subclass `CyberLogExtension`, you must override this method. Your
override method must call its inherited method.

SEE ALSO

The `CyberItem::Compare` method (page 231).
The `CyberSession::LogContainsCyberItem` method (page 366).

IsLogWindowShown

Tests whether the log window is currently displayed.

```
ODBoolean IsLogWindowShown ();
```

return value   `kODTrue` if the log window is displayed; otherwise, `kODFalse`.

DISCUSSION

This method should determine whether the log window is currently displayed. You should not call this method directly; to determine whether the log window is displayed, you should call `CyberSession::IsLogWindowShown`, which calls this method.

If you subclass `CyberLogExtension`, you must override this method. Your override must call its inherited method.

SEE ALSO

The `ShowLogWindow` method (page 255).
The `CyberSession::IsLogWindowShown` method (page 365).

SetLogFinger

Sets the log finger to a particular Cyberdog item.

```
void SetLogFinger (in CyberItem item);
```

item   A `CyberItem` object representing a location just visited by the user.

DISCUSSION

This method should set the log finger to point to a Cyberdog item. The method can assume that the Cyberdog item has already been added to the log; if the item is not in the log, this method should do nothing.

You should not call this method directly; to set the log finger, you should call `CyberSession::SetLogFinger`, which calls this method.

If you subclass `CyberLogExtension`, you must override this method. Your override must not call its inherited method; that is, your override method must implement this method's functionality completely.

SEE ALSO

The ClearLogFinger method (page 252).
The CyberSession::SetLogFinger method (page 372).

ShowLogWindow

Displays the log window.

```
void ShowLogWindow ();
```

DISCUSSION

This method should display the log window if it is not already displayed. You should not call this method directly; to show the log window, you should call CyberSession::ShowLogWindow, which calls this method.

If you subclass CyberLogExtension, you must override this method. Your override must call its inherited method.

SEE ALSO

The IsLogWindowShown method (page 253).
The CyberSession::ShowLogWindow method (page 374).

7

Classes and Methods

CyberNavigatorExtension

Superclasses	`CyberOpenerPartExtension` → `CyberProgressPartExtension` → `CyberExtension` → `ODExtension` → `ODRefCntObject` → `ODObject`
Subclasses	none

The `CyberNavigatorExtension` class defines extra behaviors for a part that is to be used as a navigator.

Description

The `CyberNavigatorExtension` class is an abstract class that you can subclass to create an extension that allows a part to be used as a navigator. Cyberdog provides a fully implemented navigator; to use this navigator, you do not need to subclass this class.

A navigator serves as a container part for display parts that display content referenced by Cyberdog items. The Cyberdog-provided Gopher, FTP, and HTML display parts are displayed embedded in the navigator. If you want to display your Cyberdog display part embedded in a navigator, you should override the display part's `OpenCyberItem` method to call the navigator's `GoToCyberItem` method.

A navigator keeps track of its visitation history, the sequence of Cyberdog items, and associated display parts that it displays. A navigator adds a Cyberdog item to its visitation history when the location the item represents is visited. The navigator provides a user interface that allows the user to view the history of the items visited and to open an item in the history.

`CyberNavigatorExtension` is derived from `CyberProgressPartExtension`; in other words, the navigator is a progress part. The navigator can display progress information to the user when Cyberdog items are resolved and downloaded.

Methods

This section presents summary descriptions of the `CyberNavigatorExtension` methods grouped according to purpose, followed by detailed descriptions.

Initialization and Cleanup

ICyberNavigatorExtension

Initializes this `CyberNavigatorExtension` object.

Detecting Changes

CurrentCyberItemChanged

Notifies this navigator that the current Cyberdog item has changed.

Navigation

GetHistory	Retrieves the visitation history for this navigator.
GoToCyberItem	Displays the content referenced by a Cyberdog item in this navigator.
NavigateToCyberItem	Displays the content referenced by a Cyberdog item that has been shown in this navigator.
NextCyberItem	Displays the content referenced by the next Cyberdog item in this navigator's visitation history.
PreviousCyberItem	Displays the content referenced by the previous Cyberdog item in this navigator's visitation history.

CurrentCyberItemChanged

Notifies this navigator that the current Cyberdog item has changed.

```
void CurrentCyberItemChanged (in CyberItem item);
```

item   The new or changed `CyberItem` object.

DISCUSSION

A display part embedded in this navigator calls this method to notify the navigator that some aspect of the Cyberdog item that is currently displayed, such as its default name or icon, has changed. The specified Cyberdog item may be a different item than the one that is currently displayed. The navigator should refresh any user interface elements that depend on the Cyberdog item.

If you subclass `CyberNavigatorExtension`, you must override this method. Your override must not call its inherited method; that is, your override method must implement this method's functionality completely.

GetHistory

Retrieves the visitation history for this navigator.

```
void GetHistory (out CyberItemList cyberItems,
                 out long curIndex);
```

cyberItems   On return, the list of `CyberItem` objects visited by the navigator part.

curIndex   The zero-based index of the currently displayed Cyberdog item in the visitation history.

DISCUSSION

This method increments the reference counts for the items in the list; the caller is responsible for releasing the items in the list and disposing of the list's buffer.

If you subclass `CyberNavigatorExtension`, you must override this method. Your override must not call its inherited method; that is, your override method must implement this method's functionality completely.

GoToCyberItem

Displays the content referenced by a Cyberdog item in this navigator.

```
void GoToCyberItem (in CyberItem item,
                    in ODPart part,
                    in ParameterSet openParams);
```

item   The Cyberdog item to display.

part   The part that displays the contents of the Cyberdog item.

openParams   The `ParameterSet` object associated with the opening process.

DISCUSSION

This method opens a Cyberdog item in a navigator. The navigator embeds the display part that displays the content referenced by the Cyberdog item in its content area. The navigator also adds the Cyberdog item to its visitation history.

Typically, this method is called by a Cyberdog display part's implementation of the `CyberPartExtension::OpenCyberItem` method. It is up to the developer of a display part to determine whether the display part will appear embedded in a navigator.

If you subclass `CyberNavigatorExtension`, you must override this method. Your override must not call its inherited method; that is, your override method must implement this method's functionality completely.

SEE ALSO

The `NavigateToCyberItem` method (page 260).
The `CyberPartExtension::OpenCyberItem` method (page 291).

ICyberNavigatorExtension

Initializes this `CyberNavigatorExtension` object.

```
void ICyberNavigatorExtension (in ODPart basePart);
```

`basePart`   The OpenDoc part extended by this object.

DISCUSSION

You call this method to initialize a newly created `CyberNavigatorExtension` object.

If you subclass `CyberNavigatorExtension` and override this method, your override must call its inherited method.

NavigateToCyberItem

Displays the content referenced by a Cyberdog item that has been shown in this navigator.

```
void NavigateToCyberItem (in CyberItem item);
```

item   The Cyberdog item to revisit.

DISCUSSION

This method notifies a navigator part to navigate to a Cyberdog item that is already in its visitation history. If the specified item is not in the visitation history, this method calls the item's `Open` method. The navigator embeds the display part associated with the Cyberdog item and updates the visitation history. This method is typically called when the user selects a Cyberdog item from the navigator's visitation history.

If you subclass `CyberNavigatorExtension`, you must override this method. Your override must not call its inherited method; that is, your override method must implement this method's functionality completely.

SEE ALSO

The `GoToCyberItem` method (page 258).
The `CyberItem::Open` method (page 241).

NextCyberItem

Displays the content referenced by the next Cyberdog item in this navigator's visitation history.

```
void NextCyberItem ();
```

DISCUSSION

This method notifies a navigator to select the next Cyberdog item in its visitation history and display the item's content. If there is no next item in the visitation history, the navigator does nothing. The navigator embeds the display part associated with the Cyberdog item and updates the visitation history.

If you subclass `CyberNavigatorExtension`, you must override this method. Your override must call its inherited method.

SEE ALSO

The `NavigateToCyberItem` method (page 260).
The `PreviousCyberItem` method (page 261).

PreviousCyberItem

Displays the content referenced by the previous Cyberdog item in this navigator's visitation history.

```
void PreviousCyberItem ();
```

DISCUSSION

This method notifies a navigator to select the previous Cyberdog item in its visitation history and display the item's content. If there is no previous item in the visitation history, the navigator does nothing. The navigator embeds the display part associated with the Cyberdog item and updates the visitation history.

If you subclass `CyberNavigatorExtension`, you must override this method. Your override must call its inherited method.

SEE ALSO

The `NavigateToCyberItem` method (page 260).
The `NextCyberItem` method (page 260).

CyberNotebookExtension

Superclasses	CyberExtension → ODExtension → ODRefCntObject → ODObject
Subclasses	none

The `CyberNotebookExtension` class defines extra behaviors for a part that is to be used as a notebook.

Description

The `CyberNotebookExtension` class defines an extension that allows a part to be used as a notebook. `CyberNotebookExtension` is an abstract superclass that you must subclass and implement to create your own custom notebook part. However, Cyberdog provides a fully implemented notebook; to use that Cyberdog notebook, you do not need to subclass this class.

The Cyberdog notebook implementation is divided between two parts: a notebook manager and a notebook part. The Cyberdog notebook manager (`kNotebookManagerKind`) is composed of an object of an `ODPart` subclass extended with a subclass of `CyberNotebookExtension`. The notebook manager does not provide a user interface. The notebook user interface is provided by the notebook part (`kNotebookKind`), an object of an `ODPart` subclass.

You never need to call `CyberNotebookExtension` methods directly; the `CyberSession` class provides the methods you should use to interact with the notebook.

Methods

This section presents summary descriptions of the `CyberNotebookExtension` methods grouped according to purpose, followed by detailed descriptions.

Initialization and Cleanup

Cleanup	Shuts down this notebook.

Adding Items to the Notebook

AddCyberItemsToNotebook

> Adds a set of Cyberdog items to this notebook.

AddCyberItemToNotebook

> Adds a Cyberdog item to this notebook.

Accessing Cyberdog Items

CountCyberItems Retrieves the number of Cyberdog items in this notebook.

GetNthCyberItem Retrieves a Cyberdog item displayed in this notebook.

Showing the Notebook

IsNotebookWindowShown

> Tests whether this notebook's window is currently displayed.

ShowNotebookWindow Displays this notebook's window.

The Address Browser

PromptForAddresses Displays the Cyberdog address browser.

AddCyberItemsToNotebook

Adds a set of Cyberdog items to this notebook.

```
void AddCyberItemsToNotebook (in CyberItemList items);
```

items   The CyberItem objects to be added.

DISCUSSION

This method should add a set of Cyberdog items to the notebook. The method displays a dialog box that prompts the user for a notebook. You could override this method, for example, to display a different dialog box.

You should not call this method directly. To add Cyberdog items to the notebook, you should call CyberSession::AddCyberItemsToNotebook, which calls this method.

Classes and Methods

If you subclass `CyberNotebookExtension`, you must override this method. Your override must not call its inherited method; that is, your override method must implement this method's functionality completely.

SEE ALSO

The `AddCyberItemToNotebook` method (page 264).
The `CyberSession::AddCyberItemsToNotebook` method (page 349).

AddCyberItemToNotebook

Adds a Cyberdog item to this notebook.

```
void AddCyberItemToNotebook (in CyberItem item);
```

item   The `CyberItem` object to be added.

DISCUSSION

This method should add a Cyberdog item to the notebook. The method displays a dialog box that prompts the user for a notebook. You could override this method, for example, to display a different dialog box.

You should not call this method directly. To add a Cyberdog item to the notebook, you should call `CyberSession::AddCyberItemToNotebook`, which calls this method.

If you subclass `CyberNotebookExtension`, you must override this method. Your override must call its inherited method.

SEE ALSO

The `AddCyberItemsToNotebook` method (page 263).
The `CyberSession::AddCyberItemToNotebook` method (page 350).

Cleanup

Shuts down this notebook.

```
void Cleanup ();
```

DISCUSSION

The global Cyberdog session object calls this method before closing Cyberdog to give the notebook the opportunity to deallocate its structures.

If you subclass `CyberNotebookExtension`, you must override this method. Your override must not call its inherited method; that is, your override method must implement this method's functionality completely.

CountCyberItems

Retrieves the number of Cyberdog items in this notebook.

```
long CountCyberItems ();
```

return value   The number of `CyberItem` objects in this notebook.

DISCUSSION

This method should return the number of Cyberdog items in this notebook. This method is used in conjunction with the `GetNthCyberItem` method to iterate through the Cyberdog items in a notebook.

If you subclass `CyberNotebookExtension`, you must override this method. Your override must not call its inherited method; that is, your override method must implement this method's functionality completely.

SEE ALSO

The `GetNthCyberItem` method (page 266).

7

Classes and Methods

GetNthCyberItem

Retrieves a Cyberdog item displayed in this notebook.

```
CyberItem GetNthCyberItem (in long n);
```

n   The zero-based index of the CyberItem object to be retrieved.

return value   The CyberItem object specified by n.

DISCUSSION

This method should return the Cyberdog item indicated by the specified index. This method is used in conjunction with the CountCyberItems method to iterate through the Cyberdog items in a notebook.

If the specified index is out of range, the return value of this method is undefined.

If you subclass CyberNotebookExtension, you must override this method. Your override must not call its inherited method; that is, your override method must implement this method's functionality completely.

SEE ALSO

The CountCyberItems method (page 265).

IsNotebookWindowShown

Tests whether this notebook's window is currently displayed.

```
ODBoolean IsNotebookWindowShown ();
```

return value   kODTrue if the notebook's window is displayed; otherwise, kODFalse.

DISCUSSION

This method should determine whether the notebook's window is currently displayed. You should not call this method directly; to determine whether the notebook window is displayed, you should call `CyberSession::IsNotebookWindowShown`, which calls this method.

If you subclass `CyberNotebookExtension`, you must override this method. Your override must call its inherited method.

SEE ALSO

The `ShowNotebookWindow` method (page 268).
The `CyberSession::IsNotebookWindowShown` method (page 366).

PromptForAddresses

Displays the Cyberdog address browser.

```
void PromptForAddresses (in CyberNotebookAddressUPP proc,
                in Ptr procData);
```

proc   A pointer to a programmer-defined function that handles addresses selected by the user in the address browser.

procData   A pointer to data that is passed to the callback function. For example, it could point to a data structure representing the mail message being created.

DISCUSSION

This method displays the Cyberdog address browser, which is a part that displays a selectable list of the Cyberdog items in the notebook that are mail addresses. This method is called by a message editor in the Cyberdog mail system.

When the user selects a set of addresses and clicks a button in the address browser (such as the "To:" button), this method passes the information to the callback function. The callback function should handle inserting the addresses in the appropriate address field of the mail message.

7

Classes and Methods

The `proc` parameter specifies a pointer to a callback function that is called to handle addresses that the user selects in the address browser. The following type is used for a notebook address function. The function takes three parameters: a constant, a list of Cyberdog items, and a pointer to data. The function returns no value.

```
typedef void (* CyberNotebookAddressProcPtr) (
          CDAddressField whichField,
          void* cyberItemsList,
          Ptr userDataPtr);
```

The `MyNotebookAddressHandler` programmer-defined function (page 194) illustrates the form of a notebook address function.

If you subclass `CyberNotebookExtension`, you must override this method. Your override must not call its inherited method; that is, your override method must implement this method's functionality completely.

ShowNotebookWindow

Displays this notebook's window.

```
void ShowNotebookWindow ();
```

DISCUSSION

This method should display this notebook's window if it is not already displayed. You should not call this method directly; to show the notebook window, you should call `CyberSession::ShowNotebookWindow`, which calls this method.

If you subclass `CyberNotebookExtension`, you must override this method. Your override must call its inherited method.

SEE ALSO

The `IsNotebookWindowShown` method (page 266).
The `CyberSession::ShowNotebookWindow` method (page 375).

CyberOpenerPartExtension

Superclasses   `CyberProgressPartExtension` → `CyberExtension` →
`ODExtension` → `ODRefCntObject` → `ODObject`

Subclasses   `CyberNavigatorExtension`

`CyberOpenerPartExtension` defines extra behaviors for a part that is to be used
as an opener part.

Description

The `CyberOpenerPartExtension` class is a part extension that allows a part to be
used as an opener part. `CyberOpenerPartExtension` is an abstract superclass that
you must subclass and implement to create your own custom opener part.
However, Cyberdog provides a fully implemented opener part; to use this
opener part, you do not need to subclass this class.

When a Cyberdog item is opened, the type of data the Cyberdog item
references is not always known immediately. In some situations—for instance,
when a user is dragging a Cyberdog item or embedding a Cyberdog item in a
document—OpenDoc needs to create a part immediately, sometimes before the
type of data the Cyberdog item references is known.

An opener part is a temporary part used during the process of opening a
Cyberdog item; it is used until the Cyberdog display part for the item can be
opened. If, during opening, OpenDoc must have a part, the opener part acts as
a placeholder in a document until the display part can be created. Once the
display part has been created, it is swapped into the embedded frames that
contain the opener part.

The opener part is a kind of progress part; you can use it to display status
information to the user while the Cyberdog display part is being opened.

The opener part is the editor that OpenDoc binds to data whose kind is
`kCyberItemKind`; hence, if you are developing a Cyberdog item, you should
store your Cyberdog items as kind `kCyberItemKind`. When reading a storage
unit that contains a Cyberdog item (`kCyberItemKind`), the opener part creates
the Cyberdog item and calls its `Open` method. The Cyberdog item must
determine the right part kind to bind to itself. If this process is time consuming,

the opener part can display status and progress information. Once the right display part is created, either it is opened in its own window or the opener part calls `ChangePart` to replace itself with display part.

For more information on how the opener part is used during the Cyberdog item opening process, see "Cyberdog Item Opening Process" (page 71).

Methods

This section presents summary descriptions of the `CyberOpenerPartExtension` methods grouped according to purpose, followed by detailed descriptions.

Initialization and Cleanup

`ICyberOpenerPartExtension`
                    Initializes this `CyberOpenerPartExtension` object.

Getting Opener Part Information

`GetDestinationDraft` Retrieves the draft in which this opener part is embedded.

`GetWindow`   Retrieves the window of this opener part.

Opening a Cyberdog Item

`BeginOpening`   Informs this opener part that the process of opening a Cyberdog item is asynchronous.

`EndOpening`   Informs this opener part that the process of opening a Cyberdog item is complete.

`OpenFile`   Opens a file that contains a Cyberdog item's downloaded content.

`OpenPart`   Opens a Cyberdog item in the specified part.

BeginOpening

Informs this opener part that the process of opening a Cyberdog item is asynchronous.

```
ODPart BeginOpening (in CyberItem item,
                     in ODType openerKind,
                     in ParameterSet openParams);
```

item   The `CyberItem` object that is being opened.

openerKind   The part kind for the opener part if you have a preference; otherwise, `kODNULL`.

openParams   The parameter set associated with the opening process.

return value The opener part.

DISCUSSION

The `CyberSession::ObtainOpener` method calls this method when the opening process for a Cyberdog item is asynchronous. `BeginOpening` adds the opener part to the `ParameterSet` object with a parameter destructor that will call the `CyberOpenerPartExtension::EndOpening` method when the `ParameterSet` object is released.

You should not call this method directly; instead, to obtain an opener part, you should call the `CyberSession::ObtainOpener` method.

If you subclass `CyberOpenerPartExtension`, you must override this method. Your override must not call its inherited method; that is, your override method must implement this method's functionality completely.

SEE ALSO

The `EndOpening` method (page 272).
The `CyberSession::ObtainOpener` method (page 368).

EndOpening

Informs this opener part that the process of opening a Cyberdog item is complete.

```
void EndOpening ();
```

DISCUSSION

You should not call this method directly; this method is called when the `ParameterSet` object associated with a Cyberdog item's opening process is released. By convention, an opener part's `BeginOpening` method adds the opener part to the `ParameterSet` object with a parameter destructor that will call `EndOpening`.

If you subclass `CyberOpenerPartExtension`, you must override this method. Your override must not call its inherited method; that is, your override method must implement this method's functionality completely.

SEE ALSO

The `BeginOpening` method (page 271).

GetDestinationDraft

Retrieves the OpenDoc draft in which this opener part is embedded.

```
ODDraft GetDestinationDraft ();
```

return value   The opener part's draft if the opener part is embedded; otherwise, kODNULL.

DISCUSSION

The `CyberSession::CreateCyberPart` method calls this method to determine in which document to create a Cyberdog display part. If `GetDestinationDraft` returns a draft, the opener part is embedded in an OpenDoc document and the display part should be as well. If `GetDestinationDraft` returns kODNULL, the opener part is not embedded in an OpenDoc document; in this case, CreateCyberPart calls CreatePartInCyberDocument to create the display part in the Cyberdog session document.

If you subclass CyberOpenerPartExtension, you must override this method. Your override must call its inherited method.

SEE ALSO

The CyberSession::CreateCyberPart method (page 354).
The CyberSession::CreatePartInCyberDocument method (page 355).

GetWindow

Retrieves the window of this opener part.

```
ODWindow GetWindow ();
```

return value   The opener part's window if the opener part is the root part; otherwise, kODNULL.

DISCUSSION

You call this method to retrieve an opener part's window. If you are developing a Cyberdog item or a Cyberdog display part, you should call this method to determine the screen position and the window layer at which to open new windows.

If you subclass CyberOpenerPartExtension, you must override this method. Your override must not call its inherited method; that is, your override method must implement this method's functionality completely.

ICyberOpenerPartExtension

Initializes this `CyberOpenerPartExtension` object.

```
void ICyberOpenerPartExtension (in ODPart basePart);
```

basePart   The OpenDoc part extended by this object.

DISCUSSION

You call this method to initialize a newly created `CyberOpenerPartExtension` object.

If you subclass `CyberOpenerPartExtension` and override this method, your override must call its inherited method.

OpenFile

Opens a file that contains a Cyberdog item's downloaded content.

```
void OpenFile     (in CyberItem item,
                   in FSSpecPtr file,
                   in ParameterSet openParams);
```

item   The `CyberItem` object that is being opened.
file   The file specification of the file that contains the Cyberdog item's downloaded content.
openParams The parameter set associated with the opening process.

DISCUSSION

This method may be called during a Cyberdog item's opening process. If a Cyberdog item is unable to create a Cyberdog display part for the data it references, it can create a download part to download the data and save it to disk. The Cyberdog download part calls this method after downloading and saving to a file a Cyberdog item that was passed to its `OpenCyberItem` method. The specified file contains the Cyberdog item's downloaded content. The opener part attempts to find an OpenDoc part editor for the file according to its file type.

- If an appropriate OpenDoc part editor is available, the opener part creates a new part. Then, the opener part calls its own `OpenPart` method. The specified file is bound to the part editor.

- If an appropriate OpenDoc part editor is not available, a new part cannot be created. The opener part sends an Apple event to the Finder process telling it to open the file.

If you subclass `CyberOpenerPartExtension`, you must override this method. Your override must not call its inherited method; that is, your override method must implement this method's functionality completely.

SEE ALSO

The `OpenPart` method (page 275).
The `CyberPartExtension::OpenCyberItem` method (page 291).

OpenPart

Opens a part to display the data referenced by the specified Cyberdog item.

```
void OpenPart        (in CyberItem item,
                      in ODPart part,
                      in ParameterSet openParams);
```

item   The `CyberItem` object that is being opened.

part   The part that is to display the content associated with the Cyberdog item.

openParams The parameter set associated with the opening process.

DISCUSSION

A Cyberdog display part calls this method to open a part to display the content associated with a Cyberdog item. The opener part displays the specified part either by assigning the part to its own frames or by opening the part in its own window.

- If the opener part is embedded in an OpenDoc draft and the display part resides in the same draft, the opener part assigns the display part to its own frames by calling the `ChangePart` method for each of its frames.

- Otherwise, the opener part calls the display part's `Open` method to open the part in its own window.

An opener part may also call this method from its `OpenFile` method after creating an OpenDoc part to display the content of a Cyberdog item downloaded by the download part.

If you subclass `CyberOpenerPartExtension`, you must override this method. Your override must not call its inherited method; that is, your override method must implement this method's functionality completely.

SEE ALSO

The `OpenFile` method (page 274).

CyberPanelExtension

Superclasses	`CyberExtension` → `ODExtension` → `ODRefCntObject` → `ODObject`
Subclasses	`CyberConnectExtension`, `CyberPrefsExtension`

The `CyberPanelExtension` class defines extra behaviors for parts that will be embedded as panels in dialog box containers, such as the Connect To dialog box or the Preferences dialog box.

Description

A panel is part that is embedded in a dialog box container. In Cyberdog, panels are parts with extensions subclassed from `CyberPanelExtension`. A panel is embedded in a dialog box container, a part extended with a subclass of `CyberContainerExtension`.

The Cyberdog Connect To dialog box contains panels with extensions subclassed from `CyberConnectExtension`. The Cyberdog Preferences dialog box contain panels with extensions subclassed from `CyberPrefsExtension`. Both `CyberConnectExtension` and `CyberPrefsExtension` are subclasses of `CyberPanelExtension`.

`CyberPanelExtension` is an abstract superclass that you can subclass to create embeddable panels with custom behaviors. However, if you want to create a custom Connect To or Preferences panel, do not subclass `CyberPanelExtension` directly; instead, you should subclass either `CyberConnectExtension` or `CyberPrefsExtension`.

Methods

This section presents summary descriptions of the `CyberPanelExtension` methods grouped according to purpose, followed by detailed descriptions.

Setting the Containing Part

`SetContainingPart`   Embeds this panel in the specified dialog box.

Acquiring and Losing Focus

TabIn	Notifies this panel that it has received the keyboard focus.
TabOut	Notifies this panel that it has lost the keyboard focus.

Enabling Buttons

EnableOKButton	Enables or disables the OK button of this panel's dialog box.

Closing the Containing Part

FlashCancelButton	Highlights the Cancel button of this panel's dialog box and closes the dialog box.
FlashOKButton	Highlights the OK button of this panel's dialog box and closes the dialog box.

EnableOKButton

Enables or disables the OK button of this panel's dialog box.

```
void EnableOKButton (in ODBoolean enabled);
```

enabled   kODTrue if the OK button should be enabled; kODFalse if the OK button should be disabled.

DISCUSSION

You call this method to notify this panel's dialog box to enable or disable its OK button. The superclass's implementation of this method calls the dialog box's EnableOKButton method.

If you subclass CyberPanelExtension, do not override this method.

SEE ALSO

The FlashOKButton method (page 279).
The CyberContainerExtension::EnableOKButton method (page 209).

FlashCancelButton

Highlights the Cancel button of this panel's dialog box and closes the dialog box.

```
void FlashCancelButton ();
```

DISCUSSION

You call this method to notify the panel's dialog box to highlight its Cancel button and then close. For example, you might call this method when the user presses the Escape key while the cursor is in a panel. This method calls the dialog box's FlashCancelButton method.

If you subclass CyberPanelExtension, do not override this method.

SEE ALSO

The FlashOKButton method (page 279).
The CyberContainerExtension::FlashCancelButton method (page 210).

FlashOKButton

Highlights the OK button of this panel's dialog box and closes the dialog box.

```
void FlashOKButton ();
```

DISCUSSION

You call this method to notify the panel's dialog box to highlight its OK button and then close. For example, you might call this method when the user presses the Return key while the cursor is in a panel. This method calls the dialog box's FlashOKButton method.

If you subclass CyberPanelExtension, do not override this method.

The `FlashCancelButton` method (page 279).
The `CyberContainerExtension::FlashOKButton` method (page 210).

SetContainingPart

Embeds this panel in the specified dialog box.

```
void SetContainingPart (in ODPart containingPart);
```

`containingPart`
    The dialog box in which to embed the panel.

DISCUSSION

You call this method to specify the containing dialog box in which a panel
is embedded.

If you subclass `CyberPanelExtension` and override this method, your override
must call its inherited method.

TabIn

Notifies this panel that it has received the keyboard focus.

```
void TabIn (in ODBoolean reverse);
```

`reverse`   `kODTrue` if reverse tab order should be used; otherwise, `kODFalse`.

DISCUSSION

You call this method to notify this panel that the keyboard focus should be
transferred to it. Typically, you call this method when the user tabs into a panel
from the dialog box in which it is embedded.

If you subclass `CyberPanelExtension`, you must override this method. Your override must not call its inherited method; that is, your override method must implement this method's functionality completely.

SEE ALSO

The `TabOut` method (page 281).

TabOut

Notifies this panel that it has lost the keyboard focus.

```
void TabOut (in ODBoolean reverse);
```

reverse   kODTrue if reverse tab order should be used; otherwise, kODFalse.

DISCUSSION

You call this method to notify a panel that the keyboard focus should be transferred to its containing part. Typically, you call this method when the user tabs from a panel to the dialog box container in which it is embedded. This method calls the dialog box container's `TabIn` method.

If you subclass `CyberPanelExtension`, do not override this method.

SEE ALSO

The `CyberContainerExtension::TabIn` method (page 211).

7

Classes and Methods

CyberPartExtension

Superclasses   CyberExtension → ODExtension → ODRefCntObject → ODObject

Subclasses   none

CyberPartExtension defines extra behaviors for Cyberdog display parts, parts that display content referenced by a Cyberdog item.

Description

The CyberPartExtension class is a part extension that allows an OpenDoc part to be a Cyberdog display part, a part that displays content referenced by a Cyberdog item. CyberPartExtension is an abstract superclass that you must subclass and implement to create a Cyberdog display part. Any part that displays content referenced by a Cyberdog item must be composed of an object of class ODPart (or one of its subclasses) paired with an object of a class derived from the CyberPartExtension class.

The CyberPartExtension object is the public interface for a Cyberdog display part. External entities that want to communicate with a Cyberdog display part obtain the part's CyberPartExtension object and send the Cyberdog-related messages to it.

A Cyberdog item's Open method creates a Cyberdog display part to display the content referenced by the Cyberdog item and calls the display part's OpenCyberItem method. Typically, the OpenCyberItem method performs the following tasks:

■ It calls SetCyberItem to store a reference to the Cyberdog item in the display part.

■ It performs any tasks necessary to prepare to display the data referenced by the Cyberdog item. For example, the display part might request a stream from the Cyberdog item and use it to download the data referenced by the Cyberdog item.

■ Calls its inherited OpenCyberItem method. If an opener part was passed in as a parameter to OpenCyberItem, the inherited method calls the opener part's OpenPart method to open the display part. If no opener part was passed in, OpenCyberItem calls the display part's Open method.

The display part's `ShowCyberItem` method, on the other hand, assumes that the display part is already displaying the content referenced by the Cyberdog item. You call `ShowCyberItem` once you have determined (by calling `CanShowCyberItem` or `GetCyberItemWindow`) that the display part is already displaying a Cyberdog item equal to (or, for example, on the same page as) the Cyberdog item whose referenced content you want to display. Typically, you call `ShowCyberItem` when you want a display part to scroll to display a particular Cyberdog item.

Methods

This section presents summary descriptions of the `CyberPartExtension` methods grouped according to purpose, followed by detailed descriptions.

Initialization and Cleanup

`ICyberPartExtension` Initializes this `CyberPartExtension` object.

Displaying Cyberdog Items

`CanShowCyberItem`	Tests whether this part is displaying content referenced by the specified Cyberdog item.
`GetCyberItem`	Retrieves the Cyberdog item whose referenced content is displayed by this part.
`GetCyberItemWindow`	Retrieves the window in which a Cyberdog item's referenced content is displayed.
`OpenCyberItem`	Opens a Cyberdog item in this display part.
`SetCyberItem`	Assigns the specified Cyberdog item to this display part.
`ShowCyberItem`	Displays the content referenced by the specified Cyberdog item in this display part.

Embedding Cyberdog Items

`AcquireSelectedCyberItems`
Acquires references to the selected Cyberdog items.

`IsCyberItemSelected`
Tests whether any Cyberdog items are selected in this part.

Opening a Selected URL

GetSelectedURL   Retrieves the selected URL.

IsURLSelected   Tests whether the selected text in this part is a URL.

Adding Commands

HandleCommand   Handles semantic events for this Cyberdog display part.

AcquireSelectedCyberItems

Acquires references to the selected Cyberdog items.

```
void AcquireSelectedCyberItems (in ODFrame frame,
                 out CyberItemList cyberItems);
```

frame   The frame to check for selected Cyberdog items.

cyberItems   A CyberItemList object. On return, the CyberItemList structure contains the acquired CyberItem objects.

DISCUSSION

This method should return a CyberItemList structure containing acquired references to the selected Cyberdog items in the specified frame. The superclass implementation of this method returns an empty list. If a Cyberdog display part displays Cyberdog items as part of its content model and allows the user to select them, the part's CyberPartExtension subclass must override this method.

If you subclass CyberPartExtension and override this method, your override may call its inherited method.

SEE ALSO

The IsCyberItemSelected method (page 289).

CanShowCyberItem

Tests whether this part is displaying content referenced by the specified Cyberdog item.

```
ODBoolean CanShowCyberItem (in CyberItem item);
```

item   The Cyberdog item for this operation.

return value   kODTrue if the part is displaying the content referenced by the specified Cyberdog item; otherwise, kODFalse.

DISCUSSION

This method is called by the CyberSession::FindCyberItemWindow and CyberSession::SelectCyberItemWindow methods to determine whether the content referenced by the specified Cyberdog item is already being shown in a window.

The superclass implementation of this method returns kODTrue if the specified item is equal to the Cyberdog item returned by the GetCyberItem method. In some cases, you may wish to use a less stringent test. For example, it is possible for two URLs to reference different locations in the same web page. An HTML display part's CanShowCyberItem method might return kODTrue if the specified Cyberdog item references the page that the display part is currently displaying, even though the item's URL is different.

SEE ALSO

The GetCyberItem method (page 286).
The CyberSession::FindCyberItemWindow method (page 357).
The CyberSession::SelectCyberItemWindow method (page 370).

GetCyberItem

Retrieves the Cyberdog item whose referenced content is displayed by this part.

```
CyberItem GetCyberItem ();
```

return value   The `CyberItem` object.

DISCUSSION

This method is called by the `CyberSession::FindCyberItemWindow` and `CyberSession::SelectCyberItemWindow` methods to retrieve the Cyberdog item whose referenced content the part is displaying. The superclass implementation returns the Cyberdog item last set by the `SetCyberItem` method. If you are going to hold a reference to the Cyberdog item returned by this method, you must follow a call to this method by a call to the object's `Acquire` method.

If you subclass `CyberPartExtension` and override this method, your override must call its inherited method.

SEE ALSO

The `CanShowCyberItem` method (page 285).
The `SetCyberItem` method (page 292).
The `CyberSession::FindCyberItemWindow` method (page 357).
The `CyberSession::SelectCyberItemWindow` method (page 370).

GetCyberItemWindow

Retrieves the window in which a Cyberdog item's referenced content is displayed.

```
ODWindow GetCyberItemWindow (in CyberItem item);
```

`item`   The `CyberItem` object for this operation.

return value   The `ODWindow` object if the Cyberdog item is displayed; otherwise, `kODNULL`.

DISCUSSION

This method is called by the `CyberSession::FindCyberItemWindow` and `CyberSession::SelectCyberItemWindow` methods to retrieve the `ODWindow` object in which this display part is displaying the content referenced by the specified Cyberdog item. The superclass implementation of this method returns `kODNULL`.

This method should use the same algorithm that the `CanShowCyberItem` method uses to determine whether a Cyberdog item is displayed in a window.

If you subclass `CyberPartExtension` and override this method, your override must not call its inherited method; that is, your override method must implement this method's functionality completely.

SEE ALSO

The `CanShowCyberItem` method (page 285).
The `CyberSession::FindCyberItemWindow` method (page 357).
The `CyberSession::SelectCyberItemWindow` method (page 370).

GetSelectedURL

Retrieves the selected URL.

```
char* GetSelectedURL (in ODFrame frame);
```

frame   The frame to check for selected text.

return value A pointer to a string that contains the selected URL.

DISCUSSION

This method should return a string copy of the URL selected in the specified frame. The superclass implementation of this method returns `kODNULL`. If a Cyberdog display part allows the user to select and open a URL, its `CyberPartExtension` subclass must override this method.

You should call this method after calling the `IsURLSelected` method to test whether the selected text is a URL.

If you subclass `CyberPartExtension` and override this method, your override must not call its inherited method; that is, your override method must implement this method's functionality completely.

SEE ALSO

The `IsURLSelected` method (page 290).

HandleCommand

Handles semantic events for this Cyberdog display part.

```
ODBoolean HandleCommand (in long commandCreator,
                         in long commandID,
                         in ODFrame frame,
                         in void* commandData);
```

`commandCreator`
> The creator of the display part.

`commandID`   The ID of the command to execute.

`frame`   The frame to which the command applies.

`commandData`   A pointer to data associated with the command.

return value   `kODTrue` if the method handled the command; otherwise, `kODFalse`.

DISCUSSION

This method should handle any additional semantic events defined by the display part. The superclass implementation returns `kODFalse`.

You can avoid command-ID conflicts by qualifying your display part's command IDs with a creator; you need only worry about making all of your command IDs unique. You should register your creator with Developer Technical Support.

Cyberdog defines some command IDs in `Cyberdog.h`. The creator associated with Cyberdog's commands is `kCyberdogCreator`.

ICyberPartExtension

Initializes this `CyberPartExtension` object.

```
void ICyberPartExtension (in ODPart part);
```

part   The OpenDoc part extended by this object.

DISCUSSION

This method should initialize a newly created `CyberPartExtension` object. As a side effect, this method should make sure that a global `CyberSession` object exists.

If you subclass `CyberPartExtension` and override this method, your override must call its inherited method.

IsCyberItemSelected

Tests whether any Cyberdog items are selected in this part.

```
ODBoolean IsCyberItemSelected (in ODFrame frame);
```

frame   The frame to check for a selection.

return value   `kODTrue` if one or more Cyberdog items are selected; otherwise, `kODFalse`.

DISCUSSION

This method should return `kODTrue` if there are any Cyberdog items selected in the specified frame. The superclass implementation of this method returns `kODFalse`. If a Cyberdog display part displays Cyberdog items as part of its content model and allows the user to select them, the part's `CyberPartExtension` subclass must override this method.

If you subclass `CyberPartExtension` and override this method, your override must not call its inherited method; that is, your override method must implement this method's functionality completely.

SEE ALSO

The `AcquireSelectedCyberItems` method (page 284).

IsURLSelected

Tests whether the selected text in this part is a URL.

```
ODBoolean IsURLSelected (in ODFrame frame);
```

frame   The frame to check for selected text.

return value   `kODTrue` if a URL is selected; otherwise, `kODFalse`.

DISCUSSION

This method should return `kODTrue` if a URL is selected in the specified frame. The superclass implementation of this method returns `kODFalse`. If a Cyberdog display part allows the user to select and open a URL, its `CyberPartExtension` subclass must override this method.

If you subclass `CyberPartExtension` and override this method, your override must not call its inherited method; that is, your override method must implement this method's functionality completely.

SEE ALSO

The `GetSelectedURL` method (page 287).

OpenCyberItem

Opens a Cyberdog item in this display part.

```
void OpenCyberItem  (in CyberItem item,
                     in ODPart openerPart,
                     in ParameterSet openParams);
```

item   The Cyberdog item to be opened.

openerPart   The opener part to use in the opening process, if any; otherwise,
                kODNULL.

openParams   The ParameterSet object to use in the opening process, if any;
                otherwise, kODNULL.

DISCUSSION

This method notifies this Cyberdog display part that it is being opened to display the content referenced by the specified Cyberdog item. The superclass implementation first calls SetCyberItem to store a reference to the Cyberdog item. Then, if an opener part is passed in as a parameter, the method calls the opener part's OpenPart method to open the Cyberdog item. If no opener part is passed in, OpenCyberItem calls the display part's Open method.

If you are creating a Cyberdog display part, you would override this method in your CyberPartExtension subclass to insert additional code in the opening process. For example, your override might take these actions:

- Notify the extension's associated part of the Cyberdog item to be opened.

- Create a progress broadcaster and attach it to a navigator or opener part to show the status of the opening process.

- Embed the display part in a navigator part.

- Retrieve a stream for downloading the data referenced by the Cyberdog item and initiate the download.

SEE ALSO

The SetCyberItem method (page 292).
The CyberOpenerPartExtension::OpenPart method (page 275).

SetCyberItem

Assigns the specified Cyberdog item to this display part.

```
void SetCyberItem    (in CyberItem item,
                       in ParameterSet openParams);
```

item   The Cyberdog item to be displayed.

openParams   The ParameterSet object to use in the opening process, if any;
                otherwise, kODNULL.

DISCUSSION

This method is called by the OpenCyberItem method; this method should store a
reference to the specified Cyberdog item. The superclass implementation of this
method releases the old Cyberdog item, if any, and acquires the new Cyberdog
item. Subsequent calls to GetCyberItem will return the specified Cyberdog item.

If you subclass CyberPartExtension and override this method, your override
must call its inherited method.

SEE ALSO

The GetCyberItem method (page 286).
The OpenCyberItem method (page 291).

ShowCyberItem

Displays the content referenced by the specified Cyberdog item in this
display part.

```
void ShowCyberItem (in CyberItem item);
```

item   The Cyberdog item to display.

DISCUSSION

This method is called by the `CyberSession::SelectCyberItemWindow` method to notify a Cyberdog display part to display the specified Cyberdog item. This method differs from `OpenCyberItem`; you call `ShowCyberItem` once you have determined (by calling `CanShowCyberItem` or `GetCyberItemWindow`) that the display part is already displaying a Cyberdog item equal to (or, for example, on the same page as) the specified Cyberdog item. Typically, you call `ShowCyberItem` when you want the display part to scroll to display a particular Cyberdog item.

If you subclass `CyberPartExtension` and override this method, your override must not call its inherited method; that is, your override method must implement this method's functionality completely.

SEE ALSO

The `CanShowCyberItem` method (page 285).
The `GetCyberItemWindow` method (page 286).
The `OpenCyberItem` method (page 291).
The `CyberSession::SelectCyberItemWindow` method (page 370).

Classes and Methods

CyberPrefsExtension

Superclasses   CyberPanelExtension → CyberExtension → ODExtension →
                  ODRefCntObject → ODObject

Subclasses   none

The CyberPrefsExtension class defines extra behaviors for parts that will be
embedded as panels in the Preferences dialog box.

Description

The CyberPrefsExtension class is a part extension that allows a part to be
embedded as a panel in the Preferences dialog box. A preferences panel allows
the user to specify preferences for a particular service. For example, a
preferences panel for a Cyberdog HTTP service might allow the user to specify
the colors to be used for displaying links in an HTML document.

CyberPrefsExtension is an abstract superclass you can subclass and implement
to create a custom preferences panel. Cyberdog stores preferences using
Internet Config, software that many Internet access programs use to store and
recall user preferences. If you add a new service to Cyberdog that has
preferences associated with it and you do not store those preferences using
Internet Config, you do not need to extend your preferences panel with a
CyberPrefsExtension subclass.

For more information on Internet Config, see the Internet Config documentation
located at the FTP site ftp://redback.cs.uwa.edu.au//Others/PeterLewis/
InternetConfig1.2.sit or search on the Internet for "Internet Config".

Methods

This section presents summary descriptions of the CyberPrefsExtension
methods, followed by detailed descriptions.

ExternalizeIC   Writes the preferences associated with this preferences
                       panel to storage.
InternalizeIC   Reads the preferences associated with this preferences
                       panel from storage.

ExternalizeIC

Writes the preferences associated with this preferences panel to storage.

```
void ExternalizeIC (in ICInstance inst);
```

inst   The ICInstance object for the preferences to be stored.

DISCUSSION

This method stores the preferences associated with this preferences panel.
Typically, you call this method when the user dismisses the dialog box that
contains the preferences panel. A preferences panel should write all of its
preference settings. It is recommended that developers use Internet Config to
store preferences.

If you subclass CyberPrefsExtension, you must override this method. Your
override must not call its inherited method; that is, your override method must
implement this method's functionality completely.

SEE ALSO

The InternalizeIC method (page 296).

InternalizeIC

Reads the preferences associated with a preferences panel from storage.

```
void InternalizeIC (in ICInstance inst);
```

inst   The ICInstance object for the preferences to be read.

DISCUSSION

You call this method to read the preferences represented by this preferences panel when the panel is created. A preferences panel should read all of its preference settings. It is recommended that developers use Internet Config to store preferences.

If you subclass CyberPrefsExtension, you must override this method. Your override must not call its inherited method; that is, your override method must implement this method's functionality completely.

SEE ALSO

The ExternalizeIC method (page 295).

CyberProgressBroadcaster

Superclasses	ODObject
Subclasses	none

An object of the CyberProgressBroadcaster class is used to represent the progress of a process that occurs asynchronously.

Description

When you initiate an asynchronous operation, such as opening a Cyberdog stream, you can create a corresponding CyberProgressBroadcaster object to represent the progress of the process. You use the progress broadcaster object together with a progress receiver (page 317) and a progress part (page 312) to monitor and display the progress and status of the asynchronous process.

A progress broadcaster has attributes that describe the current status and progress of the process. The broadcaster keeps track of the total amount of work to be performed by the process and the amount that has been performed so far. The **progress mode** of the process indicates whether the total amount of work to be performed is known and can be measured. A progress broadcaster has accessor methods that allow you to get and set its attributes.

The object initiating an asynchronous process attaches a progress broadcaster to a progress part that displays the progress of the process to the user. The progress part, in turn, attaches its progress receiver to the progress broadcaster. When the display part calls one of the broadcaster's accessor methods to set an attribute, the broadcaster caches the value and calls a corresponding method to set the value in each of its attached progress receivers. The progress receiver updates the display of the progress part.

In Cyberdog, this progress reporting mechanism is used in two situations.

- When a Cyberdog item is opened, if either a Cyberdog item's Open method or a Cyberdog display part's OpenCyberItem method is asynchronous, the method should display the progress of the asynchronous operation to the user. To do this, the asynchronous method should obtain an opener part and attach a broadcaster that represents the asynchronous operation to the obtained opener part.

- When a Cyberdog display part is embedded in a navigator, the display part should attach a broadcaster object to the navigator; the broadcaster represents the process of downloading the content referenced by the display part's Cyberdog item.

Typically, there is a one-to-one relationship between a progress broadcaster object and a progress receiver object. However, if necessary, you can attach multiple receivers to a broadcaster, or vice versa. For example, if you were downloading multiple images located on a web page, you might represent the downloading of each image as a separate broadcaster, and attach one progress receiver to all the broadcasters to monitor the progress of all the download operations.

You can use the CyberProgressBroadcaster class as is or subclass it to customize its behavior. The CyberProgressBroadcaster class is fully functional with the exception of the Abort method. The Abort method calls the callback function registered by the ICyberProgressBroadcaster method. You implement the Abort method's behavior with this function. This allows you to customize the behavior of the CyberProgressBroadcaster class's Abort method without creating a subclass.

For more information on using progress parts to display progress, see the description of the CyberProgressPartExtension class (page 312).

Methods

This section presents summary descriptions of the CyberProgressBroadcaster methods grouped according to purpose, followed by detailed descriptions.

Initialization and Cleanup

ICyberProgressBroadcaster
                Initializes this progress broadcaster.

Aborting a Process

Abort   Terminates this progress broadcaster.

Attaching and Detaching Progress Receivers

AttachReceiver   Attaches a progress receiver to this progress broadcaster.

DetachReceiver   Detaches a progress receiver from this progress broadcaster.

Accessing Progress Receivers

CountReceivers   Retrieves the number of progress receivers attached to this progress broadcaster.

GetReceiver   Retrieves a progress receiver attached to this progress broadcaster.

Polling for Progress

GetAmountDone   Retrieves a value representing what portion of an asynchronous process has been completed.

GetAmountTotal   Retrieves a value representing the total amount of work to be completed by an asynchronous process.

GetErrorString   Retrieves the error string associated with an asynchronous process.

GetProgressMode   Retrieves the progress mode for an asynchronous process.

GetProgressPercent   Retrieves the percentage of an asynchronous process that has been completed.

GetStatusString   Retrieves the status string associated with an asynchronous process.

Broadcasting Progress

ResetProgress   Resets the status and progress attributes of this progress broadcaster to their default values.

SetAmountDone   Sets a value representing what portion of an asynchronous process has been completed.

SetAmountTotal   Sets a value representing the total amount of work to be completed by an asynchronous process.

SetErrorString   Sets the error string associated with an asynchronous process.

SetProgressMode   Sets the progress mode for an asynchronous process.

SetProgressPercent   Sets the percentage of an asynchronous process that has been completed.

SetStatusString   Sets the status string associated with an asynchronous process.

7

Classes and Methods

Abort

Terminates this progress broadcaster.

```
void Abort ();
```

DISCUSSION

You call this method when you want to terminate a progress broadcaster object, typically when you are also terminating the actual asynchronous process that the object represents. This method calls the programmer-defined function registered by the `ICyberProgressBroadcaster` method, passing the `kAbortMessage` constant as a parameter. This callback mechanism is provided to allow you to customize the `Abort` method of the superclass without having to subclass `CyberProgressBroadcaster`.

SEE ALSO

The `ICyberProgressBroadcaster` method (page 306).

AttachReceiver

Attaches a progress receiver to this progress broadcaster.

```
void AttachReceiver (in CyberProgressReceiver receiver);
```

`receiver`   The `CyberProgressReceiver` object to attach to the process.

DISCUSSION

Once a progress receiver has been attached to a broadcaster, the broadcaster notifies the receiver of status and progress changes.

If you subclass `CyberProgressBroadcaster` and override this method, your override must call its inherited method.

SEE ALSO

The `DetachReceiver` method (page 301).
The `CyberProgressReceiver::BroadcasterAttached` method (page 319).

CountReceivers

Retrieves the number of progress receivers attached to this progress broadcaster.

```
long CountReceivers ();
```

return value   The number of `CyberProgressReceiver` objects attached to the progress broadcaster.

DISCUSSION

You can use this method in conjunction with the `GetReceiver` method to iterate through the progress receivers attached to this broadcaster.

SEE ALSO

The `GetReceiver` method (page 305).

DetachReceiver

Detaches a progress receiver from this progress broadcaster.

```
void DetachReceiver (in CyberProgressReceiver receiver);
```

`receiver`   The `CyberProgressReceiver` object to detach from the process.

DISCUSSION

Once a progress receiver has been detached from a broadcaster, the broadcaster no longer notifies the receiver of status and progress changes.

If you subclass `CyberProgressBroadcaster` and override this method, your override must call its inherited method.

SEE ALSO

The `AttachReceiver` method (page 300).
The `CyberProgressReceiver::BroadcasterDetached` method (page 319).

GetAmountDone

Retrieves a value representing what portion of an asynchronous process has been completed.

```
void GetAmountDone (out long amtDone);
```

amtDone   A numeric indication of the portion of the process that has been completed.

DISCUSSION

This method returns the last value set by the SetAmountDone method or 0 if SetAmountDone has not been called since the object was initialized or reset. The amount done is relative to the total amount as set by the SetAmountTotal method.

The value in the amtDone parameter is a numeric indication of the amount done. For example, consider the process of downloading 200 bytes of data. If you have downloaded 100 bytes, the amount done is 100.

SEE ALSO

The GetAmountTotal method (page 302).
The GetProgressPercent method (page 304).
The SetAmountDone method (page 308).
The SetAmountTotal method (page 308).
The SetProgressPercent method (page 310).

GetAmountTotal

Retrieves a value representing the total amount of work to be completed by an asynchronous process.

```
void GetAmountTotal (out long amtTotal);
```

amtTotal   The total amount of work to be completed.

DISCUSSION

The GetAmountTotal method returns a value that represents the total amount of work to be performed by the process. GetAmountTotal returns the last value set by the SetAmountTotal method or 0 if SetAmountTotal has not been called since the object was initialized or reset. The amount done, set by the SetAmountDone method, is specified relative to the total amount as set by the SetAmountTotal method.

The value in the amtTotal parameter is a numeric indication of the total amount of work to be performed. For example, consider the process of downloading 200 bytes of data. In this case, the total amount is 200.

SEE ALSO

The GetAmountDone method (page 302).
The GetProgressPercent method (page 304).
The SetAmountDone method (page 308).
The SetAmountTotal method (page 308).
The SetProgressPercent method (page 310).

GetErrorString

Retrieves the error string associated with an asynchronous process.

```
void GetErrorString (in StringPtr errorStr);
```

errorStr   A pointer to a string buffer. On return, the buffer contains the error string.

DISCUSSION

The GetErrorString method returns a pointer to the last error string set by the SetErrorString method or an empty string if SetErrorString has not been called since the object was initialized or reset.

SEE ALSO

The SetErrorString method (page 309).

Classes and Methods

GetProgressMode

Retrieves the progress mode for an asynchronous process.

```
void GetProgressMode (out short mode);
```

mode   The progress mode of the process. Valid values for this
                parameter are `kUnmeteredProgress` and `kMeteredProgress`.

DISCUSSION

The `GetProgressMode` method returns the last value set by the `SetProgressMode` method or `kUnmeteredProgress` if `SetProgressMode` has not been called since the object was initialized or reset.

The progress mode of the process indicates whether the total amount of work to be performed is known and can be measured. For example, if you know in advance the number of bytes to be downloaded, the progress mode is metered. In contrast, if you don't know in advance the number of bytes to be downloaded, the progress mode is unmetered. The default progress mode is unmetered.

SEE ALSO

The `SetProgressMode` method (page 310).

GetProgressPercent

Retrieves the percentage of an asynchronous process that has been completed.

```
void GetProgressPercent (out short percentDone);
```

percentDone   The percentage of the process that has been completed.

DISCUSSION

You can call the `GetProgressPercent` method to determine the percentage of the process that has been completed. For example, consider the process of downloading 200 bytes of data. If you have downloaded 100 bytes, 50% has been completed.

GetProgressPercent returns the last value set by the SetProgressPercent method or 0 if SetProgressPercent has not been called since the object was initialized or reset.

SEE ALSO

The GetAmountDone method (page 302).
The GetAmountTotal method (page 302).
The SetAmountDone method (page 308).
The SetAmountTotal method (page 308).
The SetProgressPercent method (page 310).

GetReceiver

Retrieves a progress receiver attached to this progress broadcaster.

```
CyberProgressReceiver GetReceiver (in long index);
```

index   The zero-based index of the CyberProgressReceiver object to be retrieved.

return value   The CyberProgressReceiver object specified by index.

DISCUSSION

This method retrieves by index a progress receiver that is attached to this broadcaster. You can use this method in conjunction with the CountReceivers method to iterate through the progress receivers attached to a broadcaster.

If the value supplied in the index parameter is out of range, the return value of this method is undefined.

SEE ALSO

The CountReceivers method (page 301).

GetStatusString

Retrieves the status string associated with an asynchronous process.

```
void GetStatusString (in StringPtr statusStr);
```

statusStr   A pointer to a string buffer. On return, the buffer contains the status string.

DISCUSSION

The GetStatusString method returns a pointer to the last status string set by the SetStatusString method or an empty string if SetStatusString has not been called since the object was initialized or reset.

Typically, the status string describes what the process is currently doing. For example, if an asynchronous process is downloading data, GetStatusString might return the string "Downloading".

SEE ALSO

The SetStatusString method (page 311).

ICyberProgressBroadcaster

Initializes this progress broadcaster.

```
void ICyberProgressBroadcaster (in CyberAbortUPP proc,
                    in Ptr procData);
```

proc   A pointer to a programmer-defined function that implements the abort behavior for the progress broadcaster object.

procData   A pointer to data that is to be passed to the callback function.

DISCUSSION

You should call the ICyberProgressBroadcaster method to initialize a newly created CyberProgressBroadcaster object.

The callback function you register implements the behavior of the Abort method; the Abort method calls this function. This allows you to customize the behavior of the Abort method without creating a subclass. You can set the procData parameter to point to some data that you want Cyberdog to pass to the callback function. For example, you might set this parameter to point to the CyberStream object whose progress the progress broadcaster is reporting so that the callback function can call the stream's Abort method.

The following type is used for abort functions. The function takes three parameters: a message code, a pointer to a progress broadcaster, and a pointer to some data; the function returns no value.

```
typedef void (* CyberAbortProcPtr) (
            CDAbortProcMessage msgCode,
            CyberProgressBroadcaster* broadcaster,
            Ptr userDataPtr);
```

The MyAbortFunction programmer-defined function (page 191) illustrates the form of an abort function.

If you subclass CyberProgressBroadcaster and override this method, your override must call its inherited method.

ResetProgress

Resets the status and progress attributes of this progress broadcaster to their default values.

```
void ResetProgress ();
```

DISCUSSION

This method resets all status and progress attributes of the broadcaster to their default values and calls the ResetProgress method of the CyberProgressReceiver class to broadcast the change to all attached progress receivers.

If you subclass CyberProgressBroadcaster and override this method, your override must call its inherited method.

SEE ALSO

The CyberProgressReceiver::ResetProgress method (page 322).

SetAmountDone

Sets a value representing what portion of an asynchronous process has been completed.

```
void SetAmountDone (in long amtDone);
```

amtDone   A numeric indication of the portion of the process that has been completed.

DISCUSSION

You can call the `SetAmountDone` method to set the progress of a process and broadcast the change to all attached progress receivers. The amount done is relative to the total amount set by the `SetAmountTotal` method.

The value in the `amtDone` parameter is a numeric indication of the amount done. For example, consider the process of downloading 200 bytes of data. If you have downloaded 100 bytes, the amount done is 100.

If you subclass `CyberProgressBroadcaster` and override this method, your override must call its inherited method.

SEE ALSO

The `GetAmountDone` method (page 302).
The `GetAmountTotal` method (page 302).
The `GetProgressPercent` method (page 304).
The `SetAmountTotal` method (page 308).
The `SetProgressPercent` method (page 310).

SetAmountTotal

Sets a value representing the total amount of work to be completed by an asynchronous process.

```
void SetAmountTotal (in long amtTotal);
```

amtTotal   The total amount to be done by the process.

DISCUSSION

The SetAmountTotal method sets a numeric value that represents the total amount of work to be performed by the process and broadcasts the change to all attached progress receivers. The amount done, set by the SetAmountDone method, is specified relative to the total amount as set by the SetAmountTotal method.

The value in the amtTotal parameter is a numeric indication of the total amount of work to be performed. For example, consider the process of downloading 200 bytes of data. In this case, the total amount is 200.

If you subclass CyberProgressBroadcaster and override this method, your override must call its inherited method.

SEE ALSO

The GetAmountDone method (page 302).
The GetAmountTotal method (page 302).
The GetProgressPercent method (page 304).
The SetAmountDone method (page 308).
The SetProgressPercent method (page 310).

SetErrorString

Sets the error string associated with an asynchronous process.

```
void SetErrorString (in StringPtr errorStr);
```

errorStr   A pointer to a string buffer that contains the error string.

DISCUSSION

You can call the SetErrorString method to set an error string for an asynchronous process and broadcast the change to all attached progress receivers.

If you subclass CyberProgressBroadcaster and override this method, your override must call its inherited method.

SEE ALSO

The GetErrorString method (page 303).

SetProgressMode

Sets the progress mode for an asynchronous process.

```
void SetProgressMode (in short mode);
```

mode   The progress mode of the process. Valid values for this
                    parameter are kUnmeteredProgress or kMeteredProgress.

DISCUSSION

You can call the SetProgressMode method to set the progress mode of a process and broadcast the change to all attached progress receivers.

The progress mode of the process indicates whether the total amount of work to be performed is known and can be measured. For example, if you know in advance the number of bytes to be downloaded, the progress mode is metered. In contrast, if you don't know in advance the number of bytes to be downloaded, the progress mode is unmetered. The default progress mode is unmetered.

If you subclass CyberProgressBroadcaster and override this method, your override must call its inherited method.

SEE ALSO

The GetProgressMode method (page 304).

SetProgressPercent

Sets the percentage of an asynchronous process that has been completed.

```
void SetProgressPercent (in short percentDone);
```

percentDone   The percentage of the process that has been completed.

DISCUSSION

You can call the `SetProgressPercent` method to set the percentage of a process that has been completed and broadcast the change to all attached progress receivers. For example, consider the process of downloading 200 bytes of data. If you have downloaded 100 bytes, 50% has been completed.

If you subclass `CyberProgressBroadcaster` and override this method, your override must call its inherited method.

SEE ALSO

The `GetAmountDone` method (page 302).
The `GetAmountTotal` method (page 302).
The `GetProgressPercent` method (page 304).
The `SetAmountDone` method (page 308).
The `SetAmountTotal` method (page 308).

SetStatusString

Sets the status string associated with an asynchronous process.

```
void SetStatusString (in StringPtr statusStr);
```

statusStr   A pointer to a string buffer that contains the status string.

DISCUSSION

You can call the `SetStatusString` method to set a status string for an asynchronous process and broadcast the change to all attached progress receivers.

If you subclass `CyberProgressBroadcaster`, you must override this method. Your override must call its inherited method.

SEE ALSO

The `GetStatusString` method (page 306).

CyberProgressPartExtension

Superclasses CyberExtension → ODExtension → ODRefCntObject → ODObject

Subclasses CyberOpenerPartExtension

The CyberProgressPartExtension class defines extra behaviors for parts that display the progress and status of an asynchronous process.

Description

The CyberProgressPartExtension class is a part extension that allows a part to monitor and display the status and progress of an asynchronous operation, such as a download operation performed by a Cyberdog stream or the opening of a Cyberdog item. You use a progress part together with a progress broadcaster (page 297) and a progress receiver (page 317) to monitor and display the progress and status of an asynchronous operation.

The Cyberdog navigator and opener parts are both fully implemented progress parts. In most situations, you will use these to display progress. However, CyberProgressPartExtension is an abstract superclass that you can subclass and implement to create your own custom progress part. If you create a custom progress part, you also need to implement a corresponding CyberProgressReceiver subclass.

A progress part has two main uses in Cyberdog:

■ The navigator displays status and progress information while a display part embedded in the navigator performs an asynchronous operation.

■ The opener part displays status and progress information while a Cyberdog item is opened asynchronously.

When an object initiates an asynchronous operation, such as the opening of a Cyberdog stream, the object can create a corresponding CyberProgressBroadcaster object to represent that process and attach it to a progress part, such as the navigator. The progress part, in turn, attaches its progress receiver to the broadcaster. The display part calls the broadcaster's accessor methods periodically to notify it of the status and progress of the actual asynchronous operation; the broadcaster broadcasts these changes in status and progress to the progress receiver.

For example, consider an HTML display part that is embedded in the Cyberdog navigator. While the display part downloads and parses the content referenced by a Cyberdog item, the display part shows the progress of the operation using the Cyberdog navigator. This is the sequence of steps:

1. The HTML display part creates a broadcaster object.

2. The HTML display part acquires its containing navigator.

3. The HTML display part attaches the broadcaster to the navigator.

4. The navigator attaches an object of its associated progress receiver subclass to the broadcaster.

5. The HTML display part calls accessor methods on the broadcaster to update its progress attributes. The broadcaster broadcasts the changes to the progress receiver.

6. The progress receiver receives the changes and updates the navigator's progress display.

Methods

This section presents summary descriptions of the `CyberProgressPartExtension` methods grouped according to purpose, followed by detailed descriptions.

Initialization and Cleanup

`ICyberProgressPartExtension`
>   Initializes this `ICyberProgressPartExtension` object.

Attaching and Detaching Processes

`AttachProgressBroadcaster`
>   Attaches a progress broadcaster to this progress part.

`DetachProgressBroadcaster`
>   Detaches a progress broadcaster from this progress part.

Retrieving Processes

`GetAttachedProgressBroadcaster`
>   Retrieves the progress broadcaster attached to this progress part.

AttachProgressBroadcaster

Attaches a progress broadcaster to this progress part.

```
void AttachProgressBroadcaster (in CyberProgressBroadcaster broadcaster);
```

broadcaster   The progress broadcaster to attach to the progress part.

DISCUSSION

Typically, the progress part creates an object of its corresponding
CyberProgressReceiver subclass and attaches the object to the broadcaster.

If you subclass CyberProgressPartExtension, you must override this method.
Your override must not call its inherited method; that is, your override method
must implement this method's functionality completely.

SEE ALSO

The DetachProgressBroadcaster method (page 314).
The CyberProgressBroadcaster::AttachReceiver method (page 300).

DetachProgressBroadcaster

Detaches a progress broadcaster from this progress part.

```
void DetachProgressBroadcaster (in CyberProgressBroadcaster broadcaster);
```

broadcaster   The progress broadcaster to detach from the progress part.

DISCUSSION

Once a broadcaster has been detached from a progress part, the progress part
no longer monitors the process and no longer displays status and progress to
the user. If the progress part was using a progress receiver object, it should
detach the progress receiver object from the broadcaster by calling
CyberProgressBroadcaster:DetachReceiver.

If you subclass `CyberProgressPartExtension`, you must override this method. Your override must not call its inherited method; that is, your override method must implement this method's functionality completely.

SEE ALSO

The `AttachProgressBroadcaster` method (page 314).
The `CyberProgressBroadcaster::DetachReceiver` method (page 301).

GetAttachedProgressBroadcaster

Retrieves the progress broadcaster attached to this progress part.

```
CyberProgressBroadcaster GetAttachedProgressBroadcaster ();
```

return value   The progress broadcaster attached to the progress part.

DISCUSSION

This method returns the broadcaster that is currently attached to a progress part, if any.

If you subclass `CyberProgressPartExtension`, you must override this method. Your override must not call its inherited method; that is, your override method must implement this method's functionality completely.

SEE ALSO

The `AttachProgressBroadcaster` method (page 314).
The `DetachProgressBroadcaster` method (page 314).

ICyberProgressPartExtension

Initializes this `CyberProgressPartExtension` object.

```
void ICyberProgressPartExtension (in ODPart basePart);
```

basePart   The OpenDoc part extended by this object.

DISCUSSION

You should call the `ICyberProgressPartExtension` method to initialize a newly created `CyberProgressPartExtension` object.

If you subclass `CyberProgressPartExtension` and override this method, your override must call its inherited method.

CyberProgressReceiver

Superclasses   ODObject

Subclasses   none

An object of the CyberProgressReceiver class is used to monitor the progress of an asynchronous process.

Description

The CyberProgressReceiver class is an abstract class for monitoring the progress of an asynchronous operation, such as a download operation performed by a Cyberdog stream. You use a progress receiver object together with a progress broadcaster (page 297) and a progress part (page 312) to monitor and display the progress and status of an asynchronous operation.

When an object initiates an asynchronous operation, such as a Cyberdog display part opening a Cyberdog stream, the object can create a corresponding CyberProgressBroadcaster object to represent that process and attach it to a progress part, such as the navigator. The progress part, in turn, attaches a progress receiver to the progress broadcaster object. The object calls the broadcaster's accessor methods periodically to notify it of the status and progress of the asynchronous operation; the broadcaster broadcasts these changes in status and progress to the progress receiver.

Typically, there is a one-to-one relationship between a progress broadcaster object and a progress receiver object. However, if necessary, you can attach multiple progress receivers to a progress broadcaster, or vice versa. For example, if you were downloading multiple images located on a web page, you might represent the downloading of each image as a separate broadcaster and attach one progress receiver to all the broadcasters to monitor the progress of all the download operations.

The CyberProgressReceiver class is an abstract superclass that you must subclass and implement to create a progress receiver. If you subclass the CyberProgressPartExtension class to create a custom progress part, you must create a corresponding CyberProgressReceiver subclass.

For more information on using progress parts to display progress, see the description of the CyberProgressPartExtension class (page 312).

Methods

This section presents summary descriptions of the `CyberProgressReceiver` methods grouped according to purpose, followed by detailed descriptions.

Initialization and Cleanup

`ICyberProgressReceiver`
> Initializes this progress receiver.

Attaching and Detaching Processes

`BroadcasterAttached`
> Notifies this progress receiver that it has been attached to a progress broadcaster.

`BroadcasterDetached`
> Notifies this progress receiver that it has been detached from a progress broadcaster.

Retrieving Processes

`CountBroadcasters`
> Retrieves the number of progress broadcasters attached to this progress receiver.

`GetBroadcaster`
> Retrieves a progress broadcaster attached to this progress receiver.

Receiving Progress

`ResetProgress`
> Resets the status and progress attributes of this progress receiver to their default values.

`SetAmountDone`
> Sets a value representing what portion of an asynchronous process has been completed.

`SetAmountTotal`
> Sets a value representing the total amount of work to be completed by an asynchronous process.

`SetErrorString`
> Sets the error string associated with an asynchronous process.

`SetProgressMode`
> Sets the progress mode associated with an asynchronous process.

`SetProgressPercent`
> Sets the percentage of an asynchronous process that has been completed.

`SetStatusString`
> Sets the status string associated with an asynchronous process.

BroadcasterAttached

Notifies this progress receiver that it has been attached to a progress broadcaster.

```
void BroadcasterAttached (in CyberProgressBroadcaster broadcaster);
```

broadcaster   The progress broadcaster to which the progress receiver has been attached.

DISCUSSION

When the `CyberProgressBroadcaster::AttachReceiver` method is called to attach a progress receiver to a progress broadcaster, that method calls `BroadcasterAttached` to notify the progress receiver that it has been attached to the broadcaster. Once a progress receiver has been attached to a broadcaster, the broadcaster notifies it of status and progress changes.

SEE ALSO

The `BroadcasterDetached` method (page 319).
The `CyberProgressBroadcaster::AttachReceiver` method (page 300).

BroadcasterDetached

Notifies this progress receiver that it has been detached from a progress broadcaster.

```
void BroadcasterDetached (in CyberProgressBroadcaster broadcaster);
```

broadcaster   The progress broadcaster from which the progress receiver has been detached.

DISCUSSION

When the `CyberProgressBroadcaster::DetachReceiver` method is called to detach a progress receiver from a progress broadcaster, that method calls `BroadcasterDetached` to notify the progress receiver that it has been detached from the broadcaster. Once a progress receiver has been detached from a broadcaster, the broadcaster no longer notifies it of status and progress changes.

SEE ALSO

The BroadcasterAttached method (page 319).
The CyberProgressBroadcaster::DetachReceiver method (page 301).

CountBroadcasters

Retrieves the number of progress broadcasters attached to this progress receiver.

```
long CountBroadcasters ();
```

return value   The number of progress broadcasters attached to the progress receiver.

DISCUSSION

You can use this method in conjunction with the GetBroadcaster method to iterate through the broadcasters attached to a progress receiver.

If you subclass CyberProgressReceiver, you must override this method. Your override must call its inherited method.

SEE ALSO

The GetBroadcaster method (page 321).

GetBroadcaster

Retrieves a progress broadcaster attached to this progress receiver.

```
CyberProgressBroadcaster GetBroadcaster (in long index);
```

index | The zero-based index of the process to be retrieved.
return value | The progress broadcaster specified by index.

DISCUSSION

This method retrieves by index a progress broadcaster that is attached to a progress receiver. You can use this method in conjunction with the CountBroadcasters method to iterate through the broadcasters attached to a progress receiver.

If the value supplied in the index parameter is out of range, the return value of this method is undefined.

If you subclass CyberProgressReceiver, you must override this method. Your override must call its inherited method.

SEE ALSO

The CountBroadcasters method (page 320).

ICyberProgressReceiver

Initializes this progress receiver.

```
void ICyberProgressReceiver ();
```

DISCUSSION

You should call the ICyberProgressReceiver method to initialize a newly created CyberProgressReceiver object.

If you subclass CyberProgressReceiver, you must override this method. Your override must call its inherited method.

ResetProgress

Resets the status and progress attributes of this progress receiver to their default values.

```
void ResetProgress (in CyberProgressBroadcaster broadcaster);
```

broadcaster   The progress broadcaster whose progress receivers should be reset.

DISCUSSION

The `CyberProgressBroadcaster::ResetProgress` method calls this method to reset the status and progress attributes of this progress receiver.

SEE ALSO

The `CyberProgressBroadcaster::ResetProgress` method (page 307).

SetAmountDone

Sets a value representing what portion of an asynchronous process has been completed.

```
void SetAmountDone  (in long amtDone,
                     in CyberProgressBroadcaster broadcaster);
```

amtDone   The amount of the process that has been completed.
broadcaster   The progress broadcaster broadcasting the change.

DISCUSSION

This method is called by the `CyberProgressBroadcaster::SetAmountDone` method to broadcast a new value to all progress receivers attached to the broadcaster. The amount done is relative to the total amount by the `SetAmountTotal` method.

The value in the `amtDone` parameter is a numeric indication of the amount done. For example, consider the process of downloading 200 bytes of data. If you have downloaded 100 bytes, the amount done is 100.

If you subclass `CyberProgressReceiver`, you must override this method. Your override must not call its inherited method; that is, your override method must implement this method's functionality completely.

SEE ALSO

The `CyberProgressBroadcaster::SetAmountDone` method (page 308).

SetAmountTotal

Sets a value representing the total amount of work to be completed by an asynchronous process.

```
void SetAmountTotal (in long amtTotal,
                     in CyberProgressBroadcaster broadcaster);
```

amtTotal   The total amount to be done by the process.

broadcaster   The progress broadcaster broadcasting the change.

DISCUSSION

This method is called by the `CyberProgressBroadcaster::SetAmountTotal` method to broadcast a new total amount value to all progress receivers attached to the broadcaster. The amount done, set by the `SetAmountDone` method, is specified relative to the total amount by the `SetAmountTotal` method.

The value in the `amtTotal` parameter is a numeric indication of the total amount of work to be performed. For example, consider the process of downloading 200 bytes of data. In this case, the total amount is 200.

If you subclass `CyberProgressReceiver`, you must override this method. Your override must not call its inherited method; that is, your override method must implement this method's functionality completely.

SEE ALSO

The `CyberProgressBroadcaster::SetAmountTotal` method (page 308).

SetErrorString

Sets the error string associated with an asynchronous process.

```
void SetErrorString (in StringPtr errorStr,
                     in CyberProgressBroadcaster broadcaster);
```

errorStr   A pointer to a string buffer that contains the error string.

broadcaster   The progress broadcaster broadcasting the change.

DISCUSSION

This method is called by the `CyberProgressBroadcaster::SetErrorString`
method to broadcast a new error string to all progress receivers attached to
the broadcaster.

If you subclass `CyberProgressReceiver`, you must override this method. Your
override must not call its inherited method; that is, your override method must
implement this method's functionality completely.

SEE ALSO

The `CyberProgressBroadcaster::SetErrorString` method (page 309).

SetProgressMode

Sets the progress mode associated with an asynchronous process.

```
void SetProgressMode (in short mode,
                      in CyberProgressBroadcaster broadcaster);
```

mode   The progress mode of the process. Valid values for this
                parameter are `kUnmeteredProgress` or `kMeteredProgress`.

broadcaster   The progress broadcaster broadcasting the change.

DISCUSSION

This method is called by the `CyberProgressBroadcaster::SetProgressMode` method to broadcast a new progress mode to all progress receivers attached to the broadcaster.

The progress mode of the process indicates whether the total amount of work to be performed is known and can be measured. For example, if you know in advance the number of bytes to be downloaded, the progress mode is metered. In contrast, if you don't know in advance the number of bytes to be downloaded, the progress mode is unmetered. The default progress mode is unmetered.

If you subclass `CyberProgressReceiver`, you must override this method. Your override must not call its inherited method; that is, your override method must implement this method's functionality completely.

SEE ALSO

The `CyberProgressBroadcaster::SetProgressMode` method (page 310).

SetProgressPercent

Sets the percentage of an asynchronous process that has been completed.

```
void SetProgressPercent (in short percentDone,
                    in CyberProgressBroadcaster broadcaster);
```

percentDone   An integer value indicating the percentage of the process that has been completed.

broadcaster   The progress broadcaster broadcasting the change.

DISCUSSION

This method is called by the `CyberProgressBroadcaster::SetProgressPercent` method to broadcast a new percent done amount to all progress receivers attached to the broadcaster.

For example, consider the process of downloading 200 bytes of data. If you have downloaded 100 bytes, 50% is completed.

If you subclass `CyberProgressReceiver`, you must override this method. Your override must not call its inherited method; that is, your override method must implement this method's functionality completely.

SEE ALSO

The `CyberProgressBroadcaster::SetProgressPercent` method (page 310).

SetStatusString

Sets the status string associated with an asynchronous process.

```
void SetStatusString (in StringPtr statusStr,
                      in CyberProgressBroadcaster broadcaster);
```

statusStr   A pointer to a string buffer that contains the status string.

broadcaster   The progress broadcaster broadcasting the change.

DISCUSSION

This method is called by the `CyberProgressBroadcaster::SetStatusString` method to broadcast a new status string to all progress receivers attached to the broadcaster.

If you subclass `CyberProgressReceiver`, you must override this method. Your override must not call its inherited method; that is, your override method must implement this method's functionality completely.

SEE ALSO

The `CyberProgressBroadcaster::SetStatusString` method (page 311).

CyberService

Superclasses   ODObject

Subclasses   none

An object of the CyberService class represents a network service or protocol.

Description

A CyberService object represents a Cyberdog service, an object that, along with companion objects, provides support for accessing data using a particular network protocol. The CyberService class is an abstract superclass that you subclass and implement to provide a service. Cyberdog includes CyberService subclasses to support common network protocols, such as HTTP, Gopher, and FTP. You can use the existing CyberService subclasses or create a new CyberService subclass to support a new service.

Cyberdog determines which services are supported by checking for 'srvc' resources. When a Cyberdog session is initialized, it creates a Cyberdog service for each 'srvc' resource in your shared library. The 'srvc' resource identifies the SOM class of the Cyberdog service to create as well as other configuration attributes of the service. Cyberdog selects the appropriate service object as needed to access network data. Cyberdog services are deleted when the Cyberdog session is deleted.

If you are developing a Cyberdog display part, you should not need to access service objects directly. In most cases, other classes in Cyberdog mediate between Cyberdog display parts and service objects. For example, to create a Cyberdog item from a URL, a display part calls the CyberSession::CreateCyberItemFromURL method. This method iterates over all of the CyberService objects, determines which service owns the particular URL scheme, and asks that service to create a Cyberdog item for the URL.

A CyberService subclass may have companion CyberItem and CyberStream subclasses that address and download data using the protocol. Each service may have its own Connect To and Preferences panels, displayed in the Connect To and Preferences dialog boxes, respectively.

In addition, the Cyberdog service interacts with Cyberdog service menu objects (page 339) to display its service-related menu items for Cyberdog display parts. A service's menu commands are specified as offsets from a service menu object's base command ID. As a display part developer, you specify the base menu command ID to be used for a service menu object when you call `CyberServiceMenu::ICyberServiceMenu` to initialize the object. For more information on registering menu command IDs with OpenDoc, see the chapter on windows and menus in *OpenDoc Programmer's Guide*.

Methods

This section presents summary descriptions of the `CyberService` methods grouped according to purpose, followed by detailed descriptions.

Initialization and Cleanup

`ICyberService`   Initializes this Cyberdog service.

Creating Cyberdog Items

`CreateCyberItem`   Creates a Cyberdog item for the specified URL.

`OwnsURL`   Tests whether this Cyberdog service can create a Cyberdog item for the specified URL.

Managing Menus

`AdjustCyberMenu`   Adjusts the menu items of this Cyberdog service.

`AppendCyberMenuCommands`
                         Appends the menu items of this Cyberdog service to a Cyberdog service menu object.

`CyberMenuFocusAcquired`
                         Notifies this Cyberdog service that the part associated with a Cyberdog service menu object has acquired the focus.

`CyberMenuFocusLost`   Notifies this Cyberdog service that the part associated with a Cyberdog service menu object has lost the focus.

`DoCyberMenuCommand`   Performs a menu command.

Accessing Display Information

`GetIconSuite`   Retrieves the icon suite for this Cyberdog service.

`GetName`   Retrieves the name of this Cyberdog service.

Preferences and Connect To Panels

GetConnectPartKind	Retrieves the part kind of the Connect To panel for this Cyberdog service.
GetPrefsPartKind	Retrieves the part kind of the Preferences panel for this Cyberdog service.

AdjustCyberMenu

Adjusts the menu items of this Cyberdog service.

```
void AdjustCyberMenu (in ODMenuBar menuBar,
                      in ODFrame frame,
                      in long baseCommandID,
                      in CyberMenuData menuData);
```

menuBar	The current ODMenuBar object.
frame	The frame that has the menu focus.
baseCommandID	
	The Cyberdog service menu object's base command ID for service-related commands.
menuData	A pointer to the service's menu data.

DISCUSSION

This method is called by a Cyberdog service menu object's Adjust method, which adjusts all of a display part's service-related menus when the display part gets the menu focus. This method should enable and disable this service's menu items for the specified frame. This method is responsible for adjusting all of the menu items added to the menu bar by the AppendCyberMenuCommands method.

If you subclass CyberService and override this method, your override must not call its inherited method; that is, your override method must implement this method's functionality completely.

SEE ALSO

The `AppendCyberMenuCommands` method (page 330).
The `CyberServiceMenu::Adjust` method (page 340).

AppendCyberMenuCommands

Appends the menu items of this Cyberdog service to a Cyberdog service menu object.

```
void AppendCyberMenuCommands (in ODMenuBar menuBar,
                in ODPart part,
                in MenuHandle menuHnd,
                in long baseCommandID,
                out CyberMenuData menuData,
                out CyberMenuDataDestructorUPP menuDataDestructor);
```

menuBar   The `ODMenuBar` object to which the service should add its menus.

part   The part associated with the Cyberdog service menu object.

menuHnd   A handle to the menu to which the menu items should be added.

baseCommandID
                    The Cyberdog service menu object's base command ID for service-related commands.

menuData   A pointer to menu data that is passed to the function specified by `menuDataDestructor`.

menuDataDestructor
                    A pointer to a programmer-defined function that destroys the service's menu data when the `CyberServiceMenu` object is deleted.

DISCUSSION

This method should add this service's menu items to a Cyberdog service menu object. This method should append the service's menu items to the menu handle and register the service's commands with the menu bar.

The output parameters `menuData` and `menuDataDestructor` provide a means for the service to associate data with a service menu object. The service menu object stores the service's menu data and destructor. The service menu object passes the menu data to the service when it calls any of the service's menu-related methods. The menu data destructor is called when the service menu object is deleted. The destructor should deallocate the data pointed to by `menuData`. The superclass implementation of this method sets `menuData` and `menuDataDestructor` to `nil`.

The following type is used to define a menu data destructor. The function takes one parameter: a pointer of type `void*`; the function returns no value.

```
typedef void (* CyberMenuDataDestructorProcPtr) (
            void* menuData);
```

The `MyMenuDataDestructor` programmer-defined function (page 194) illustrates the form of a menu data destructor function.

If you subclass `CyberService` and override this method, your override must not call its inherited method; that is, your override method must implement this method's functionality completely.

CreateCyberItem

Creates a Cyberdog item for the specified URL.

```
CyberItem CreateCyberItem (in char* url);
```

url   A pointer to a string that contains the URL for this operation.

return value   The newly created `CyberItem` object.

DISCUSSION

If this service supports the URL scheme of the specified URL, this method should create and initialize a Cyberdog item for the specified URL. The superclass implementation of this method returns `kODNULL`.

If you subclass `CyberService` and override this method, your override must not call its inherited method; that is, your override method must implement this method's functionality completely.

SEE ALSO

The OwnsURL method (page 337).

CyberMenuFocusAcquired

Notifies this Cyberdog service that the part associated with a Cyberdog service menu object has acquired the focus.

```
void CyberMenuFocusAcquired (in ODFrame frame,
                    in CyberMenuData menuData);
```

frame   The frame that is acquiring the menu focus.

menuData   A pointer to the service's menu data.

DISCUSSION

When a display part gets the menu focus and needs to display its menus, it calls its Cyberdog service menu object's MenuFocusAcquired method, which, in turn, calls this method. You can override this method to install the menu items for this service when the display part acquires the focus.

If you subclass CyberService and override this method, your override must not call its inherited method; that is, your override method must implement this method's functionality completely.

SEE ALSO

The CyberMenuFocusLost method (page 333).
The CyberServiceMenu::MenuFocusAcquired method (page 342).

CyberMenuFocusLost

Notifies this Cyberdog service that the part associated with a Cyberdog service menu object has lost the focus.

```
void CyberMenuFocusLost (in ODFrame frame,
                    in CyberMenuData menuData);
```

frame   The frame that is losing the menu focus.

menuData   A pointer to the service's menu data.

DISCUSSION

When a display part loses the menu focus and needs to display its menus, it calls its Cyberdog service menu object's MenuFocusLost method, which, in turn, calls this method. You can override this method to remove the menu items for this service when the display part loses the focus.

If you subclass CyberService and override this method, your override must not call its inherited method; that is, your override method must implement this method's functionality completely.

SEE ALSO

The CyberMenuFocusAcquired method (page 332).
The CyberServiceMenu::MenuFocusLost method (page 343).

DoCyberMenuCommand

Performs a menu command.

```
ODBoolean DoCyberMenuCommand (in long commandID,
                    in ODFrame frame,
                    in long baseCommandID,
                    in CyberMenuData menuData);
```

commandID   The command ID of the menu item.

frame   The frame that has the menu focus.

Classes and Methods

baseCommandID

The Cyberdog service menu object's base command ID for
service-related commands.

menuData   A pointer to the service's menu data.

return value   kODTrue if the menu command was handled; otherwise,
kODFalse.

DISCUSSION

When a display part has the menu focus and the user selects a menu command,
the part's HandleMenuEvent method calls the Cyberdog service menu object's
DoCommand method, which, in turn, calls this method.

If you subclass CyberService and override this method, your override must not
call its inherited method; that is, your override method must implement this
method's functionality completely.

SEE ALSO

The AppendCyberMenuCommands method (page 330).
The CyberServiceMenu::DoCommand method (page 341).

GetConnectPartKind

Retrieves the part kind of the Connect To panel for this Cyberdog service.

ODType GetConnectPartKind ();

return value   The part kind of the Connect To panel.

DISCUSSION

This method should return the part kind of this service's associated Connect To
panel or kODNULL if this service does not have a Connect To panel. The
superclass implementation of this method returns kODNULL.

The string returned by this method is owned by the service object; you should
not alter it or dispose of it.

If you subclass `CyberService` and override this method, your override must not call its inherited method; that is, your override method must implement this method's functionality completely.

GetIconSuite

Retrieves the icon suite for this Cyberdog service.

```
Handle GetIconSuite ();
```

return value   A handle to the icon suite.

DISCUSSION

This method should retrieve a handle to the icon suite for this Cyberdog service. This icon is used in the scrolling lists of services in the Connect To and Preferences dialog boxes. The superclass implementation of this method returns `nil`. You should override this method if your service defines a Connect To panel or a Preferences panel.

The service object owns the handle returned by this method; you should not alter the handle in any way.

If you subclass `CyberService` and override this method, your override must not call its inherited method; that is, your override method must implement this method's functionality completely.

GetName

Retrieves the name of this Cyberdog service.

```
void GetName (in Str255 menuName);
```

menuName   A string buffer. On return, the buffer contains the name of the service.

DISCUSSION

This method should retrieve a user-readable name of this Cyberdog service. This name appears in the scrolling lists of services in the Connect To and Preferences dialog boxes. You should override this method if your service defines a Connect To panel or a Preferences panel.

If you subclass CyberService and override this method, your override must not call its inherited method; that is, your override method must implement this method's functionality completely.

GetPrefsPartKind

Retrieves the part kind of the Preferences panel for this Cyberdog service.

```
ODType GetPrefsPartKind ();
```

return value   The part kind of the Preferences panel.

DISCUSSION

This method should return the part kind of this service's associated Preferences panel or kODNULL if this service does not have a Preferences panel. The superclass implementation of this method returns kODNULL.

The string returned by this method is owned by the service object; you should not alter it or dispose of it.

If you subclass CyberService and override this method, your override must not call its inherited method; that is, your override method must implement this method's functionality completely.

SEE ALSO

The GetConnectPartKind method (page 334).

ICyberService

Initializes this Cyberdog service.

```
void ICyberService  (in Handle serviceDataHnd,
                      in long menuCommandOffset,
                      out short numMenuCommands);
```

serviceDataHnd
> A handle to the 'srvc' resource associated with the Cyberdog service.

menuCommandOffset
> The offset of the service's commands from the Cyberdog service menu object's base command ID.

numMenuCommands
> The number of menu items this service defines.

DISCUSSION

This method should initialize a newly created Cyberdog service object. The Cyberdog session calls this method when it loads the Cyberdog service.

If you subclass CyberService and override this method, your override must call its inherited method.

OwnsURL

Tests whether this Cyberdog service can create a Cyberdog item for the specified URL.

```
ODBoolean OwnsURL (in char* url);
```

url
> A pointer to a string that contains the URL for this operation.

return value
> kODTrue if the service can create a Cyberdog item from the URL; otherwise, kODFalse.

DISCUSSION

This method should parse the specified URL and return kODTrue if this service supports the URL scheme and can manufacture a Cyberdog item from the URL. The superclass implementation returns kODFalse.

If you subclass CyberService and override this method, your override must not call its inherited method; that is, your override method must implement this method's functionality completely.

SEE ALSO

The CreateCyberItem method (page 331).

CyberServiceMenu

Superclasses   ODObject

Subclasses   none

An object of the CyberServiceMenu class is used to represent the Cyberdog service-related menus that a Cyberdog display part adds to the menu bar.

Description

The CyberServiceMenu class represents the Cyberdog menu and all of the menus added to the menu bar by all Cyberdog services. A single service menu object represents the Cyberdog menu as well as all of the menus added to the menu bar by all Cyberdog services.

A Cyberdog display part can choose to add these service-related menus to the menu bar when the part gets the menu focus. If you want to display the Cyberdog menu and service-specific menus when your Cyberdog display part has the menu focus, you should create and initialize a single CyberServiceMenu object when you initialize your display part. Every display part that wants to display the service-related menus must create a service menu object. In addition, your display part needs to do the following things:

■ When your display part handles kODEvtMenu events, it should call DoCommand to give Cyberdog services the opportunity to handle their own menu commands.

■ When your display part adjusts menus, it should call Adjust to allow Cyberdog services to adjust their menus.

■ When your display part acquires the menu focus, it should call MenuFocusAcquired to allow Cyberdog services to install their menus. When your display part loses the menu focus, it should call MenuFocusLost to allow Cyberdog services to remove their menus.

Each service menu object has a base menu command ID, which should be in the range allowed by OpenDoc. All service-related menu commands are specified as offsets from a service menu object's base command ID. As a display part developer, you specify the base menu command ID to be used for the service menu object when you call ICyberServiceMenu to initialize the object.

For more information on registering menu command IDs with OpenDoc, see the chapter on windows and menus in *OpenDoc Programmer's Guide*.

Do not subclass this class.

Methods

This section presents summary descriptions of the `CyberServiceMenu` methods grouped according to purpose, followed by detailed descriptions.

Initialization and Cleanup

ICyberServiceMenu   Initializes this Cyberdog service menu object.

Modifying Menus

Adjust   Adjusts the menus represented by this Cyberdog service menu object.

MenuFocusAcquired   Notifies this Cyberdog service menu object that its associated display part has acquired the focus.

MenuFocusLost   Notifies this Cyberdog service menu object that its associated display part has lost the focus.

Performing Menu Commands

DoCommand   Handles a menu event for this Cyberdog service menu object.

Adjust

Adjusts the menus represented by this Cyberdog service menu object.

```
void Adjust (in ODFrame frame);
```

frame   The frame that has the menu focus.

DISCUSSION

You call this method to allow Cyberdog to enable and disable all service-related menu items for the specified frame. Any Cyberdog display part that displays service-related menus should call this method from within its AdjustMenus implementation to allow the Cyberdog services to adjust their menus. Adjust iterates through all the Cyberdog services, calling each service's AdjustCyberMenu method.

Do not subclass this class.

SEE ALSO

The CyberService::AdjustCyberMenu method (page 329).

DoCommand

Handles a menu event for this Cyberdog service menu object.

```
ODBoolean DoCommand (in long commandID,
                     in ODFrame frame);
```

commandID   The command ID from the ODMenuBar object.

frame   The frame associated with this menu event.

return value   kODTrue if Cyberdog handles the menu event; otherwise, kODFalse.

DISCUSSION

This method handles Cyberdog service-related menu commands. A display part that displays service-related menus should call this method from within its HandleMenu method to allow the Cyberdog services to handle their menu commands. DoCommand iterates through all the Cyberdog services, calling each service's DoCyberMenuCommand method until a service's method returns kODTrue.

Do not subclass this class.

SEE ALSO

The CyberService::DoCyberMenuCommand method (page 333).

ICyberServiceMenu

Initializes this Cyberdog service menu object.

```
void ICyberServiceMenu (in ODMenuBar menuBar,
                        in ODPart part,
                        in long baseCommandID);
```

menuBar   The menu bar to be modified.

part   The display part that owns the menu bar.

baseCommandID

                The base command ID for this service menu object.

DISCUSSION

You call this method to initialize a newly created `CyberServiceMenu` object. This method installs all of the Cyberdog service-related menu items and registers their command numbers with the `ODMenuBar` object.

As a display part developer, you specify the base menu command ID to be used for the service menu object; however, the base command ID you choose should be in a range allowed by OpenDoc. For more information on registering menu command IDs with OpenDoc, see the chapter on windows and menus in *OpenDoc Programmer's Guide*.

Any display part that displays service-related menus should call this method from within its `InitPart` and `InitPartFromStorage` methods.

Do not subclass this class.

MenuFocusAcquired

Notifies this Cyberdog service menu object that its associated display part has acquired the focus.

```
void MenuFocusAcquired (in ODFrame frame);
```

frame   The frame that acquired the menu focus.

DISCUSSION

Any Cyberdog display part that displays Cyberdog service-related menus should call this method when one of its frames acquires the menu focus. `MenuFocusAcquired` iterates through all the Cyberdog services, calling each service's `CyberMenuFocusAcquired` method.

Do not subclass this class.

SEE ALSO

The `MenuFocusLost` method (page 343).
The `CyberService::CyberMenuFocusAcquired` method (page 332).

MenuFocusLost

Notifies this Cyberdog service menu object that its associated display part has lost the focus.

```
void MenuFocusLost (in ODFrame frame);
```

`frame`   The frame that lost the menu focus.

DISCUSSION

Any Cyberdog display part that displays Cyberdog service-related menus should call this method when one of its frames loses the menu focus. `MenuFocusLost` iterates through all the Cyberdog services, calling each service's `CyberMenuFocusLost` method.

Do not subclass this class.

SEE ALSO

The `MenuFocusAcquired` method (page 342).
The `CyberService::CyberMenuFocusLost` method (page 333).

CyberSession

Superclasses	ODObject
Subclasses	none

An object of the CyberSession class represents a user's access to Cyberdog.

Description

The Cyberdog session is a single, global object whose interface provides access to various objects in Cyberdog, including the available Cyberdog services. Any part that calls Cyberdog methods should call the InitCyberdog global function (page 190) during its initialization to initialize Cyberdog and create the global session object. Once a Cyberdog session object has been created, you can retrieve it by calling the GetCyberSession global function.

When a Cyberdog session is initialized, it loads and keeps track of the available Cyberdog services (page 327). In addition, the Cyberdog session object provides methods for accessing the default notebook, the log, and the Connect To and Preferences dialog boxes. The Cyberdog session also provides access to a number of global Cyberdog utility methods.

The Cyberdog session keeps track of the user's opening of and access to a single, temporary Cyberdog session document, which has a single OpenDoc draft. The root part of the Cyberdog session document never displays itself. During a Cyberdog session, this temporary session document contains all of the display parts that are not contained in other OpenDoc documents.

The Cyberdog session document does not contain the log, the notebook, or any other Cyberdog-related document that can be opened from the Finder. Although these are also OpenDoc documents, they are separate from the session document. However, all documents created by Cyberdog, including the session document, share a single process.

Do not subclass this class.

Methods

This section presents summary descriptions of the CyberSession methods grouped according to purpose, followed by detailed descriptions.

Initialization and Cleanup

ICyberSession   Initializes this session object.

Accessing a Cyberdog Service

CountCyberServices   Retrieves the number of services available to this Cyberdog session.

GetCyberService   Retrieves a Cyberdog service by index.

Accessing the OpenDoc Session

GetODSession   Retrieves the OpenDoc session object for this Cyberdog session.

Connect To Dialog Utilities

PromptForCyberItem   Displays the Connect To dialog box and returns the Cyberdog item specified by the user.

ShowConnectDialog   Displays the Connect To dialog box.

Cyberdog Session Document Utilities

CloseCyberDraftWindow
   Closes a part window in the Cyberdog session document.

CreatePartInCyberDocument
   Creates a new part in a Cyberdog session document.

CreatePartInNewDocument
   Creates a new part as a separate OpenDoc document.

GetCyberDraft   Retrieves the draft of the Cyberdog session document.

InstallCyberDocumentMenu
   Installs a Document menu customized for Cyberdog display parts contained in the Cyberdog session document.

IsInCyberDraft   Tests whether the specified persistent object is stored in the Cyberdog session document's draft.

Classes and Methods

Cyberdog Item Utilities

`CreateCyberItemFromSU`
        Creates a Cyberdog item from a storage unit.

`CreateCyberItemFromURL`
        Creates a Cyberdog item for a URL.

`CreateProxyItemFromURL`
        Creates a proxy Cyberdog item for a URL.

`FindCyberItemWindow` Retrieves the window that displays a Cyberdog item.

`NewCyberItem`   Creates a Cyberdog item.

`SelectCyberItemWindow`
        Retrieves and selects the window that displays a
        Cyberdog item.

Log Utilities

`AddCyberItemToLog`   Adds a Cyberdog item to the log.

`ClearLogFinger`   Clears the log finger from a Cyberdog item.

`GetLog`   Retrieves the log part.

`IsLogWindowShown`   Tests whether the log window is currently displayed.

`LogContainsCyberItem`
        Tests whether a particular Cyberdog item is in the log.

`SetLog`   Sets the log part and its extension.

`SetLogFinger`   Sets the log finger to a particular Cyberdog item.

`ShowLogWindow`   Displays the log window.

Navigator Utilities

`AcquireContainingNavigatorPart`
        Retrieves a frame's containing navigator.

`IsContainedInRootNavigatorPart`
        Tests whether a frame is embedded in a navigator and
        the navigator is the root part.

Notebook Utilities

`AddCyberItemsToNotebook`
        Adds a set of Cyberdog items to the notebook.

`AddCyberItemToNotebook`
        Adds a Cyberdog item to the notebook.

GetNotebook	Retrieves the notebook part.
IsNotebookWindowShown	
	Tests whether the notebook window is currently displayed.
SetNotebook	Sets the current notebook part and its extension.
ShowNotebookWindow	Displays the notebook window.

Opener Part Utilities

CreateCyberPart	Creates a new Cyberdog display part to replace an opener part.
ObtainOpener	Retrieves an opener part to be used for the duration of the opening process for a Cyberdog item.

Preferences Dialog Utilities

AcquireICInstance	Opens an Internet Config session.
GetConfigReference	Retrieves the Internet configuration specification.
ReleaseICInstance	Releases an Internet configuration instance.
SetConfigReference	Sets the Internet configuration specification.
ShowPreferencesDialog	
	Displays the Preferences dialog box.

Type Conversion Utilities

GetCyberItemTypeFromContentType	
	Converts an OpenDoc value type to a Cyberdog item value type.
GetISOTypeFromMIMEType	
	Converts a MIME media type to an OpenDoc value type.

AcquireContainingNavigatorPart

Acquires a frame's containing navigator.

```
ODPart AcquireContainingNavigatorPart (in ODFrame frame);
```

frame	The frame where the search for a containing navigator begins.
return value	A reference to the navigator that contains the frame, if one exists; otherwise, kODNULL.

DISCUSSION

You call this method to retrieve a frame's containing navigator part, if one exists. This method traverses the frame hierarchy until it finds the navigator.

This method increments the reference count of the ODPart object that it returns; the caller is responsible for calling the ODPart object's Release method.

Do not subclass this class.

SEE ALSO

The IsContainedInRootNavigatorPart method (page 364).

AcquireICInstance

Opens an Internet Config session.

```
ICError AcquireICInstance (out ICInstance inst,
                in ODOSType creator);
```

inst   The connection instance for all subsequent calls to Internet Config.

creator   The creator that uniquely identifies your display part.

return value An Internet Config error code.

DISCUSSION

You call this method to retrieve an ICInstance object instead of calling the Internet Config functions ICStart and ICFindConfigFile. One connection instance is required per creator. Cyberdog needs to maintain a list of all the ICInstance objects in use so that when the SetConfigReference method is called, it can redirect the ICInstance objects to the new file. See InternetConfig.h for the list of possible Internet Config error codes that may be returned.

Do not subclass this class.

SEE ALSO

The SetConfigReference method (page 371).

AddCyberItemsToNotebook

Adds a set of Cyberdog items to the notebook.

```
void AddCyberItemsToNotebook (in CyberItemList cyberItems);
```

cyberItems   The CyberItem objects to be added.

DISCUSSION

This method calls the notebook part extension's AddCyberItemsToNotebook method. The Cyberdog implementation of the notebook displays a dialog box that allows the user to specify the notebook category in which to add the items.

Do not subclass this class.

SEE ALSO

The AddCyberItemToNotebook method (page 350).
The CyberNotebookExtension::AddCyberItemsToNotebook method (page 263).

AddCyberItemToLog

Adds a Cyberdog item to the log.

```
void AddCyberItemToLog (in CyberItem parent,
                        in CyberItem child);
```

parent   The CyberItem object's parent, if one exists; otherwise, kODNULL.

child   The CyberItem object to be added.

DISCUSSION

This method calls the log part extension's AddCyberItemToLog method. The log can display the hierarchical relationships among the Cyberdog items in the log. If the item to be added to the log has a parent, you should pass it in the parent parameter.

Classes and Methods

By convention, a display part is responsible for adding to the log the item whose referenced content it displays. When a display part's window gets the selection focus, the part should call `SetLogFinger` to set the log finger to point to the item.

Do not subclass this class.

SEE ALSO

The `ClearLogFinger` method (page 351).
The `LogContainsCyberItem` method (page 366).
The `SetLogFinger` method (page 372).
The `CyberLogExtension::AddCyberItemToLog` method (page 251).

AddCyberItemToNotebook

Adds a Cyberdog item to the notebook.

```
void AddCyberItemToNotebook (in CyberItem item);
```

item   The `CyberItem` object to be added.

DISCUSSION

This method calls the notebook part extension's `AddCyberItemToNotebook` method. The Cyberdog implementation of the notebook displays a dialog box that allows the user to specify the notebook category in which to add the items.

Do not subclass this class.

SEE ALSO

The `AddCyberItemsToNotebook` method (page 349).
The `CyberNotebookExtension::AddCyberItemToNotebook` method (page 264).

ClearLogFinger

Clears the log finger from a Cyberdog item.

```
void ClearLogFinger (in CyberItem item);
```

item   The `CyberItem` object to be cleared.

DISCUSSION

You call this method to remove the finger from an item in the log. This method calls the log part extension's `ClearLogFinger` method. Typically, a Cyberdog display part calls this method when its frame loses the selection focus or, more generally, when the part determines that the Cyberdog item whose referenced content it displays is no longer the current item.

Do not subclass this class.

SEE ALSO

The `SetLogFinger` method (page 372).
The `CyberLogExtension::ClearLogFinger` method (page 252).

CloseCyberDraftWindow

Closes a part window in the Cyberdog session document.

```
ODBoolean CloseCyberDraftWindow (in ODPart part);
```

part   The part whose window should be closed.

return value   `kODTrue` if the window was closed; otherwise, `kODFalse`.

DISCUSSION

You call this method to close a window of a part that was created using the `CreatePartInCyberDocument` method. Typically, you call `CloseCyberDraftWindow` in response to a Close command or a click in a window's close box.

If the specified part is in the Cyberdog session document, this method closes the part's window and returns `kODTrue`. If the part is in some OpenDoc document other than the session document, the method does not close the window and returns `kODFalse` to indicate that the window should be closed normally.

Do not subclass this class.

SEE ALSO

The `CreatePartInCyberDocument` method (page 355).

CountCyberServices

Retrieves the number of services available to this Cyberdog session.

```
long CountCyberServices ();
```

return value   The number of available `CyberService` objects.

DISCUSSION

You can use this method in conjunction with the `GetCyberService` method to iterate through the available services.

Do not subclass this class.

SEE ALSO

The `GetCyberService` method (page 360).

CreateCyberItemFromSU

Creates a Cyberdog item from a storage unit.

```
CyberItem CreateCyberItemFromSU (in ODStorageUnit su);
```

su   The persistent representation of a `CyberItem` object.

return value   The `CyberItem` object that was stored in the storage unit.

DISCUSSION

You call this method to read a Cyberdog item that was stored in the specified storage unit by the `CyberItem::StreamToStorageUnit` method or the `CyberItem::ExternalizeContent` method. This method assumes that you have already called OpenDoc methods to focus the storage unit on the appropriate property and value. After this method returns, the storage unit focus is positioned immediately after the stored Cyberdog item.

Do not subclass this class.

SEE ALSO

The `CyberItem::ExternalizeContent` method (page 233).
The `CyberItem::StreamToStorageUnit` method (page 246).

CreateCyberItemFromURL

Creates a Cyberdog item from a URL.

```
CyberItem CreateCyberItemFromURL (in char* url);
```

url   The URL to be converted to a `CyberItem` object.

return value   The newly created `CyberItem` object.

DISCUSSION

You call this method to create and initialize the appropriate kind of Cyberdog item from the specified URL.

Do not subclass this class.

CreateCyberPart

Creates a new Cyberdog display part to replace an opener part.

```
ODPart CreateCyberPart (in ODPart openerPart,
                        in ODType partType,
                        in ODEditor optionalEditor);
```

openerPart   The opener part to be replaced by the new display part.

partType   The part kind to create.

optionalEditor
              The part editor to create.

return value   The newly created part.

DISCUSSION

This method is called by a Cyberdog item during the opening process to create a new Cyberdog display part. This method determines the correct draft in which to create the new part by calling the specified opener part's GetDestinationDraft method.

If GetDestinationDraft returns a draft, the opener part is contained in some OpenDoc document other than the Cyberdog session document; CreateCyberPart creates the new part in the same draft that contains the opener part. If GetDestinationDraft returns kODNULL, the opener part is contained in the session document. In this case, CreateCyberPart calls CreatePartInCyberDocument to create the new part in the Cyberdog session document.

If you specify kODNULL for the optionalEditor parameter, CreateCyberPart creates the default editor for the part kind specified by the partType parameter.

Do not subclass this class.

SEE ALSO

The CreatePartInCyberDocument method (page 355).
The CyberOpenerPartExtension::GetDestinationDraft method (page 272).

CreatePartInCyberDocument

Creates a new part in the Cyberdog session document.

```
ODPart CreatePartInCyberDocument (in ODType partType,
                    in ODEditor optionalEditor);
```

partType   The part kind to use for the new part.

optionalEditor
                  The part editor to use for the new part.

return value   The newly created part.

DISCUSSION

This method is called by the CreateCyberPart method to create a new display part in the Cyberdog session document. This method calls the ODDraft::CreatePart method.

You cannot use the standard OpenDoc code for closing a window when closing a part created using CreatePartInCyberDocument. Instead, you should call CloseCyberDraftWindow.

Do not subclass this class.

SEE ALSO

The CloseCyberDraftWindow method (page 351).
The CreateCyberPart method (page 354).

CreatePartInNewDocument

Creates a new part as a separate OpenDoc document.

```
ODPart CreatePartInNewDocument (in ODType partType,
                    in ODEditor optionalEditor);
```

partType   The part kind to use for the new part.

optionalEditor

> The part editor to use for the new part.

return value   The newly created part.

DISCUSSION

This method creates a new OpenDoc document with a new part as the root part of the document. The document is created in a temporary file. This method calls the ODDraft::CreatePart method.

Cyberdog calls this method to create the Cyberdog session document. Cyberdog mail calls this method to create a new message.

Do not subclass this class.

SEE ALSO

The CreatePartInCyberDocument method (page 355).

CreateProxyItemFromURL

Creates a proxy Cyberdog item from a URL.

```
CyberItem CreateProxyItemFromURL (in char* url);
```

url   The URL to be converted to a CyberItem object.

return value   The newly created proxy CyberItem object.

DISCUSSION

This method creates a Cyberdog item capable of retrieving data by way of a proxy server.

Gopher and FTP Cyberdog items must be able to access data located on a proxy server; if you implement your own Gopher or FTP Cyberdog item subclass, it needs to provide for this capability. When a Gopher or FTP Cyberdog item is opened (CyberItem::Open), it should check the preferences to see whether proxy server access is enabled. If so, the Cyberdog item should call

`CyberSession::CreateProxyItemFromURL` to create a proxy Cyberdog item that can access a proxy server and then call `Open` to open the proxy item. Similarly, the Cyberdog item's other methods should pass appropriate messages through to the proxy item when proxy server access is enabled.

Likewise, to support access to proxy servers, a web service needs to include the Cyberdog proxy scheme, represented by `kCyberProxyScheme`, in the list of URL schemes that it supports. If you implement your own web service subclass, it needs to provide for this capability.

Do not subclass this class.

SEE ALSO

The `kCyberProxyScheme` constant (page 179).

FindCyberItemWindow

Retrieves the window that displays a Cyberdog item.

```
ODWindow FindCyberItemWindow (in CyberItem item);
```

item   The `CyberItem` object for this operation.

return value   The window that displays the Cyberdog item; otherwise, `kODNULL`.

DISCUSSION

This method traverses the window list, looking for each window whose root is a Cyberdog display part. This method calls each display part's `GetCyberItemWindow` method until it finds the display part that is displaying the content referenced by the specified Cyberdog item.

Do not subclass this class.

SEE ALSO

The `SelectCyberItemWindow` method (page 370).
The `CyberItem::Compare` method (page 231).
The `CyberPartExtension::GetCyberItemWindow` method (page 286).

GetConfigReference

Retrieves the Internet configuration specification.

```
ICError GetConfigReference (in ICConfigRefHandle ref);
```

ref   An Internet Config reference handle. On return, the handle
               refers to the current Internet Config specification.

return value   An Internet Config error code.

DISCUSSION

You call this method to retrieve the Internet configuration specification
currently being used by your Cyberdog session. You must create the
`ICConfigRefHandle` object and pass it to this method. The method resizes the
object appropriately and returns the configuration reference in it. When you
have finished using the `ICConfigRefHandle` object, you should dispose of it. See
`InternetConfig.h` for the list of possible Internet Config error codes that may
be returned.

Do not subclass this class.

SEE ALSO

The `SetConfigReference` method (page 371).

GetCyberDraft

Retrieves the draft of the Cyberdog session document.

```
ODDraft GetCyberDraft ();
```

return value   An `ODDraft` that represents the session document draft.

DISCUSSION

You call this method to retrieve the draft of the Cyberdog session document. If the draft does not exist, this method creates one. To determine whether a display part is contained in the Cyberdog session document, you should call `IsInCyberDraft`.

Do not subclass this class.

SEE ALSO

The `IsInCyberDraft` method (page 364).

GetCyberItemTypeFromContentType

Converts an OpenDoc value type to a Cyberdog item value type.

```
ODValueType GetCyberItemTypeFromContentType (in ODValueType contentType);
```

`contentType`   An OpenDoc value type you want to convert.

return value   The corresponding Cyberdog item value type.

DISCUSSION

You use this method to convert an OpenDoc value type to a Cyberdog item value type; typically, in order to display a Cyberdog item icon instead of a content icon. You are responsible for deallocating the returned `ODValueType` object when you have finished using it.

Do not subclass this class.

Classes and Methods

SEE ALSO

The `GetISOTypeFromMIMEType` method (page 360).

GetCyberService

Retrieves a Cyberdog service by index.

```
CyberService GetCyberService (in long index);
```

index   The zero-based index of the `CyberService` object to be retrieved.

return value   The `CyberService` object specified by the index.

DISCUSSION

This method retrieves a Cyberdog service object by index. You can use this method in conjunction with the `CountCyberServices` method to iterate through the available services.

Service objects are allocated once and are owned by the session object, so you should not delete them.

Do not subclass this class.

SEE ALSO

The `CountCyberServices` method (page 352).

GetISOTypeFromMIMEType

Converts a MIME media type to an OpenDoc value type.

```
ODValueType GetISOTypeFromMIMEType (in char* mediaType);
```

mediaType   A pointer to a null-terminated string that contains the MIME media type (for example, 'text/html').

return value   A corresponding OpenDoc value type.

DISCUSSION

Typically, you call this method when you need to determine the kind of part to create to display a Cyberdog item. You are responsible for deallocating the returned ODValueType object when you have finished using it.

Do not subclass this class.

SEE ALSO

The GetCyberItemTypeFromContentType method (page 359).
The section "Media Types and Part Kinds" (page 184).

GetLog

Retrieves the log part.

```
ODPart GetLog (in ODBoolean create);
```

create   kODTrue if the log should be created if it is not found; otherwise, kODFalse.

return value The log part.

DISCUSSION

This method returns an OpenDoc part of part kind kLogManagerKind. If the log is not found and the value of the create parameter is kODTrue, this method creates the log.

Do not subclass this class.

SEE ALSO

The SetLog method (page 372).

7

Classes and Methods

GetNotebook

Retrieves the notebook part.

```
ODPart GetNotebook (in ODBoolean create);
```

create   kODTrue if the notebook should be created if it is not found; otherwise, kODFalse.

return value   The notebook part.

DISCUSSION

This method returns an OpenDoc part of part kind kNotebookManagerKind. If a notebook is not found and the value of the create parameter is kODTrue, this method creates a notebook.

Do not subclass this class.

SEE ALSO

The SetNotebook method (page 373).

GetODSession

Retrieves the OpenDoc session object for this Cyberdog session.

```
ODSession GetODSession ();
```

return value   The ODSession object.

DISCUSSION

You call this method to retrieve a reference to the ODSession object associated with the current Cyberdog session.

Do not subclass this class.

ICyberSession

Initializes this session object.

```
void ICyberSession (in ODSession session);
```

session   The ODSession object associated with the current Mac OS process.

DISCUSSION

This method initializes a newly created session object. It detects, loads, and initializes the Cyberdog services available to the system. This method is called by Cyberdog during initialization.

Do not subclass this class.

InstallCyberDocumentMenu

Installs a Document menu customized for Cyberdog display parts contained in the Cyberdog session document.

```
Handle InstallCyberDocumentMenu (in ODPart part,
                 in ODMenuBar menuBar);
```

part   The part that owns the menu bar.

menuBar   The menu bar into which the custom Document menu should be installed.

return value   A handle to the Document menu.

DISCUSSION

You can call this method to replace the standard Document menu with a custom Document menu optimized for a Cyberdog display part contained in the session document. This method installs the custom Document menu only if the specified part is in the Cyberdog session document.

The display part is responsible for disposing of the menu handle returned by this method when the part is released.

Do not subclass this class.

7

Classes and Methods

IsContainedInRootNavigatorPart

Tests whether a frame is embedded in a navigator and the navigator is the root part.

```
ODBoolean IsContainedInRootNavigatorPart (in ODFrame frame);
```

frame   The frame for this operation.

return value   kODTrue if the frame is contained in a navigator and the navigator is the root part of its window; otherwise, kODFalse.

DISCUSSION

You call this method to determine whether the specified frame is embedded in a navigator and the navigator is the root part of its window.

Do not subclass this class.

SEE ALSO

The AcquireContainingNavigatorPart method (page 347).

IsInCyberDraft

Tests whether the specified persistent object is stored in the Cyberdog session document's draft.

```
ODBoolean IsInCyberDraft (in ODPersistentObject object);
```

object   The object to test.

return value   kODTrue if the given object is stored in a storage unit of the Cyberdog session document's draft; otherwise, kODFalse.

DISCUSSION

You should call this method to determine whether a persistent object is stored in the Cyberdog session document. You should not call `GetCyberDraft` for this purpose; `GetCyberDraft` creates the draft if it is not there.

Do not subclass this class.

SEE ALSO

The `GetCyberDraft` method (page 359).

IsLogWindowShown

Tests whether the log window is currently displayed.

```
ODBoolean IsLogWindowShown ();
```

return value   `kODTrue` if the log window is displayed; otherwise, `kODFalse`.

DISCUSSION

You call this method when you need to determine whether the log window is displayed. This method calls the log extension's `IsLogWindowShown` method.

Do not subclass this class.

SEE ALSO

The `ShowLogWindow` method (page 374).
The `CyberLogExtension::IsLogWindowShown` method (page 253).

Classes and Methods

IsNotebookWindowShown

Tests whether the notebook window is currently displayed.

```
ODBoolean IsNotebookWindowShown ();
```

return value   `kODTrue` if the notebook window is displayed; otherwise, `kODFalse`.

DISCUSSION

You call this method when you need to determine whether the notebook window is displayed. This method calls the notebook extension's `IsNotebookWindowShown` method.

Do not subclass this class.

SEE ALSO

The `ShowNotebookWindow` method (page 375).
The `CyberNotebookExtension::IsNotebookWindowShown` method (page 266).

LogContainsCyberItem

Tests whether a particular Cyberdog item is in the log.

```
ODBoolean LogContainsCyberItem (in CyberItem item);
```

item   The Cyberdog item for this operation.

return value   `kODTrue` if the log contains an equivalent Cyberdog item; otherwise, `kODFalse`.

DISCUSSION

You call this method to determine whether a particular Cyberdog item is in the log. This method calls the log extension's `ContainsCyberItem` method. Typically, a Cyberdog display part calls `LogContainsCyberItem` to see whether an item is already in the log before adding the item.

Do not subclass this class.

SEE ALSO

The `CyberItem::Compare` method (page 231).
The `CyberLogExtension::ContainsCyberItem` method (page 253).

NewCyberItem

Creates a Cyberdog item.

```
CyberItem NewCyberItem (in char* classID);
```

classID   A pointer to the SOM class ID of the Cyberdog item to create.

return value   The newly created Cyberdog item.

DISCUSSION

This method creates a Cyberdog item for the specified SOM class ID. The first time a particular class ID is passed to the method, the method calls `ODNewObject` to create a prototype Cyberdog item for that class ID, caches the prototype, and returns a clone of that prototype. On subsequent calls to the method with the same class ID, the method returns a clone of the prototype.

This method is optimized for creating large numbers of Cyberdog items at a time, for example, when reading the log from storage.

Do not subclass this class.

ObtainOpener

Retrieves an opener part to be used for the duration of the opening process for a Cyberdog item.

```
ODPart ObtainOpener (in ODPart openerPart,
                     in ODType openerKind,
                     in CyberItem item,
                     in ParameterSet openParams);
```

openerPart   The opener part to obtain.

openerKind   The desired OpenDoc part kind of the opener part to be obtained.

item   The `CyberItem` object that is being opened.

openParams   The `ParameterSet` object associated with the opening process.

return value An opener part for the `CyberItem` object.

DISCUSSION

You call this method to obtain an opener part to serve as placeholder in the user interface when the opening process for a Cyberdog item is asynchronous. This method creates an opener part if it needs to and then calls the opener part's `BeginOpening` method, which adds the opener part to the parameter set.

If you already have an opener part, you can obtain it by passing it to the method in the `openerPart` parameter. If you pass `kODNULL` for the `openerPart` parameter, the method creates a new opener part of the kind specified by the `openerKind` parameter (`kOpenerPartKind` or `kNavigatorKind`, for example). You can set the `openerKind` parameter to `kODNULL` if you have no preference for a particular part kind.

This method may return an opener part that is different from the one that is passed in as a parameter. For example, if the opener part passed into `ObtainOpener` is a navigator and the user has turned off the Browse in Place menu item, the method may return a different navigator.

Do not subclass this class.

The `CyberOpenerPartExtension::BeginOpening` method (page 271).

PromptForCyberItem

Displays the Connect To dialog box and returns the Cyberdog item specified by the user.

```
CyberItem PromptForCyberItem (in Str255 windowTitle);
```

windowTitle   The title to be used for the Connect To dialog box.

return value   The `CyberItem` object specified by the user.

DISCUSSION

You call this method to display the Connect To dialog box with the specified title; this method calls the `CyberItemPromptExtension::PromptForCyberItem` method. If you do not specify a window title, the Connect To dialog box is displayed with a default title.

The Connect To dialog box allows the user to select from any services installed in the system and to specify a Cyberdog item in the corresponding Connect To panel. This method returns the Cyberdog item specified by the user; it does not open the item.

Do not subclass this class.

SEE ALSO

The `ShowConnectDialog` method (page 374).
The `CyberItemPromptExtension::PromptForCyberItem` method (page 249).

7

Classes and Methods

ReleaseICInstance

Releases an Internet configuration instance.

```
ICError ReleaseICInstance (in ICInstance inst);
```

inst   The ICInstance object to be released.

return value   An Internet Config error code.

DISCUSSION

When you have finished using an ICInstance object, you should release it by calling the ReleaseICInstance method rather than the Internet Config function ICEnd. See InternetConfig.h for the list of possible Internet Config error codes that may be returned.

Do not subclass this class.

SEE ALSO

The AcquireICInstance method (page 348).

SelectCyberItemWindow

Retrieves and selects the window that displays a Cyberdog item.

```
ODWindow SelectCyberItemWindow (in CyberItem item);
```

item   The CyberItem object for this operation.

return value   The window that displays the CyberItem object; otherwise, kODNULL.

DISCUSSION

You call this method to retrieve and select the window that displays a specified Cyberdog item.

Do not subclass this class.

SEE ALSO

The `FindCyberItemWindow` method (page 357).

SetConfigReference

Sets the Internet configuration specification.

```
ICError SetConfigReference (in ICConfigRefHandle ref,
                    in long flags);
```

ref | A reference to the new Internet configuration specification.

flags | A set of flags whose values control the specification-setting operation, expressed as a 32-bit integer.

return value | An Internet Config error code.

DISCUSSION

You call this method to set the Internet configuration specification to be used by your Cyberdog session. All `ICInstance` objects instantiated by the `AcquireICInstance` method will reference this new specification. You are responsible for allocating and deallocating the `ICConfigRefHandle` object.

You can set the `icNoUserInteraction_bit` flag in the `flags` parameter to prevent Internet Config from displaying a modal dialog box to the user during this operation. See `InternetConfig.h` for the list of possible Internet Config error codes that may be returned.

Do not subclass this class.

SEE ALSO

The `AcquireICInstance` method (page 348).
The `GetConfigReference` method (page 358).

Classes and Methods

SetLog

Sets the log part and its extension.

```
void SetLog (in ODPart logPart);
```

logPart   The ODPart object to be used as the log. The ODPart object must
                 have an extension subclassed from CyberLogExtension.

DISCUSSION

This method designates the specified part as the log. If you develop your own
log part, you can call this method to notify the session object that your log part
should be used as the log. If the user opens a log stored as a part in the Finder,
Cyberdog calls this method to designate the part as the log.

The specified part must have an extension subclassed from CyberLogExtension
and a part kind of kLogManagerKind.

Do not subclass this class.

SEE ALSO

The GetLog method (page 361).

SetLogFinger

Sets the log finger to a particular Cyberdog item.

```
void SetLogFinger (in CyberItem item);
```

item   A CyberItem object representing a location just visited by
                 the user.

DISCUSSION

This method sets the log finger to point to the Cyberdog item that the user
visited most recently. Your Cyberdog display part should call this method
when its window acquires the selection focus or, more generally, when your

part determines that the Cyberdog item whose referenced content it displays is the current item.

This method assumes that the Cyberdog item has already been added to the log; if the item is not in the log, this method does nothing. Typically, you call this method after adding a Cyberdog item to the log (AddCyberItemToLog) or determining that a Cyberdog item is already in the log (LogContainsCyberItem).

Do not subclass this class.

SEE ALSO

The AddCyberItemToLog method (page 349).
The ClearLogFinger method (page 351).
The LogContainsCyberItem method (page 366).
The CyberLogExtension::SetLogFinger method (page 254).

SetNotebook

Sets the notebook part and its extension.

```
void SetNotebook (in ODPart notebookPart);
```

notebookPart   The ODPart object to be used as the notebook. The ODPart object must have an extension subclassed from CyberNotebookExtension.

DISCUSSION

This method designates the specified part as the notebook part. If you develop your own notebook part, you can call this method to notify the session object that your notebook part should be used as the notebook. If the user opens a notebook stored as a part in the Finder, Cyberdog calls this method to designate the part as the notebook.

The specified part must have an extension subclassed from CyberNotebookExtension and a part kind of kNotebookManagerKind.

Do not subclass this class.

SEE ALSO

The `GetNotebook` method (page 362).

ShowConnectDialog

Displays the Connect To dialog box.

```
void ShowConnectDialog ();
```

DISCUSSION

This method displays the Connect To dialog box and opens the Cyberdog item specified by the user. This method differs from `PromptForCyberItem` in that this method initiates opening the Cyberdog item specified by the user, whereas `PromptForCyberItem` simply returns the Cyberdog item.

Do not subclass this class.

SEE ALSO

The `PromptForCyberItem` method (page 369).

ShowLogWindow

Displays the log window.

```
void ShowLogWindow ();
```

DISCUSSION

This method displays the log window if it is not already displayed. This method calls the log extension's `ShowLogWindow` method.

Do not subclass this class.

SEE ALSO

The `IsLogWindowShown` method (page 365).
The `CyberLogExtension::ShowLogWindow` method (page 255).

ShowNotebookWindow

Displays the notebook window.

```
void ShowNotebookWindow ();
```

DISCUSSION

This method displays the notebook window if it is not already displayed. This method calls the notebook extension's `ShowNotebookWindow` method.

Do not subclass this class.

SEE ALSO

The `IsNotebookWindowShown` method (page 366).
The `CyberNotebookExtension::ShowNotebookWindow` method (page 268).

ShowPreferencesDialog

Displays the Preferences dialog box.

```
void ShowPreferencesDialog ();
```

DISCUSSION

You call this method to display the Preferences dialog box so that the user can specify preferences.

Do not subclass this class.

CyberStream

Superclasses	ODObject
Subclasses	none

An object of class CyberStream downloads the data referenced by a
CyberItem object.

Description

The CyberStream class is an abstract class that you can subclass and implement
to provide downloading support for a particular service. A stream object
interacts with a server to download the data referenced by a Cyberdog item,
given its location. A Cyberdog display part uses a stream object to download
the data referenced by its Cyberdog item.

Cyberdog provides implemented CyberStream subclasses for some common
protocols: HTTP, Gopher, and FTP. You can use any of these existing
CyberStream subclasses or create a new CyberStream subclass to support a new
network protocol.

A stream subclass usually has a companion Cyberdog item subclass that
references data on that type of server. For example, an object of the WebItem
class (an implemented CyberItem subclass supplied with Cyberdog) references
data located on a web (HTTP) server. An object of the companion WebStream
class (an implemented CyberStream subclass supplied with Cyberdog) interacts
with the web server to download the data.

If a stream is to be used to download the data referenced by a Cyberdog item,
the Cyberdog item is responsible for creating a stream. A Cyberdog display
part calls the CyberItem::CreateCyberStream method to create a new stream
object initialized to download the data referenced by the Cyberdog item. The
Cyberdog item performs any initialization necessary to communicate the
address of its resources to the stream object.

When a Cyberdog display part is ready to download the data referenced by
its Cyberdog item, it calls the stream's Open method, which always returns
immediately; however, a stream object may download data either
asynchronously or synchronously. In either case, the display part checks the

status of the download operation periodically by calling the `GetStreamStatus` method, which returns a set of flags indicating the current status.

A stream object allocates memory buffers to hold incoming data. If the stream has data (if the `kCDDataAvailable` flag is set to `true`), the display part can call the stream's `GetBuffer` method to retrieve a buffer. This scheme minimizes the repeated copying of data during the download process and allows the stream to proceed with the download operation instead of waiting for the first call to `GetBuffer`. When it has finished using a buffer, the display part should call the `ReleaseBuffer` method to return the buffer to the stream object.

There is no `Close` method in the stream interface; when the stream object detects that the download operation is complete (when the `kCDDownloadComplete` flag is set to `true`), it closes the connection on its own.

`GetStreamStatus`, `GetBuffer`, and `ReleaseBuffer` are all synchronous methods; they return immediately no matter whether the stream object is downloading asynchronously or synchronously. For this reason, a stream object should not postpone the reading of data until the display part calls the `GetBuffer` method. The stream should read the data on its own time and set the `kCDDataAvailable` flag to `true` when data has been read successfully. A simple stream implementation might read data until its buffers are full when `Open` is called, and then whenever `ReleaseBuffer` is called.

A simple stream implementation might also keep the `kCDBuffersAreLow` flag set to `true` at all times. To proceed with asynchronous downloading, the stream object needs memory to store the incoming data. To maximize stream performance, make sure that the stream always has memory available to store data as it comes in.

Methods

This section presents summary descriptions of the `CyberStream` methods grouped according to purpose, followed by detailed descriptions.

Controlling a Stream

`Open`	Opens this Cyberdog stream and initiates the downloading process.
`Abort`	Terminates a download operation being performed by this Cyberdog stream.

Managing Buffers

GetBuffer	Retrieves a buffer from this Cyberdog stream.
ReleaseBuffer	Releases a buffer to this Cyberdog stream.

Retrieving Stream Information

GetLastModTime	Retrieves the last modification time for the data in this Cyberdog stream.
GetStatusString	Retrieves a string describing the current status of this Cyberdog stream.
GetStreamError	Retrieves the first nontrivial error encountered by this Cyberdog stream.
GetStreamStatus	Retrieves the current status flags for this Cyberdog stream.
GetTotalDataSize	Retrieves the total size, in bytes, of the data available to be downloaded by this Cyberdog stream.
IsLastModTimeAvailable	
	Tests whether the last modification time is available for data in this Cyberdog stream.
IsTotalDataSizeAvailable	
	Tests whether the total size of this Cyberdog stream is available.

Abort

Terminates a download operation being performed by this Cyberdog stream.

```
void Abort ();
```

DISCUSSION

This method should notify this stream object to terminate a download operation. Abort is potentially an asynchronous operation. You can determine whether the abort operation has completed by calling the GetStreamStatus method and testing the value of the kCDAbortComplete flag.

You should not delete the stream object until you have determined that the abort operation has completed.

If you subclass CyberStream, you must override this method. Your override must not call its inherited method; that is, your override method must implement this method's functionality completely.

SEE ALSO

The StreamStatus type (page 179).
The GetStreamStatus method (page 382).

GetBuffer

Retrieves a buffer from this Cyberdog stream.

```
void GetBuffer (in Ptr* buffer, in Size* bufferSize);
```

buffer   A pointer to a pointer to a memory buffer. On return, the buffer contains the downloaded data.

bufferSize   A pointer to the length of the buffer. On return, the length is set to the number of bytes in the buffer.

DISCUSSION

Each stream object has memory buffers to hold incoming data. You determine whether a stream object has data available by calling the stream's GetStreamStatus method and checking the kCDDataAvailable flag. If the kCDDataAvailable flag is set, the stream has been opened successfully and there is at least one buffer of non-zero length available.

When the stream object has data available, you can call GetBuffer to retrieve a buffer from the stream. The contents of the buffer are read only; you cannot modify them. You can retrieve more than one buffer at a time. If the call to GetBuffer cannot be completed, the method sets buffer to kODNULL and bufferSize to 0.

When you call GetStreamStatus and the value of the kCDDownloadComplete flag is true, you have retrieved all of the data and you do not need to call GetBuffer again. You release a buffer when you have finished using it by calling the ReleaseBuffer method.

GetBuffer may be called at interrupt time.

If you subclass CyberStream, you must override this method. Your override must not call its inherited method; that is, your override method must implement this method's functionality completely.

SEE ALSO

The StreamStatus type (page 179).
The ReleaseBuffer method (page 386).
The GetStreamStatus method (page 382).

GetLastModTime

Retrieves the last modification time for the data in this Cyberdog stream.

```
ODTime GetLastModTime ();
```

return value   The time the stream was last modified.

DISCUSSION

This method should return the time that the data downloaded by this stream object was last modified. You can determine whether the last modification time is available by calling the IsLastModTimeAvailable method.

GetLastModTime should return the constant kCDLastModTimeUnknowable if the last modification time will never be available or if last modification time does not make sense for the protocol implemented by the stream. GetLastModTime should return the constant kCDLastModTimeUnknown if the last modification time is not known but may be known at a later time.

If you subclass CyberStream, you must override this method. Your override method must not call its inherited method; that is, your override method must implement this method's functionality completely.

SEE ALSO

The IsLastModTimeAvailable method (page 384).

GetStatusString

Retrieves a string describing the current status of this Cyberdog stream.

```
void GetStatusString (in Str255 message);
```

message   A 255-character buffer. On return, the buffer contains the status string.

DISCUSSION

This method should retrieve a string that describes the current status of the stream. This method may return an error string if the `kCDErrorOccurred` flag is set to `true`. If you are using a progress part to display status and progress of the stream, you can pass the status string to `CyberProgressBroadcaster::SetStatusString`.

You can detect whether a stream's status string has changed by calling the `GetStreamStatus` method and testing the value of the `kCDStatusStringChanged` flag.

If you subclass `CyberStream`, you must override this method. Your override must not call its inherited method; that is, your override method must implement this method's functionality completely.

SEE ALSO

The `StreamStatus` type (page 179).
The `GetStreamStatus` method (page 382).
The `CyberProgressBroadcaster::SetStatusString` method (page 311).

GetStreamError

Retrieves the first nontrivial error encountered by this Cyberdog stream.

```
OSErr GetStreamError ();
```

return value   The error code for the stream error.

DISCUSSION

This method should return a network error code for the first nontrivial error that the stream encountered, if any. The returned error code should be in the allowable range for Mac OS errors (including the Cyberdog and OpenDoc error ranges). If possible, you should use existing error codes instead of creating new error codes.

You determine whether an error has occurred in a stream by calling the GetStreamStatus method and testing the value of the kCDErrorOccurred flag. Typically, if a stream detects an error while downloading data, your display part should call the stream's Abort method to terminate the download and notify the user that the operation failed.

If you subclass CyberStream, you must override this method. Your override must not call its inherited method; that is, your override method must implement this method's functionality completely.

SEE ALSO

The StreamStatus type (page 179).
The Abort method (page 378).
The GetStreamStatus method (page 382).

GetStreamStatus

Retrieves the current status flags for this Cyberdog stream.

```
StreamStatus GetStreamStatus ();
```

return value   A set of status flags, expressed as a 16-bit integer.

DISCUSSION

This method returns the current status of the stream as a set of flags. You can use the logical & operator to determine whether a particular flag is

set. The following example calls `GetStreamStatus` and then tests the
`kCDDataAvailable` flag:

```
StreamStatus status;

status = fStream->GetStreamStatus (ev);
if (status & kCDDataAvailable)
{
    ...
}
```

`GetStreamStatus` may be called at interrupt time.

If you subclass `CyberStream`, you must override this method. Your override
must not call its inherited method; that is, your override method must
implement this method's functionality completely.

SEE ALSO

The `StreamStatus` type (page 179).

GetTotalDataSize

Retrieves the total size, in bytes, of the data available to be downloaded by this
Cyberdog stream.

```
long GetTotalDataSize ();
```

return value   The number of bytes downloaded by the stream.

DISCUSSION

This method should return the total number of bytes downloaded by a stream
object. You can determine whether the total size is available by calling the
`IsTotalDataSizeAvailable` method.

`GetTotalDataSize` should return the constant `kCDTotalDataSizeUnknowable` if
the number of bytes to be downloaded will never be available or if total
data size does not make sense for the protocol implemented by the stream.

GetTotalDataSize should return the constant kCDTotalDataSizeUnknown if the number of bytes to be downloaded is not known but may be known at a later time.

If you subclass CyberStream, you must override this method. Your override method must not call its inherited method; that is, your override method must implement this method's functionality completely.

SEE ALSO

The IsTotalDataSizeAvailable method (page 385).

IsLastModTimeAvailable

Tests whether the last modification time is available for data in this Cyberdog stream.

ODBoolean IsLastModTimeAvailable ();

return value   kODTrue if the last modification time is available; otherwise, kODFalse.

DISCUSSION

You call this method to determine whether the last modification time is available for data downloaded by a stream object. If the last modification time is available, you can retrieve it by calling the GetLastModTime method. If GetLastModTime returns kCDLastModTimeUnknowable, you do not need to continue to poll IsLastModTimeAvailable.

If you subclass CyberStream, you must override this method. Your override method must not call its inherited method; that is, your override method must implement this method's functionality completely.

SEE ALSO

The GetLastModTime method (page 380).

IsTotalDataSizeAvailable

Tests whether the total size of this Cyberdog stream is available.

```
ODBoolean IsTotalDataSizeAvailable ();
```

return value   kODTrue if the total data size is available; otherwise, kODFalse.

DISCUSSION

You call this method to determine whether the total number of bytes to be downloaded by a stream object is available. If the total size is available, you can retrieve it by calling the GetTotalDataSize method. If GetTotalDataSize returns kCDTotalDataSizeUnknowable, you do not need to continue to poll IsTotalDataSizeAvailable.

If you subclass CyberStream, you must override this method. Your override method must not call its inherited method; that is, your override method must implement this method's functionality completely.

SEE ALSO

The GetTotalDataSize method (page 383).

Open

Opens this Cyberdog stream and initiates the downloading process.

```
void Open ();
```

DISCUSSION

This method should initiate the download operation and return immediately. You should open a stream object only once.

You check the status of the download and the availability of data by calling GetStreamStatus. Once a stream object has been opened, at least one of the following three status flags must eventually be set to true: kCDDownloadComplete, kCDErrorOccurred, or kCDAbortComplete.

If you subclass `CyberStream`, you must override this method. Your override must not call its inherited method; that is, your override method must implement this method's functionality completely.

SEE ALSO

The `StreamStatus` type (page 179).
The `GetStreamStatus` method (page 382).

ReleaseBuffer

Releases a buffer to this Cyberdog stream.

```
void ReleaseBuffer (in Ptr buffer);
```

buffer   A pointer to the buffer that is to be released.

DISCUSSION

This method returns a memory buffer that was retrieved by calling `GetBuffer`. If you do not release buffers for reuse by the stream, it may eventually run out of space for incoming packets and begin dropping them, degrading download performance.

You can determine whether a stream's supply of buffers is low by calling the `GetStreamStatus` method and checking the value of the `kCDBuffersAreLow` flag.

When a stream object is destroyed, its buffers are deallocated.

`ReleaseBuffer` may be called at interrupt time.

If you subclass `CyberStream`, you must override this method. Your override must not call its inherited method; that is, your override method must implement this method's functionality completely.

SEE ALSO

The `StreamStatus` type (page 179).
The `GetBuffer` method (page 379).

ParameterSet

Superclasses   `ODRefCntObject` → `ODObject`

Subclasses   none

An object of the `ParameterSet` class manages a heterogeneous collection of parameters.

Description

The `ParameterSet` class is a Cyberdog class that maintains pointers to a heterogeneous collection of objects. A parameter set is a general-purpose object; you can use a parameter set in any way you want. In Cyberdog, a parameter set is used to keep track of the variety of cooperating objects that may play a role during the opening of a Cyberdog item.

A parameter set encapsulates an arbitrary number of parameters. Each parameter has a name or **parameter key** that identifies it. Cyberdog defines some parameter keys (page 172); developers can define additional parameter keys.

When used for opening a Cyberdog item, a parameter set contains pointers to parameters that may affect the behavior of the opening Cyberdog item or the display part created to display the content referenced by the Cyberdog item, including

- the parent Cyberdog item whose content contains the Cyberdog item being opened

- an initial or an obtained opener part

- the draft in which the opener part is embedded

- a navigator part

- the desired height and width of the frame that will display the content referenced by the Cyberdog item

The `CyberItem::Open` method takes one parameter, a `ParameterSet` object. You add parameters that may be used during the opening process to the set before calling `CyberItem::Open`. For more information about how a parameter set is used during the opening of a Cyberdog item, see "Cyberdog Item Opening Process" (page 71).

You add a parameter to a `ParameterSet` object by calling the `PutParameter` method, passing the parameter's key and a pointer to a destructor function for the parameter. A `ParameterSet` object is a reference-counted object; when a `ParameterSet` object's reference count becomes 0, each parameter in the parameter set is destroyed, and the `ParameterSet` object is deleted.

In addition, the `ParameterSet` class defines several methods that return pointers to implemented destructor functions for various types of objects. For example, `GetODPtrDestructor` returns an implemented destructor function for an `ODPtr` object. These methods return Universal Procedure Pointers (UPP) rather than simple C/Pascal function pointers.

Methods

This section presents summary descriptions of the `ParameterSet` methods grouped according to purpose, followed by detailed descriptions.

Initialization and Cleanup

`IParameterSet`	Initializes this parameter set.

Managing Parameters

`ExtractParameter`	Removes the specified parameter from this parameter set without calling the parameter's destructor.
`GetParameter`	Retrieves the specified parameter from this parameter set.
`PutParameter`	Adds the specified parameter to this parameter set.
`RemoveParameter`	Removes the specified parameter from this parameter set and calls the parameter's destructor.

Parameter Destructors

`GetODHandleDestructor`	
	Retrieves a destructor for an `ODHandle` object.
`GetODPtrDestructor`	Retrieves a destructor for an `ODPtr` object.
`GetODRefCntObjectDestructor`	
	Retrieves a destructor for a reference-counted object.
`GetSOMObjectDestructor`	
	Retrieves a destructor for a SOM object.

ExtractParameter

Removes the specified parameter from this parameter set without calling the parameter's destructor.

```
ODBoolean ExtractParameter (in ParameterKey key,
                    out void* param,
                    out ParamDestructorUPP destructor);
```

key   The name of the parameter to remove.

param   A pointer to the parameter.

destructor   A pointer to a programmer-defined destructor for the parameter.

return value   kODTrue if the parameter is in the set; otherwise, kODFalse.

DISCUSSION

You call this method to remove a parameter from a ParameterSet object. Unlike RemoveParameter, this method does not call the destructor associated with the parameter.

The following type is used for parameter destructor functions. A parameter destructor takes two parameters: an environment pointer and a pointer of type void*; the function returns no value.

```
typedef void (* ParamDestructorProcPtr)(Environment* ev,
        void* param);
```

The MyParamDestructor programmer-defined function (page 195) illustrates the form of a parameter destructor.

SEE ALSO

The ParameterKey type (page 172).
The GetParameter method (page 392).
The PutParameter method (page 393).
The RemoveParameter method (page 395).

Classes and Methods

GetODHandleDestructor

Retrieves a destructor for an ODHandle object.

```
ParamDestructorUPP GetODHandleDestructor ();
```

return value   A pointer to a destructor function that takes two parameters: an environment pointer and a pointer of type ODPtr*; the function returns no value.

DISCUSSION

You call this method to retrieve a destructor function suitable for an ODHandle object. The function has the following form:

```
void ODHandleDestructor (Environment* ev, ODPtr* odHandle);
```

The destructor function disposes of the ODHandle object, as shown in the following example:

```
ODHandleDestructor (Environment* ev, ODPtr* odHandle)
{
    ODDisposeHandle (odHandle);
}
```

If you subclass ParameterSet, do not override this method.

GetODPtrDestructor

Retrieves a destructor for an ODPtr object.

```
ParamDestructorUPP GetODPtrDestructor ();
```

return value   A pointer to a destructor function that takes two parameters: an environment pointer and a pointer of type ODPtr*; the function returns no value.

DISCUSSION

You call this method to retrieve a destructor function suitable for an ODPtr object. The function has the following form:

```
void ODPtrDestructor (Environment* ev, ODPtr* odPtr);
```

The destructor function disposes of the ODPtr object, as shown in the following example:

```
ODPtrDestructor (Environment* ev, ODPtr* odPtr)
{
    ODDisposePtr(odPtr);
}
```

If you subclass ParameterSet, do not override this method.

GetODRefCntObjectDestructor

Retrieves a destructor for a reference-counted object.

```
ParamDestructorUPP GetODRefCntObjectDestructor ();
```

return value   A pointer to a destructor function that takes two parameters: an environment pointer and a pointer of type ODRefCntObject*; the function returns no value.

DISCUSSION

You call this method to retrieve a destructor function suitable for an ODRefCntObject object. The function has the following form:

```
void ODRefCntObjectDestructor (Environment* ev,ODRefCntObject* refCntObj);
```

The destructor function releases the object, as shown in the following example:

```
ODRefCntObjectDestructor (Environment* ev, ODRefCntObject* refCntObj)
{
    refCntObj->Release(ev);
}
```

If you subclass ParameterSet, do not override this method.

GetParameter

Retrieves the specified parameter from this parameter set.

```
ODBoolean GetParameter (in ParameterKey key,
                        out void* param);
```

key   The name of the parameter to retrieve.

param   A pointer to the parameter.

return value kODTrue if the parameter is in the set; otherwise, kODFalse.

DISCUSSION

You call this method to retrieve a parameter by name from a ParameterSet object. If this method returns kODFalse, the value of param is undefined.

SEE ALSO

The ParameterKey type (page 172).
The ExtractParameter method (page 389).
The PutParameter method (page 393).
The RemoveParameter method (page 395).

GetSOMObjectDestructor

Retrieves a destructor for a SOM object.

```
ParamDestructorUPP GetSOMObjectDestructor ();
```

return value A pointer to a destructor function that takes two parameters: an environment pointer and a pointer to a SOMObject; the function returns no value.

DISCUSSION

You call this method to retrieve a suitable destructor function for a SOM object. The function has the following form:

```
void SOMObjectDestructor (Environment* ev, SOMObject* somObject);
```

The destructor function deletes the object, as shown in the following example:

```
SOMObjectDestructor (Environment* ev, SOMObject* somObject)
{
    delete somObject;
}
```

If you subclass `ParameterSet`, do not override this method.

IParameterSet

Initializes this parameter set.

```
void IParameterSet ();
```

DISCUSSION

You call this method to initialize a newly created `ParameterSet` object.

If you subclass `ParameterSet` and override this method, your override must call its inherited method.

PutParameter

Adds the specified parameter to this parameter set.

```
void PutParameter    (in ParameterKey key,
                      in void* param,
                      in ParamDestructorUPP destructor);
```

7

Classes and Methods

key   The name of the parameter to add.

param   A pointer to the parameter.

destructor   A pointer to a programmer-defined destructor for the
                parameter.

DISCUSSION

You call this method to add a parameter and its destructor to a `ParameterSet` object. If the parameter set already contains a parameter of the same name, the method throws the `kCDErrParamAlreadyExists` exception.

The following type is used for parameter destructor functions. A parameter destructor takes two parameters: an environment pointer and a pointer of type `void*`; the function returns no value.

```
typedef void (* ParamDestructorProc)(Environment* ev,
            void* param);
```

The `MyParamDestructor` programmer-defined function (page 195) illustrates the form of a parameter destructor.

If you do not specify a destructor function for a parameter in a parameter set, the parameter is not destroyed when the parameter set is disposed of.

SEE ALSO

The `ParameterKey` type (page 172).
The `ExtractParameter` method (page 389).
The `GetParameter` method (page 392).
The `RemoveParameter` method (page 395).

RemoveParameter

Removes the specified parameter from this parameter set and calls the parameter's destructor.

```
ODBoolean RemoveParameter (in ParameterKey key);
```

key   The name of the parameter to remove.

return value   kODTrue if the parameter is in the set; otherwise, kODFalse.

DISCUSSION

You call this method to remove a parameter from a ParameterSet object. This method calls the destructor function associated with the parameter.

SEE ALSO

The ParameterKey type (page 172).
The ExtractParameter method (page 389).
The GetParameter method (page 392).
The PutParameter method (page 393).

SimpleCyberService

Superclasses   CyberService

Subclasses   none

An object of the SimpleCyberService class represents a simple implementation of a service.

Description

The SimpleCyberService class provides a simple, resource-driven implementation of a Cyberdog service. SimpleCyberService is a fully implemented class that you can use as is or subclass. It overrides every method of CyberService except for CyberMenuFocusAcquired and CyberMenuFocusLost. SimpleCyberService has one method that is not an override of a CyberService method, DoMenuItemSelected.

The SimpleCyberService override of the ICyberService method reads and caches data from the various resources referenced by the 'srvc' resource; the other overrides of SimpleCyberService use those cached values. See the description of the format of the 'srvc' resource (page 178). The file CyberService.r contains an example of the 'srvc' format.

The only SimpleCyberService behavior that is not fully implemented is the handling of menu item selections. The SimpleCyberService object appends each of the strings specified in the menu 'STR#' resource to the Cyberdog menu, registers each menu item with the menu bar, and enables each menu item. When one of the service's menu items is selected, Cyberdog calls the SimpleCyberService override of the DoCyberMenuCommand method, which translates the menu command ID into a index and calls the DoMenuItemSelected method.

Methods

The SimpleCyberService class has a single method, DoMenuItemSelected. A detailed description of the method follows.

DoMenuItemSelected   Performs the selected menu command.

DoMenuItemSelected

Performs the selected menu command.

```
void DoMenuItemSelected (in long index,
                         in ODFrame frame,
                         in CyberMenuData menuData);
```

index   The zero-based index of the command.

frame   The frame associated with the menu event.

menuData   A pointer to the service's menu data.

DISCUSSION

This method is called by the SimpleCyberService override of the DoCyberMenuCommand method to perform the selected menu command. The value specified by index should be in the range 0...(*numitems* - 1), where *numitems* is the number of menu items the service defines.

If you subclass SimpleCyberService and your service has menu commands, your subclass should override DoMenuItemSelected.

If you subclass SimpleCyberService and override this method, your override must not call its inherited method; that is, your override method must implement this method's functionality completely.

SEE ALSO

The CyberService::DoCyberMenuCommand method (page 333).

Glossary

abstract class   A class used only to derive other classes. An abstract class is never instantiated. Compare **concrete class.**

address browser   An OpenDoc part that displays a list of e-mail and newsgroup addresses contained in a notebook. The address browser allows the user to select addresses to be added to an address field, such as the To: or CC: field, in a mail message.

asynchronous process   A process, potentially time consuming, that is performed in a separate thread from the process that initiated it. The initiating process starts the asynchronous process and does not wait for the process to complete before continuing. Compare **synchronous process.**

BinHex   A file format in which binary data is stored as ASCII text. This is useful for transferring 8-bit data over 7-bit networks or data paths.

browser   See **navigator.**

concrete class   A class designed to be instantiated. Compare **abstract class.**

Connect To dialog box   A dialog box with which the user can specify information for connecting to a remote location. It is an OpenDoc part with extensions subclassed from `CyberContainerExtension` and `CyberItemPromptExtension`.

Connect To panel   A dialog-box panel, embedded in the Connect To dialog box, with which the user can specify connection information for a particular service. The Connect To panel is an OpenDoc part with an extension subclassed from `CyberConnectExtension`. See also **panel.**

Cyberdog   An extensible architecture for searching and browsing networks, accessing Internet mail and newsgroups, and embedding network content in OpenDoc documents and container applications.

Cyberdog display part   A part that displays the content referenced by a Cyberdog item. It is an OpenDoc part with an extension subclassed from `CyberPartExtension`.

Cyberdog draft   See **Cyberdog session document.**

Cyberdog item   A small, portable reference to data. A Cyberdog item does not store actual data. Instead, it stores enough information about the location and protocol of the data so that it can be retrieved when it is needed. It is an object of a `CyberItem` subclass.

Cyberdog menu   A menu that contains commands for accessing Cyberdog supporting parts such as the Connect To dialog box, the log, and the default notebook.

Cyberdog service   An object of a `CyberService` subclass that represents support for accessing remotely located data using a particular protocol. Cyberdog developers subclass `CyberService` to add support for new protocols to Cyberdog.

Cyberdog service menus   A single object that represents all the menus added to the menu bar by all Cyberdog services. It is an object of the `CyberServiceMenu` class. A Cyberdog display part creates a `CyberServiceMenu` object if it wants Cyberdog services to display their menus when the display part is active.

Cyberdog session   An object of the `CyberSession` class that represents a user's access to Cyberdog. It keeps track of global objects such as the supported Cyberdog services, the notebook, and the log.

Cyberdog session document   An OpenDoc document associated with the Cyberdog session that contains all Cyberdog display parts and navigators opened by Cyberdog. (The session document does not contain Cyberdog display parts that are embedded in other OpenDoc documents.) The session document's root part never displays itself. The session document has a single draft.

Cyberdog Starting Point   An OpenDoc document window that contains buttons giving the user access to the primary Cyberdog features.

Cyberdog stream   An object of a `CyberStream` subclass that encapsulates the protocol knowledge required to download data referenced by objects of its companion `CyberItem` subclass.

dialog box part   An OpenDoc container part used as a dialog box. For Cyberdog, it has an extension subclassed from `CyberContainerExtension`. A dialog box part embeds panels. See **Connect To dialog box** and **Preferences dialog box**.

display part   See **Cyberdog display part**.

download icon   A Finder icon that represents the content referenced by a Cyberdog item. The content is downloaded and saved on disk as the data's native file type. Compare **part icon** and **reference icon**.

download part   An OpenDoc part used to download the content referenced by a Cyberdog item and save it to disk. A download part is used when the user drags a Cyberdog item to the Finder or when a Cyberdog item is opening and is unable to bind to a part editor. A download part is an OpenDoc part with extensions subclassed from `DownloadExtension` and `CyberPartExtension`.

environment parameter   A parameter used by all methods of SOM objects to pass exceptions.

extension   An OpenDoc object that extends the programming interface of another OpenDoc object. Cyberdog provides a number of extension classes that you can subclass and implement to allow your part editors to work with Cyberdog.

File Transfer Protocol (FTP)   A protocol for transferring files from one computer to another.

form   In HTML, a page that allows the user to specify information that is then submitted to the HTTP server. The HTTP server can use the form information to dynamically construct the next page to be downloaded and displayed.

FTP   See **File Transfer Protocol.**

Gopher   A hierarchical means of exploring information resources.

HTML   See **Hypertext Markup Language.**

HTTP   See **Hypertext Transfer Protocol.**

Hypertext Markup Language (HTML)   A protocol for tagging formatting attributes in a document, indicating to a Cyberdog display part how text and graphics should be displayed as well as indicating any links to other files or documents.

Hypertext Transfer Protocol (HTTP)   The protocol used by World Wide Web browsers and client programs to communicate with web servers.

IC   See **Internet Config.**

IDL   See **Interface Definition Language.**

Info window   See **Item Info window.**

initial opener part   An opener part, passed as a parameter in a parameter set, that is used during the opening of a Cyberdog item. Before you can use an initial opener part, you must obtain it by calling `CyberSession::ObtainOpener`. See also **obtained opener part.**

Interface Definition Language (IDL)   A syntax created by IBM to describe the interface of classes that can be compiled by the SOM compiler.

Internet Config (IC)   A software package used by Cyberdog to store and recall a user's Internet-related preferences, such as the user's name, e-mail address, news host, and so on.

Internet Config key   A string constant used to refer to a particular Internet Config preference setting.

ISO string   A null-terminated 7-bit ASCII string used to uniquely identify a storage unit property or data type.

item   See **Cyberdog item.**

Item Info window   A window that displays information about a Cyberdog item, including its URL.

JPEG   A compressed image format useful for transferring graphics. An abbreviation for Joint Photographic Experts Group.

log   An OpenDoc part that displays a list of the Cyberdog items visited by the user. The log displays Cyberdog items in one of three formats: alphabetical, chronological, or hierarchical.

log finger   In the log, an icon pointing to the Cyberdog item that the user is currently visiting.

log manager   In the Cyberdog log implementation, the component that handles operations performed on the log. The Cyberdog log manager is an OpenDoc part with an extension subclassed from `CyberLogExtension`.

MIME media type   A text string used in MIME transmissions to indicate the type of the data being transmitted. See **Multipurpose Internet Mail Extensions.**

Multipurpose Internet Mail Extensions (MIME)   A standard protocol for transmitting binary data, such as images or sounds, across the Internet.

name-mapping resource   A Mac OS resource, of type `'nmap'`, that contains information used for part binding.

navigator   A part that supports navigation among Cyberdog items; Cyberdog display parts can be embedded in a navigator. A navigator is an OpenDoc part with an extension subclassed from `CyberNavigatorExtension`.

notebook   An OpenDoc part in which a user can store Cyberdog items that refer to network locations of interest.

notebook manager   In the Cyberdog notebook implementation, the component that handles operations performed on the notebook. The Cyberdog notebook manager is an OpenDoc part with an extension subclassed from `CyberNotebookExtension`.

obtain   To retrieve an opener part from the Cyberdog session object by calling `CyberSession::ObtainOpener` method. See also **initial opener part** and **obtained opener part.**

obtained opener part   An opener part, passed as a parameter in a parameter set, that is used during the opening of a Cyberdog item. An obtained opener part has already been obtained by calling the `CyberSession::ObtainOpener` method. See also **initial opener part.**

OpenDoc   A multiplatform technology, implemented as a set of shared libraries, that uses component software to facilitate the construction and sharing of compound documents.

opener part   A part that acts as a placeholder and displays progress until a Cyberdog display part can be opened. If OpenDoc needs to create a part in order to open a Cyberdog item, but the item does not yet know the type of the data it references, an opener part is used as a placeholder until an appropriate Cyberdog display part for the item can be opened. An opener part is an OpenDoc part with an extension subclassed from `CyberOpenerPartExtension`. See also **initial opener part** and **obtained opener part.**

panel   A part embedded in a dialog box; typically, a panel allows the user to specify some information. For example, a panel in a Connect To dialog box allows the user to specify connection information for a remote location. For Cyberdog, a panel is an OpenDoc part with an extension subclassed from `CyberPanelExtension`.

parameter key   A string constant that identifies a parameter in a parameter set.

parameter set   A heterogeneous collection of objects. A parameter set is passed as a parameter when a Cyberdog item is opened; in this case, the parameter set contains objects that may play a role in the opening process.

part extension   See **extension.**

part icon   A Finder icon that represents the content referenced by a Cyberdog item. The content is downloaded and saved on disk as an OpenDoc part. Compare **download icon** and **reference icon.**

part kind   A specific classification of the format of data handled by a part editor. A kind specifies the specific data format handled by a part editor.

Preferences dialog box   A dialog box with which the user can specify preferences for accessing a remote location using a particular service (Gopher or FTP preferences, for example). It is an OpenDoc part with an extension subclassed from `CyberContainerExtension`.

Preferences panel   A dialog-box panel, embedded in the Preferences dialog box, that allows the user to specify preferences for a particular service. The panel is an OpenDoc part with an extension subclassed from `CyberPrefsExtension`. See also **panel.**

progress broadcaster   An object that broadcasts the status information about an asynchronous process to its attached progress receivers. It is an object of `CyberProgressBroadcaster` or one of its subclasses.

progress mode   A mode that indicates whether the amount of work to be performed by an asynchronous process is known in advance so that progress can be measured. For example, when downloading data, if you know in advance the number of bytes to be downloaded, the progress mode is metered; if you do not, the progress mode is unmetered.

progress part   A part that displays status information about an asynchronous process to the user. A progress part has an associated progress receiver that receives progress information from a progress broadcaster. A progress part is an OpenDoc part with an extension subclassed from `CyberProgressPartExtension`.

progress receiver   An object, associated with a progress part, that receives broadcasts of status information about an asynchronous process from a progress broadcaster. It is an object of a `CyberProgressReceiver` subclass.

protocol   A format for transmitting information. For example, the World Wide Web transmits data using the HTTP protocol. See also **Cyberdog service.**

reference icon   A Finder icon that represents a reference to content stored at a remote location. Compare **download icon** and **part icon.**

resolving   The process by which a Cyberdog item determines the type of data to which it refers. A Cyberdog item that can identify the type of data to which it refers is resolved.

Security Info window   A window that displays security information for a Cyberdog item referencing a secure site.

service   See **Cyberdog service.**

service menus   See **Cyberdog service menus.**

session   See **Cyberdog session.**

session document   See **Cyberdog session document.**

SOM   See **System Object Model.**

Starting Point   See **Cyberdog Starting Point.**

storage unit   In the OpenDoc storage system, an object that represents the basic unit of persistent storage. Each storage unit has a list of properties, and each property contains one or more data streams called values. A Cyberdog item is a persistent object that is stored in a storage unit.

stream   See **Cyberdog stream.**

string property   A string that describes some aspect of a Cyberdog item. A Cyberdog item's display name is an example of a string property.

synchronous process   A process that runs in the same thread as the process that initiated it.The initiating process waits for a synchronous process to complete before continuing. Compare **asynchronous process.**

System Object Model (SOM)   A technology from International Business Machines, Inc., that provides language- and platform-independent means of defining programmatic objects and handling method dispatching dynamically at runtime.

Telnet   A terminal-emulation protocol that allows users to log in remotely to other computers on the Internet using a command-line interface.

Universal Procedure Pointer (UPP)   A pointer to a function that can be called from either 68K or PowerPC code, regardless of which of the two types of code is used to implement the function.

Universal Resource Locator (URL)   A textual address used to locate, retrieve, and display remotely located data. A URL follows a standard format that includes information such as the Internet address of the data and the kind of transport protocol it requires.

user string   The user-readable name of a part editor.

visitation history   The collection of Cyberdog items visited by a navigator during a Cyberdog session.

web   See **World Wide Web.**

World Wide Web (WWW)   A hypertext-based Internet service used for browsing Internet resources.

Index

kImageJPEG constant 185
kImageJPEGKind constant 185
kImageJPEGRefKind constant 185
kImagePICT constant 185
kImagePICTKind constant 185
kImagePICTRefKind constant 185
kImageTIFF constant 185
kImageTIFFKind constant 185
kImageTIFFRefKind constant 185
kImageXBM constant 185
kImageXBMKind constant 185
kImageXBMRefKind constant 185
kImageXPM constant 185
kImageXPMKind constant 185
kImageXPMRefKind constant 185
kLogKindAlphabetical constant 176
kLogKindChronological constant 176
kLogKind constant 64, 186
kLogKindHierarchical constant 176
kLogManagerKind constant 63, 186
kMessageExternalBody constant 185
kMessageExternalBodyKind constant 185
kMessageExternalBodyRefKind constant 185
kMessagePartial constant 185
kMessagePartialKind constant 185
kMessagePartialRefKind constant 185
kMessageRFC822 constant 185
kMessageRFC822Kind constant 185
kMessageRFC822RefKind constant 185
kMeteredProgress constant 170
kMIMEPrefix constant 184
kMultipartAlternative constant 185
kMultipartAlternativeKind constant 185
kMultipartAlternativeRefKind constant 185
kMultipartDigest constant 185
kMultipartDigestKind constant 185
kMultipartDigestRefKind constant 185
kMultipartMixed constant 185
kMultipartMixedKind constant 185
kMultipartMixedRefKind constant 185
kMultipartParallel constant 185
kMultipartParallelKind constant 185
kMultipartParallelRefKind constant 185
kNavigatorCreator constant 187
kNavigatorKind constant 186

kNotebookKind constant 64, 186
kNotebookKindTagCategory constant 177
kNotebookKindTagCyberItem constant 177
kNotebookManagerKind constant 64, 187
kODEvtMenu constant 339
kOpenerPartKind constant 187
kPrefsDialogKind constant 187
kSimpleCyberServiceClassName constant 188
kTelnetPartKind constant 187
kTextEnriched constant 185
kTextEnrichedKind constant 185
kTextEnrichedRefKind constant 185
kTextHTML constant 186
kTextHTMLKind constant 186
kTextHTMLRefKind constant 186
kTextPlain constant 186
kTextPlainKind constant 186
kTextPlainRefKind constant 186
kToField constant 177
kUnmeteredProgress constant 170
kVideoAVI constant 186
kVideoAVIKind constant 186
kVideoAVIRefKind constant 186
kVideoMPEG constant 186
kVideoMPEGKind constant 186
kVideoMPEGRefKind constant 186
kVideoQuickTime constant 186
kVideoQuickTimeKind constant 186
kVideoQuickTimeRefKind constant 186

L

location banner 47
log 28, 39, 41–43, 58, 60
  adding items to 43, 80, 135, 251, 349
  checking for an item in 253, 366
  defined 41
  displaying 253, 255, 365, 374
  kinds 176
  preferences for 182
  retrieving 361
  runtime relationships of 63
  setting 372
  shutting down 252

OpenFile method 274
Open method
    of CyberItem class 68, 77–80, 100, 241
    of CyberStream class 70, 385
OpenPart method 275
OwnsURL method 337

P, Q

panels 57
    closing 279
    embedding in dialog boxes 280
    enabling the OK button 278
    keyboard focus 280, 281
parameter keys 172, 387
ParameterKey type 172
ParameterSet class 56, 101, 387
parameter sets 56, 152
    adding a parameter to 393
    destructors 195
    extracting a parameter from 389
    removing a parameter from 395
    retrieving a parameter from 392
    retrieving destructors from 390, 391, 392
part extensions, implementing 115
part kinds
    of Cyberdog components 186
    ISO prefix 184
    of items stored as parts 184
    of items stored as references 184
POP/SMTP protocol 25
PostDownloadRequest method 215
preferences 295, 296
Preferences dialog box 27, 38, 39, 60. *See also*
        Preferences panels
    displaying 109, 375
    runtime relationships of 65
Preferences panels 38, 57, 65
    part kind of 336
PreviousCyberItem method 261
progress broadcasters 55, 155
    aborting 157, 191, 300
    amount done 160, 302, 308
    amount total 302, 308

attaching receivers to 157, 300
defined 48
detaching receivers from 158, 301
error string 303, 309
initializing 155, 306
progress modes 155, 304, 310
progress percent 304, 310
resetting 307
retrieving an attached receiver from 301, 305
runtime relationships of 62
status string 160, 306, 311
progress modes 170, 297
progress parts 48–49, 58
    attaching broadcasters to 314
    defined 48
    detaching broadcasters from 314
    initializing 316
    retrieving an attached broadcaster from 315
    runtime relationships of 62
progress receivers 58
    amount done 322
    amount total 323
    attached to a broadcaster 319
    defined 48
    detached from a broadcaster 319
    error string 324
    initializing 321
    progress modes 324
    progress percent 325
    resetting 322
    retrieving an attached broadcaster from 320,
        321
    runtime relationships of 62
    status string 326
PromptForAddress method 267
PromptForCyberItem method
    of CyberItemPromptExtension class 249
    of CyberSession class 369
protocols 36
    FTP 27
    Gopher 27
    HTTP 27
    NNTP 26
    POP/SMTP 25
    Telnet 27

413

This Apple manual was written, edited, and composed on a desktop publishing system using Apple Macintosh computers and FrameMaker software. Proof pages were created on an Apple LaserWriter Pro printer. Final page negatives were output directly from text files on an Agfa Large-Format Imagesetter. Line art was created using Adobe™ Illustrator and Adobe Photoshop. PostScript™, the page-description language for the LaserWriter, was developed by Adobe Systems Incorporated.

Text type is Palatino® and display type is Helvetica®. Bullets are ITC Zapf Dingbats®. Some elements, such as program listings, are set in Adobe Letter Gothic.

Acknowledgments to Thor Anderson, Lorraine Aochi, Jim Black, Pablo Calamera, Christopher Cotton, Helen Cunningham, Trish Eastman, John Evans, Steve Fisher, Laurence Gathy, Sari Harrison, Pat Holleran, Liz Hujsak, Barb Kozlowski, Wendy Krafft, Henry Lee, Josephine Manuele, Jon Ruiz, Ed Tecot, David Williams.

WRITERS
Lori R. Stipp, Gary E. McCue

DEVELOPMENTAL EDITOR
Antonio Padial

ILLUSTRATORS
Deb Dennis, Sandee Karr

PRODUCTION EDITOR
Lorraine Findlay

COVER DESIGNER
Ruth Anderson
(Acknowledgments to Kim Webb, Webb Designs)

LEAD WRITER
Dave Bice

ONLINE PRODUCTION TEAM
Lorraine Findlay, Bill Harris, Dan Peterson, Alexandra Solinski

Special thanks to Michael Cleron, Deborah Grits, and Michael Nordman.